THE KINGFISHER ENCYCLOPEDIA OF EVERYTHING

one encyclopedia,
a world of knowledge

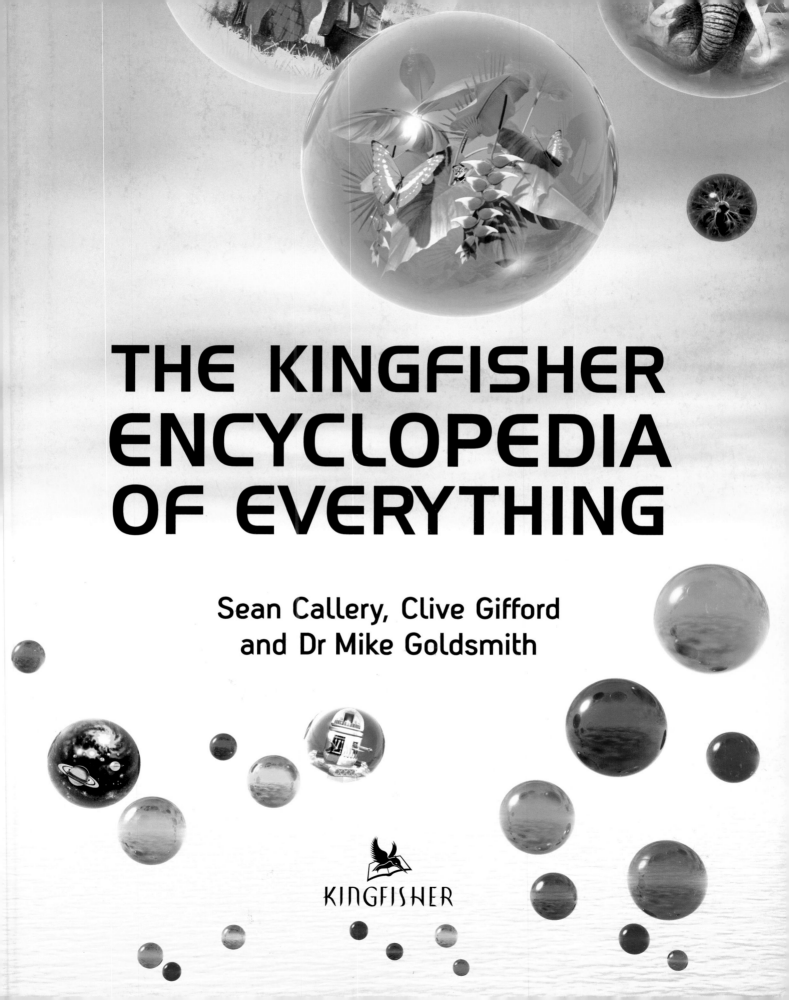

THE KINGFISHER
ENCYCLOPEDIA
OF EVERYTHING

Sean Callery, Clive Gifford
and Dr Mike Goldsmith

KINGFISHER

Contents

Earth
Science

Viewed from space, the Earth looks like a swirling blue

marble. It is the fifth largest of the eight planets in the Solar

System, and the third closest planet to the Sun, orbiting at

an average distance of 150 million kilometres. Together,

Earth's water, atmosphere and distance from the Sun help

make it the only known body in space to support life.

Formation and structure

The Earth is a planet that measures 12,742km in diameter. Made of rock, it has a core of very hot metal.

The Earth is not perfectly round, but is slightly flattened at the top and bottom, known as the poles. It also bulges at the equator, the imaginary line that runs around the middle of the planet.

Formation of the Earth

The Earth was formed about 4.5 billion years ago. Clouds of dust, rock and gas were drawn together by gravity. Over millions of years, the outer surface cooled to form solid rock, while gases formed the atmosphere around it.

Cloud of dust, rock and gas

Inner core is about 2,600km in diameter

Mantle is 2,900km thick, with a temperature of more than 1,300°C

Crust varies in thickness from 6–30km

Earth's crust

The crust is the planet's thin outer surface. It varies between 6km and 30km in depth and is made up of rocks and minerals such as silica and quartz. Over 70 per cent of this crust surface is covered by the water of seas, oceans, rivers and lakes.

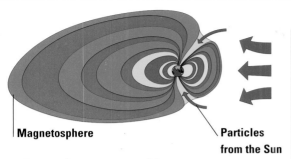

Magnetosphere

Particles from the Sun

Earth's magnetism

The Earth's outer core creates a giant magnetic field, the magnetosphere. This stretches around the Earth and reaches out far into space. It helps to prevent particles from the Sun and space harming life on Earth.

Naturally hot

In the Valley of the Geysers in Russia, steam and boiling water pour out of holes in the Earth's crust. Water is heated by hot rocks just below the Earth's surface and escapes in different ways. Fountain geysers erupt in short bursts from pools of water. Cone geysers have steady, narrow jets.

Atmosphere

Outer core is 2,250km thick

Below the surface

Beneath the Earth's crust is the mantle, which is composed of partly melted rock and metals. Beneath the mantle is the Earth's core, made of two parts: a hot, liquid metal outer core and a solid metal inner core.

SCIENTIFIC INPUT

GEOLOGICAL TIME

Geologists study the Earth, its rocks and their history. They also measure the age of rocks and fossils (*see p.19*) using geological time. This calendar of the Earth's history is divided into epochs and eras which lasted many millions of years. From the study of dinosaur fossils (above), geologists have established that dinosaurs lived during the Mesozoic Era, from 251 to 65 million years ago (mya).

Continents and mountains

A continent is a giant area of land. A third of the Earth's surface is land, divided into seven continents: Asia, Africa, North and South America, Antarctica, Europe and Australia.

Mountains are high peaks of land, often formed by movements in the Earth's crust. They are found in groups called mountain ranges. The highest mountain, Everest, is in the Himalayas.

CONTINENTAL DRIFT
These diagrams show how the continent Pangaea became today's continents.

200 million years ago

110 million years ago

Today

Continental plates
The Earth's crust is made up of a number of giant slabs of solid rock called continental plates. These float on the Earth's mantle and move very slowly.

Continental drift
At first, there was just one giant continent, Pangaea. Over many millions of years, Pangaea slowly separated into today's continents. This movement is called continental drift, and is still occurring.

Fault lines
Faults or fault lines are cracks in the Earth's crust. There are fault lines where two continental plates meet. Fault lines are often where volcanic activity and earthquakes occur.

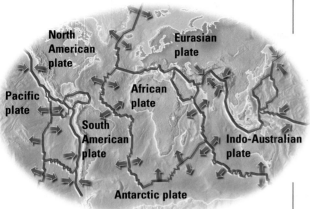

Plate activity

This map shows the world's major continental plates and the arrows show the direction in which they are currently moving. There are seven major continental plates and nine minor continental plates.

Forming mountains

The movement of the continental plates creates most of the world's mountains. Land is driven upwards, buckles and folds, often along fault lines. Volcanoes (*see pp.16–17*) can also create mountains by spewing out vast amounts of lava and ash, which harden as they cool to form rock.

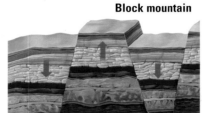

Block mountain

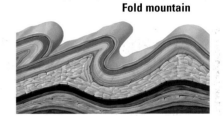

Fold mountain

Types of mountain

A large block of land can be forced upwards by plate movement to form a block mountain. Other mountains, such as the Andes in South America and Rockies in North America, are fold mountains. These are formed when softer rocks are bent into folds by immense pressure.

The Himalayas continue to move upwards.

Making a mountain range

The Himalayas mountain range was formed millions of years ago by two continental plates driving into each other. The mud and sediment on the ocean floor was squeezed together and pushed up to form the mountain range.

Earthquakes

Earthquakes are caused by movements of the Earth's crust which cause pressure in part of the crust to be released as energy.

As many as half a million earthquakes happen every year. The majority are small and harmless, but powerful earthquakes cause enormous damage.

Mobile seismograph

TYPES OF SHOCK WAVE

There are three forms of shock waves generated by an earthquake.

1
Waves travel deep underground, stretching and compressing rock.

2
Waves also travel underground, but shift rock up and down and from side to side.

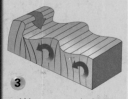

3
Waves travel along the Earth's surface, and cause the most damage.

Focus and epicentre

An earthquake begins at a point underground called the focus or hypocentre. The point on the surface directly above is called the epicentre. This is usually where the greatest force is felt.

Shock waves

From the focus, released energy spreads out quickly in the form of a series of rippling energy waves called shock waves. Their force weakens as they travel.

Tsunamis

Earthquakes can generate giant ocean waves called tsunamis. These can be devastating if they reach land. In 2004, a massive earthquake on the floor of the Indian Ocean resulted in the Asian tsunami. It killed more than 230,000 people.

Measuring earthquakes

Earthquake experts, or seismologists, study and measure earthquakes. They use a variety of scientific instruments, including satellites and seismographs, to chart the Earth's vibrations.

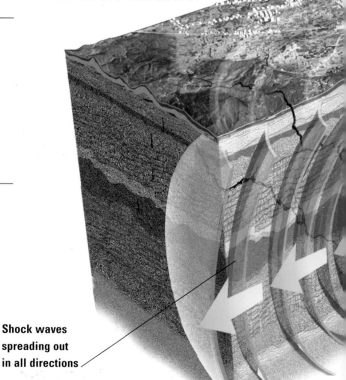

Shock waves spreading out in all directions

The Richter scale

The Richter scale indicates the magnitude or strength of an earthquake. Earthquakes above 3.5 are strong enough to be noticed, but do little damage. Major earthquakes register 7.0 or above. The earthquake that helped to generate the Asian tsunami measured over 9.0.

HISTORICAL DATA

EARTHQUAKE DAMAGE

Earthquakes in built-up areas can inflict massive damage. Roads, bridges, tunnels and buildings collapse or are torn apart, while deadly landslides, fires and explosions may be caused by broken cables and pipelines. In 1995, an earthquake measuring 7.3 on the Richter scale destroyed roads and buildings in the Japanese city of Kobe.

Epicentre directly above the focus

Fault line between two plates of the Earth's crust

Focus of earthquake deep underground

Earthquake zones

Certain parts of the planet are more likely to suffer earthquakes than the others. This map shows where major earthquakes have occurred in the past. Most of these were along existing fault lines (green), because this is where the Earth's crust is often under the most pressure.

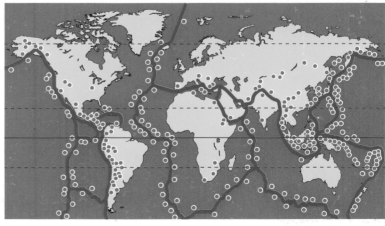

VOLCANOES

VOLCANOES ARE OPENINGS THROUGH WHICH RED-HOT, LIQUID ROCK CALLED MAGMA FORCES ITS WAY TO THE SURFACE OF THE EARTH. MAGMA COMES FROM DEEP INSIDE THE EARTH, AND THESE ERUPTIONS OCCUR WHERE THE EARTH'S CRUST IS WEAKEST.

EXPLOSIVE ERUPTIONS

On the Italian island of Sicily, Mount Etna stands 3,326m high. It is the largest active volcano in Europe. Along its slopes, magma seeps and oozes out as lava through long cracks in the rocky crust called fissures. In the past, a build-up of gases under pressure has resulted in explosive eruptions with lava, ash and gases thrown high into the air. The most explosive eruptions have blown away the top of the volcano, leaving giant craters.

A violent eruption throws out chunks of hot rock, lava, ash and a massive cloud of gas, which can be poisonous.

When magma erupts from the magma chamber, deep inside the volcano, it becomes a red-hot river of lava which flows downhill, destroying everything in its path.

Fissure volcano

Shield volcano

Ash cinder volcano

Dome volcano

Caldera volcano

Composite volcano

TYPES OF VOLCANO

Lava from an eruption eventually cools, forming rock. Thicker lava from a powerful eruption may not travel far before it hardens, forming steep, cone-shaped volcanoes. Thin, runny lava tends to travel further and may form a shallow-sided shield volcano. Some volcanoes are called composite or strato volcanoes because they form gradually from layers laid down by several eruptions.

On Mount Etna there are four summit craters.

The opening at the top of the volcano is called a vent.

Openings on the slopes through which some lava flows are called side vents.

Rocks and soil

Rocks are solid, non-living materials. They are divided into three types – igneous, metamorphic and sedimentary.

MOHS SCALE

Mohs scale rates ten minerals, from the softest to the hardest.

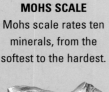

Talc is the softest mineral, rated as 1.

Gypsum is rated as 2 and can scratch talc.

Apatite is rated as 5 on Mohs scale.

Quartz is rated as 7 on Mohs scale.

Diamond is the hardest mineral, rated as 10.

Rocks are formed from chemical compounds called minerals. Minerals such as copper are single elements, while others, such as silicon, are made of many elements.

Igneous rock

Igneous rock is formed from magma or lava that has cooled and hardened. Granite is an igneous rock formed deep underground. The spectacular columns of the Giant's Causeway in Northern Ireland are basalt, which is an igneous rock formed from lava that cooled above the ground.

Metamorphic rock

'Metamorphic' means changed, and intense heat or pressure transforms this rock. For example, heat and pressure have changed some types of the sedimentary rock limestone to form marble, a metamorphic rock.

Sedimentary rock

Over millions of years, tiny particles of worn-away rock, or the skeletons and shells of creatures, were pressed together (compacted) to form solid, sedimentary rock. The sandstone and limestone of the Grand Canyon, USA, are good examples of this.

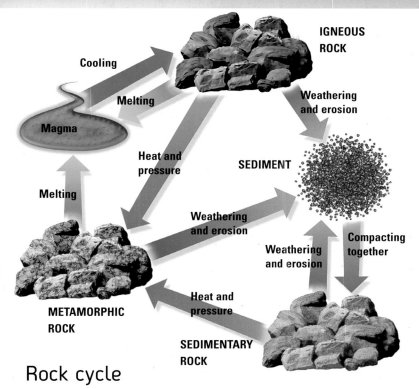

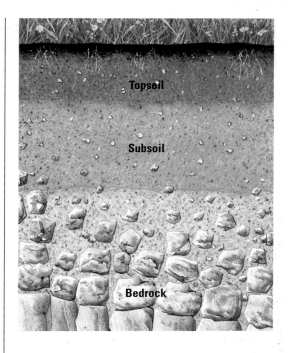

Topsoil

Subsoil

Bedrock

Rock cycle

The rock cycle is a way of showing the different ways rocks can change over long periods of time. An igneous rock, for example, can be worn away, with the particles forming a layer of sediment. Over time, these are compacted to form a sedimentary rock. This rock can then be changed again, by heat and pressure, into a metamorphic rock.

Soil composition

Soil is made up of broken particles of rock mixed with air, water, tiny holes called pores and humus, which is old plant matter. There are different soil types. Sandy soil is loose and dry. It does not usually hold water as well as thick, sticky clay soils.

Minerals under pressure

When put under pressure and at certain temperatures, some minerals form gemstones. These can be cut and polished. Many gemstones – for example, rubies, opals, emeralds and diamonds – shine with beautiful colours.

Rock strata

Geologists have discovered that many sedimentary rocks exist in layers, with the eldest rocks below layers of newer rocks. A layer of the same type of rock is called a stratum (*plural* strata). Scientists are able to examine strata to provide a record of rock formation over millions of years.

Weathering and erosion

Weathering is the gradual altering or breaking up of rocks at or very near the Earth's surface. Erosion happens when rocks and other material are worn or washed away.

Weathering can happen in different ways. Constant heating and cooling cause rock to split, while chemicals in rain and the atmosphere create a chemical reaction, weakening or dissolving rock.

Coastal erosion

Sea waves can erode coastlines dramatically. The continual action of the waves hurls fragments of rock at the land. These act as abrasives, wearing away cliffs and shores.

Waterfalls

The power of moving water erodes. Sometimes, running water travels over rock that is resistant to erosion but erodes softer rock further ahead. This creates a sharp ledge and a drop, which can form a waterfall.

Softer rock at base of cliff erodes easily.

Wind erosion

Wind erosion works most powerfully in dry regions with little water and few plants to bind soil and particles together. When carried by winds, the particles erode rock formations.

Creating dunes

Sand dunes form along coasts and in dry desert regions. Wind blowing mainly from one direction creates crescent-shaped sand dunes with a shallow sloping side nearest the wind and a steeper slope on the far side.

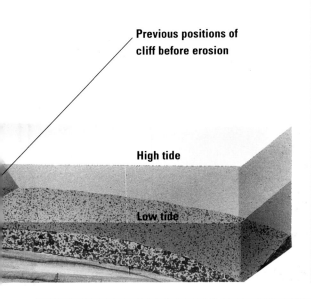

Previous positions of cliff before erosion

High tide

Low tide

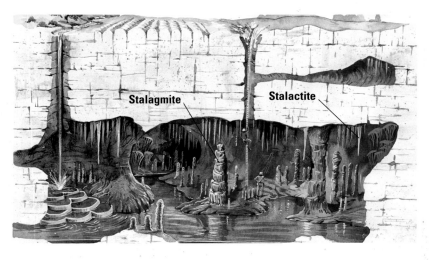

Stalagmite

Stalactite

Caves and caverns

When rain combines with carbon dioxide in the air or with decaying plant matter in the soil, it forms carbonic acid. This flows through cracks and gaps in the ground and dissolves limestone rock, creating caves full of dramatic features such as stalactites and stalagmites.

SCIENTIFIC INPUT

ACID RAIN

When polluting gases in the atmosphere from motor vehicles and industry combine with rainwater or snow, this causes acid rain. Acid raid is very harmful. The chemicals in acid rain destroy lakes and forests, and damage statues and buildings made of rocks such as sandstone and limestone.

Glaciers and ice

Ice is water that has frozen to become a solid. Ice covers over ten per cent of the Earth's surface and contains around three-quarters of the total amount of freshwater on the planet.

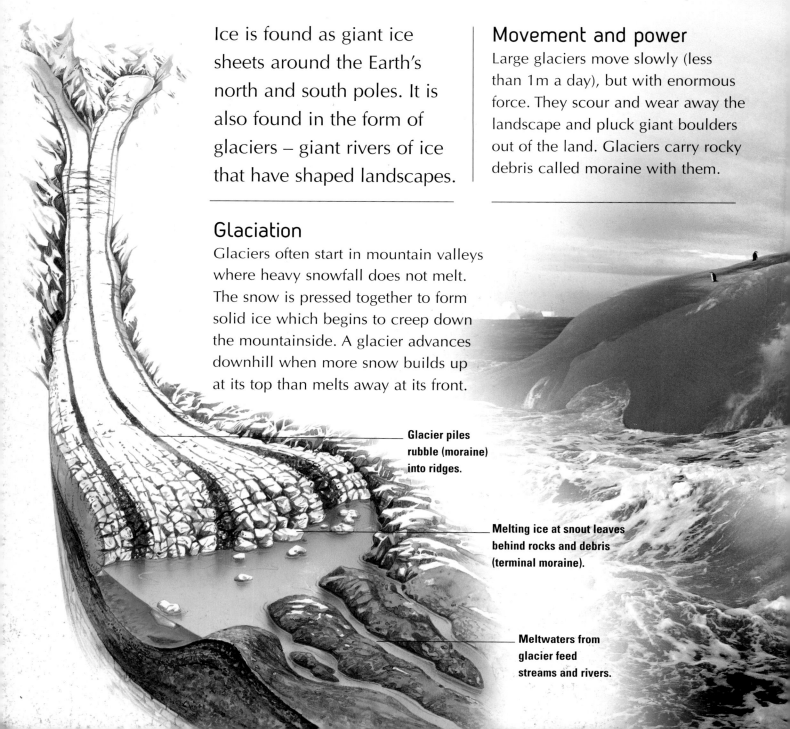

Ice is found as giant ice sheets around the Earth's north and south poles. It is also found in the form of glaciers – giant rivers of ice that have shaped landscapes.

Movement and power

Large glaciers move slowly (less than 1m a day), but with enormous force. They scour and wear away the landscape and pluck giant boulders out of the land. Glaciers carry rocky debris called moraine with them.

Glaciation

Glaciers often start in mountain valleys where heavy snowfall does not melt. The snow is pressed together to form solid ice which begins to creep down the mountainside. A glacier advances downhill when more snow builds up at its top than melts away at its front.

Glacier piles rubble (moraine) into ridges.

Melting ice at snout leaves behind rocks and debris (terminal moraine).

Meltwaters from glacier feed streams and rivers.

Glacial landscapes

Glaciers change the landscape. Bowl shapes called cirques can form high up, where the glacier begins. Lower down, broad U-shaped valleys are carved out, while the moraine carried by the glacier creates fertile farmland.

Ice sheets

Ice sheets are enormous masses of ice larger than 50,000km^2 (square kilometres) in area. The Greenland ice sheet has an area of 1.8 million km^2. The huge ice sheet that covers Antarctica is almost 14 million km^2.

Ice caves

An ice cave is any hollowed out rock structure that has ice inside all year round. Large chambers in the ice of a glacier are called 'glacier caves'. They are sometimes used by scientists to study the inside of a glacier.

Icebergs

An iceberg is a part of an ice sheet or a coastal glacier that breaks off in a process called calving. Ice is less dense than liquid water, so icebergs float in the ocean. Only around one-eighth of an iceberg is visible.

RIVERS AND LAKES

RIVERS ARE LARGE BODIES OF RUNNING WATER. THEY MAKE UP ONLY A TINY PORTION OF THE WATER ON EARTH BUT ARE INCREDIBLY IMPORTANT. RIVERS CARRY WATER TO DIFFERENT AREAS, SHAPING THE LAND THROUGH WHICH THEY RUN.

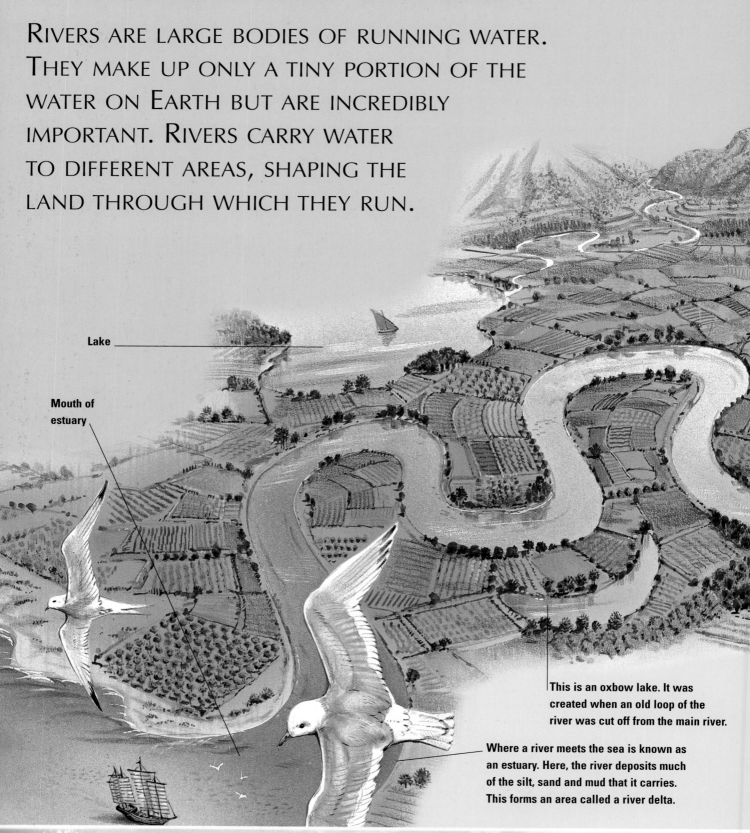

Lake

Mouth of estuary

This is an oxbow lake. It was created when an old loop of the river was cut off from the main river.

Where a river meets the sea is known as an estuary. Here, the river deposits much of the silt, sand and mud that it carries. This forms an area called a river delta.

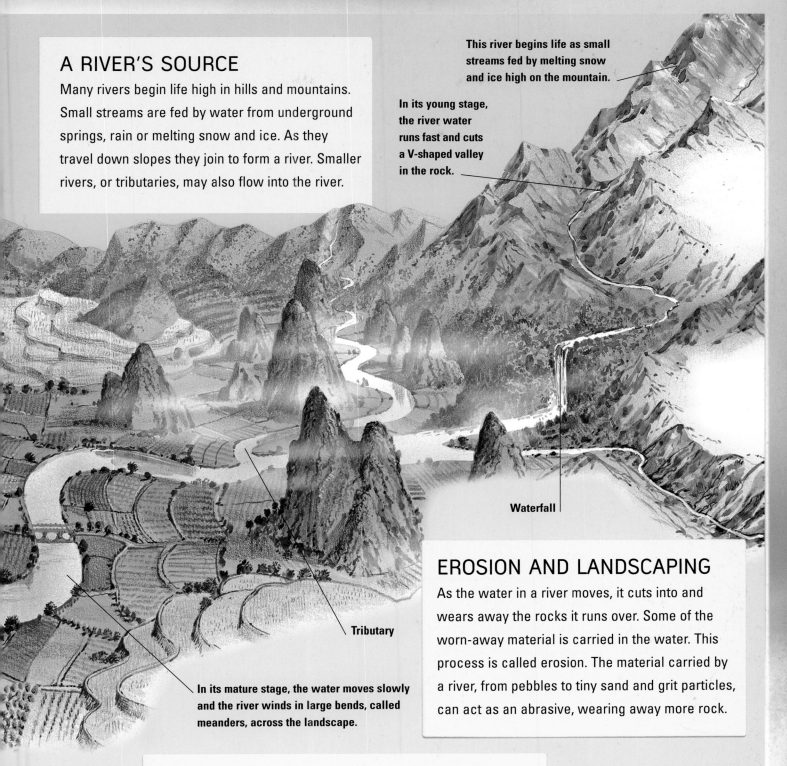

A RIVER'S SOURCE

Many rivers begin life high in hills and mountains. Small streams are fed by water from underground springs, rain or melting snow and ice. As they travel down slopes they join to form a river. Smaller rivers, or tributaries, may also flow into the river.

This river begins life as small streams fed by melting snow and ice high on the mountain.

In its young stage, the river water runs fast and cuts a V-shaped valley in the rock.

Waterfall

Tributary

In its mature stage, the water moves slowly and the river winds in large bends, called meanders, across the landscape.

EROSION AND LANDSCAPING

As the water in a river moves, it cuts into and wears away the rocks it runs over. Some of the worn-away material is carried in the water. This process is called erosion. The material carried by a river, from pebbles to tiny sand and grit particles, can act as an abrasive, wearing away more rock.

LAKES

Enclosed bodies of water are called lakes. They form wherever water collects, usually in holes or depressions in the ground. Lakes are fed by melting snow, rain and sometimes rivers or streams. They provide homes for many plants and animals.

Seas and oceans

Ninety-seven per cent of the water on Earth is found in the planet's seas and oceans. Seas are areas of the oceans that are partly cut off by land.

ATOLL FORMATION
An atoll is an island in the Indian or Pacific Ocean that encircles a lake called a lagoon.

A volcanic eruption causes the peak to poke above the water to become an island.

A coral reef grows up around the island and then rises as the island gradually sinks.

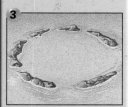

The island disappears completely, leaving only the coral atoll circling the lagoon.

There are four oceans – the Arctic, Indian, Atlantic and Pacific. The Pacific is the largest and deepest. Salt water flows between the oceans, moved by waves, currents and tides.

Ocean floor
Much of the ocean floor is made up of flat abyssal plains. However, in some places, giant mountains rise thousands of metres. A few reach the surface, where they become islands. Where the continental plates meet underwater, giant trenches form.

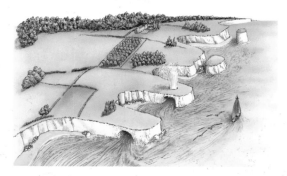

Coastlines
The coast is where the land meets the sea or ocean. The action of waves and tides can erode softer rock to leave a curved bay, while harder rock sticks out into the sea and is called a headland.

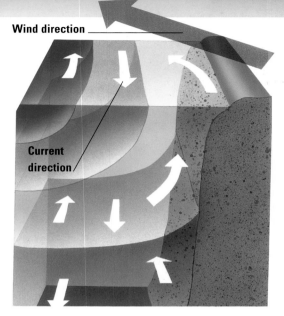

Wind direction

Current direction

Waves break on a beach

Wind direction

Peak or crest of wave

Trough of wave

Currents

Wide bands of water called currents flow around the planet's oceans. They vary in temperature, travel thousands of kilometres, and can have a great influence on climate.

The mighty Pacific

The Pacific Ocean stretches from the Bering Strait in the Arctic Circle to the edge of Antarctica. It is so large that it covers a third of the entire surface of Earth and all the land of the world could fit inside it.

Tides

Tides are the regular rise and fall of the ocean's water. They are seen when water rises up a beach at high tide and retreats at low tide. Tides are caused by the Moon's gravity pulling on the Earth (*see p.39*).

Waves

Winds travelling across the ocean's surface create circular movements in the water known as waves. The highest part of a wave is called its peak or crest. Its lowest part is the trough. On reaching shallow water, waves topple forwards and break.

Black smokers

Hydrothermal vents are openings in the ocean floor. They are nicknamed black smokers because the very hot waters that rise from them look like smoke. These waters are rich in minerals.

ATMOSPHERE

EARTH'S ATMOSPHERE IS A BODY OF
GASES THAT SURROUNDS THE PLANET.
IT PROVIDES OXYGEN TO BREATHE,
TRAPS SOME OF THE SUN'S WARMING
ENERGY, AND PROTECTS FROM HARMFUL
RADIATION AND PARTICLES FROM SPACE.

Jet airliners cruise in the lower
stratosphere, just above the
majority of the weather.

Small fragments of material in
space burn up in the mesosphere,
creating meteor showers when
viewed from Earth's surface.

Clouds form mainly in the
troposphere, where most of the
world's weather is generated.

Air currents circulate
through the troposphere.

THE COMPOSITION OF AIR

Air in the atmosphere is a mixture of different gases.
These include nitrogen (78%), oxygen (21%) and
argon (1%). Air also includes some carbon dioxide
and water vapour, which vary in amount.

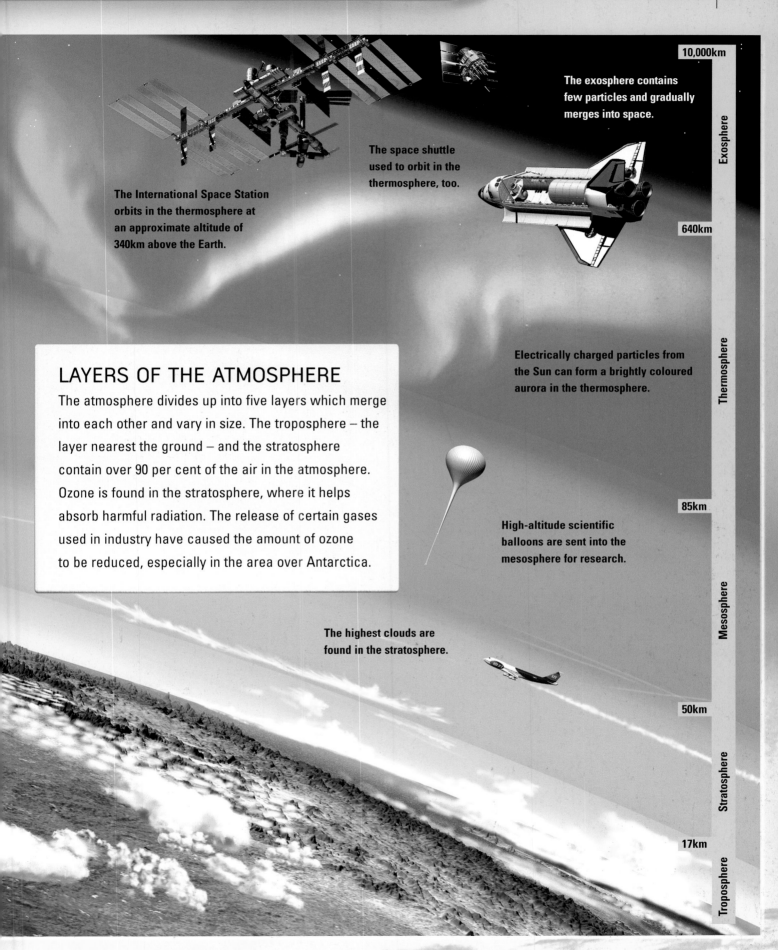

The exosphere contains few particles and gradually merges into space.

10,000km

Exosphere

The space shuttle used to orbit in the thermosphere, too.

640km

The International Space Station orbits in the thermosphere at an approximate altitude of 340km above the Earth.

Electrically charged particles from the Sun can form a brightly coloured aurora in the thermosphere.

Thermosphere

LAYERS OF THE ATMOSPHERE

The atmosphere divides up into five layers which merge into each other and vary in size. The troposphere – the layer nearest the ground – and the stratosphere contain over 90 per cent of the air in the atmosphere. Ozone is found in the stratosphere, where it helps absorb harmful radiation. The release of certain gases used in industry have caused the amount of ozone to be reduced, especially in the area over Antarctica.

85km

High-altitude scientific balloons are sent into the mesosphere for research.

The highest clouds are found in the stratosphere.

Mesosphere

50km

Stratosphere

17km

Troposphere

Earth's resources

The Earth provides the human race with an incredible abundance of different natural resources. These range from energy supplies to metals and raw materials.

Many resources, including fossil fuels, are non-renewable. This means that they cannot be replaced at the rate at which the human population is currently using them.

MAKING ALUMINIUM

Aluminium is used to make many things, from drinks cans to aircraft parts.

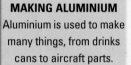

A rocky ore, bauxite, is mined from the ground.

Bauxite is processed to extract aluminium.

The aluminium is made into cans for food.

Fossil fuels

Over thousands of years, ancient plant and animal matter has been compressed under layers of rock. It has formed three vital fossil fuels – coal, oil and natural gas. These are all burned to create energy to generate electricity, provide heat and power motor vehicles. In addition, oil in particular is used to make plastics and many other products.

Deforestation

Forests provide many valuable resources from wood for building, to paper and wood chips that are made into processed wood panels. Destroying forests without replanting them is called deforestation. Over the past 40 years, almost half of the world's forests have disappeared, cut down for their wood or cleared for new farmland or settlements.

Geothermal energy

The heat beneath the Earth's surface is harnessed in certain places in the world. Hot springs on the surface are bathed in (above) or used to pipe hot water into homes. Geothermal energy plants tap into reservoirs of hot water underground, using the hot water and steam to drive power turbines that in turn generate electricity.

Renewable energies

Some energy sources on Earth are renewable. This means that they cannot be exhausted by use. These sources include the energy in sea waves and tides, and the solar energy from the Sun which can be converted into electricity by photovoltaic cells. The power of the wind can also be harnessed to create electricity by wind turbines grouped together to create a wind farm (left).

Processing metals

Metals such as gold, iron, copper and zinc exist in the Earth's crust, and can be mined and extracted. Some are heated until they melt. They are then poured into moulds to make perfect metal parts.

Steel is made by mixing three parts melted iron and one part scrap steel.

Raw materials

Rocks and minerals provide raw materials for building – from bricks made from clay used to build huts and houses, to concrete made from sand, gravel, cement and water. More than 100,000 tonnes of concrete was used in the construction of Australia's Sydney Opera House.

Earth facts

The Earth has a diameter of approximately 12,714km from North Pole to South Pole and a circumference around the equator of approximately 40,075km. It has a land area of 148 million km^2, and a water area of 362 million km^2.

HIGHEST MOUNTAINS
Asia: Mount Everest, 8,863m
South America: Aconcagua, 6,959m
North America: Mount McKinley, 6,194m
Africa: Mount Kilimanjaro, 5,963m
Europe: Mount Elbrus, 5,633m
Antarctica: Vinson Massif, 4,897m
Oceania: Puncak Jaya, 4,884m

LARGEST ISLANDS
Greenland 2,131,000km^2
New Guinea 800,000km^2
Borneo, Indonesia 726,000km^2
Madagascar, Africa 578,000km^2
Baffin Island, Canada 507,000km^2

Sumatra, Indonesia 425,000km^2
Honshu, Japan 227,000km^2
Victoria Island, Canada 217,291km^2

LONGEST RIVERS
Nile, Africa 6,670km
Amazon, South America 6,448km
Chang Jiang (Yangtze), Asia 6,300km
Mississippi–Missouri, North America 6,020km
Yenisey–Angara, Asia 5,540km
Huang (Yellow), Asia 5,464km
Ob-Irtysh, Asia 5,409km
Paraná-Rio de la Plata, South America 4,880km
Congo, Africa 4,700km

Lena, Asia 4,400km
Amur-Argun, Asia 4,345km

LARGEST LAKES
Caspian Sea, Asia and Europe 371,800km^2
Superior, North America 82,350km^2
Victoria, Africa 69,500km^2
Huron, North America 59,600km^2
Michigan, North America 57,800km^2

THE WORLD'S OCEANS
Pacific   166,240,000km^2
Atlantic   86,560,000km^2
Indian   73,430,000km^2
Arctic   13,230,000km^2

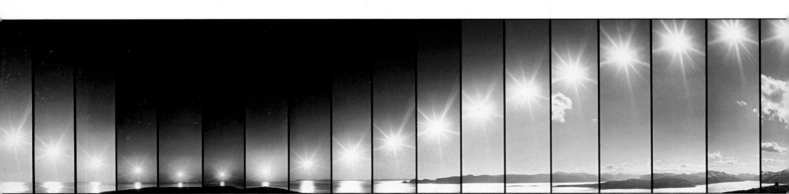

The Sun sets and rises over the Earth

USEFUL WEBSITES

www.geography4kids.com/index.html The Earth's formation, rocks and atmosphere.
http://earthquake.usgs.gov Earthquake information from the US Geological Survey.
www.geolsoc.org.uk/gsl/null/lang/en/page2673.html Fact sheets on geological topics.
http://nsidc.org/glaciers/ Glaciers, their formation and effects.

Space and the Stars

Looking up at the starlit sky, it is possible to see stars trillions of kilometres away. The Galaxy to which our Sun belongs extends many times further than this, and it is only one of countless billions that make up the Universe. Today, people have the technology to probe these distant galaxies with telescopes and to send robots to explore the Solar System.

The Solar System

The Earth and other planets, along with many smaller bodies, orbit the Sun and form our Solar System. There are eight planets, which vary greatly in size.

The Solar System contains moons, comets, asteroids, dwarf planets and meteoroids, as well as interplanetary gas and dust. Most of these objects move within a flat, round area of space which has a star, the Sun, at its centre.

The Solar System includes planets and comets in orbit around the Sun.

The birth of the Sun

The Solar System formed from a cloud in space 4.6 billion years ago. Gravity pulled part of the cloud together until it was so crushed and hot that nuclear reactions began. This part of the cloud began to glow, and became the Sun at the centre of our Solar System.

The Sun, like most stars, will shine steadily for nearly all its life.

All stars are born in dark clouds of gas and dust.

Size of the Solar System

The planets occupy an area about nine billion kilometres across, but there are many smaller objects beyond. The width of the system is probably 30,000 billion kilometres.

Formation of the planets

In other parts of the cloud, gravity gathered dust and gases together into spinning clumps. The clumps grew into giant rock chunks called planetesimals. These joined together to form dozens of planets.

The end of the Solar System

In about five billion years, the Sun will run out of fuel. It will turn red (right) and swell enormously. Its outer layers will be thrown off to leave a tiny core. The Solar System will grow cold and dark as the Sun fades.

The Great Bombardment

For about 200 million years, enormous chunks of rock smashed continuously into the newly formed planets, destroying many of them. When the bombardment ended, about 3.8 billion years ago, only eight planets remained. Many huge craters from this assault can still be seen on the surface of the Moon, as well as on Mercury and Mars.

SCIENTIFIC INPUT

GRAVITY AND THE BALANCE OF THE SOLAR SYSTEM
All objects pull on each other with the force of gravity, but this pull can only be felt if one of the objects is massive. The Sun is an enormously massive object, and its gravity holds the whole Solar System together. If the planets did not orbit the Sun, it would pull them into it. The closer they are to the Sun, the faster they have to orbit to avoid this.

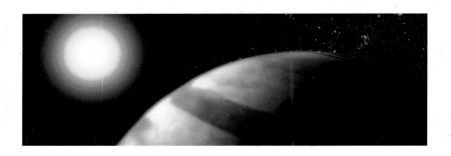

Other solar systems

Many stars have their own families of worlds orbiting around them. With so many billions of stars in the Universe, it is practically certain that many of these worlds are similar to our own.

THE SUN

THE SUN IS OUR LOCAL STAR, AND THE EARTH AND OTHER MEMBERS OF THE SOLAR SYSTEM ALL MOVE AROUND IT. WITHOUT ITS LIGHT AND HEAT, THERE WOULD BE NO LIFE ON EARTH.

THE LIFE OF OUR SUN

More than a million objects the size of Earth would fit inside the Sun, which is 4.6 billion years old. It will last for about another 5 billion years. Its surface temperature is about 5000°C and the temperature of its outer atmosphere, the corona, is several million degrees C.

Storms on the Sun sometimes throw huge masses of glowing gas called prominences high into space.

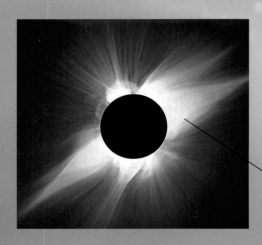

Sometimes the Moon passes directly between the Sun and the Earth. This is called a solar eclipse. During eclipses, the Sun's corona can be seen. It is a thin outer atmosphere, millions of degrees hotter than the photosphere.

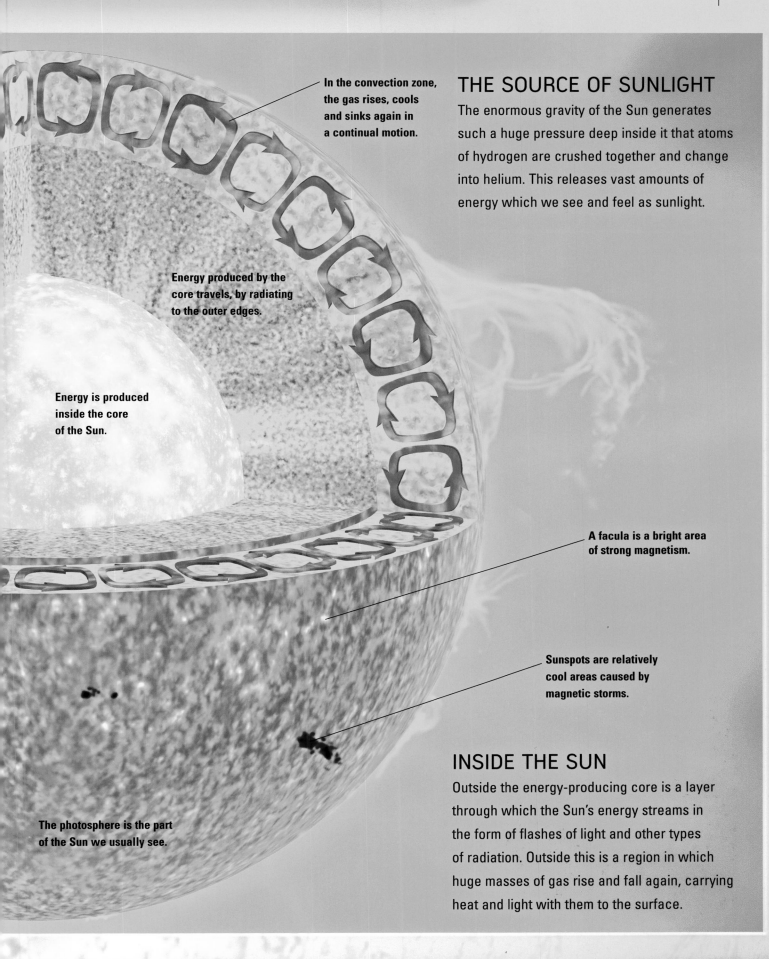

In the convection zone, the gas rises, cools and sinks again in a continual motion.

Energy produced by the core travels, by radiating to the outer edges.

Energy is produced inside the core of the Sun.

A facula is a bright area of strong magnetism.

Sunspots are relatively cool areas caused by magnetic storms.

The photosphere is the part of the Sun we usually see.

THE SOURCE OF SUNLIGHT

The enormous gravity of the Sun generates such a huge pressure deep inside it that atoms of hydrogen are crushed together and change into helium. This releases vast amounts of energy which we see and feel as sunlight.

INSIDE THE SUN

Outside the energy-producing core is a layer through which the Sun's energy streams in the form of flashes of light and other types of radiation. Outside this is a region in which huge masses of gas rise and fall again, carrying heat and light with them to the surface.

The Moon

The Moon is about 384,400km away. It is by far the closest world to Earth, the only one whose surface is clearly visible in the night sky, and the only one humans have visited.

Although it is close, the Moon is still a mysterious place. It takes the same time to spin round as it does to orbit the Earth. This means we always see the same area of the Moon, and that some of it is always hidden.

The birth of the Moon
The Moon was born about 4.5 billion years ago. A body the size of Mars smashed into the Earth, and some of the fragments formed the Moon.

The far side of the Moon
Unlike the side we see, the far side of the Moon has no large 'seas', which are actually plains of ancient lava. However, there are more craters on the far side.

New Moon **Waxing crescent** **First quarter** **Waxing gibbous**

Full Moon **Waning gibbous** **Last quarter** **Waning crescent**

Phases of the Moon
The Moon seems to change shape over the course of a month, as sunlight falls on different amounts of the half that is visible from Earth. The whole cycle takes one month ('moonth').

Astronauts on the Moon

Twelve astronauts landed on the Moon between 1969 and 1972. On some missions they took an electric car called a lunar rover, which meant they were able to explore larger areas than they could on foot.

The Moon and the tides

As the Earth turns under the Moon, the Moon pulls at the Earth and its oceans. As a result, the seas rise and fall on the world's coasts, and these motions are called tides. The Sun has a similar, but lesser, effect.

The rocky planets

Planet Earth is one of the four rocky planets. All of these have metal centres covered by thick layers of rock.

The rocky or 'inner' planets all orbit close to the Sun. Mercury is almost airless, while Venus has a thick atmosphere, the Earth has oceans and Mars has a rusty-coloured surface.

Mercury

Venus

Earth

Mars

Venus

Venus has a thick atmosphere that traps the Sun's heat, making it the hottest planet. A rain of acid falls constantly from the clouds. These clouds hide the surface from view. Spacecraft have made radar maps of the landscape, like this one.

Mercury

The sunlit side of Mercury is hot enough to melt metal, but the lack of a protective thick atmosphere means that the planet loses heat quickly at night. So the dark side is colder than anywhere on Earth.

Venusian weather

On Venus, the thick air is constantly on the move. These two spinning hurricane-like shapes (above) have been seen at the north and south poles of the planet.

Mars

Martian soil contains iron, which rusts to give the reddish colour seen from Earth. Like Earth, the planet has polar icecaps and many dead volcanoes. Dry riverbeds show that water once flowed on Mars.

Earth

The planet we live on is about 4.5 billion years old, and life has existed here for more than three-quarters of that time. Life on Earth is dependent on the presence of liquid water on the surface of the planet. The water itself, because of the water cycle (*see pp.72–73*), is as ancient as the life on Earth.

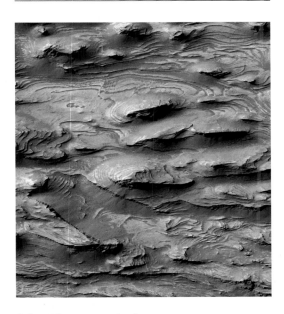

Martian rock layers

This satellite image of part of the surface of Mars shows a pattern of rock layers. Each layer is about 10m thick, and there are more than 100 of them. These layers may be the bottoms of ancient seas that dried up thousands of millions of years ago.

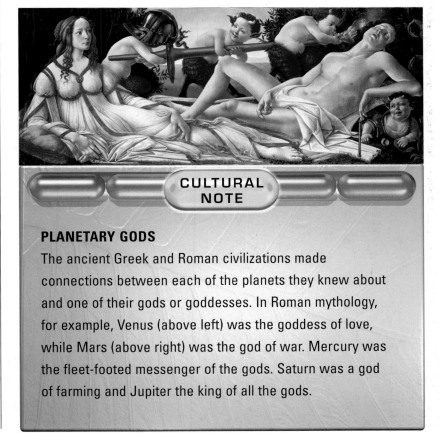

CULTURAL NOTE

PLANETARY GODS

The ancient Greek and Roman civilizations made connections between each of the planets they knew about and one of their gods or goddesses. In Roman mythology, for example, Venus (above left) was the goddess of love, while Mars (above right) was the god of war. Mercury was the fleet-footed messenger of the gods. Saturn was a god of farming and Jupiter the king of all the gods.

The giant planets

More than 580 million kilometres from Earth, the giant planets Jupiter, Saturn, Uranus and Neptune slowly orbit the Sun.

The giant planets have deep, cold atmospheres and each is orbited by a system of rings and many moons. Jupiter and Saturn often shine brightly in the night sky, but Uranus and Neptune are too faint to see.

THE GIANT PLANETS
The relative sizes of the giant planets are shown below.

Neptune

Uranus

Saturn

Jupiter

Neptune

Neptune is the most distant planet. It is also the coldest and windiest planet in the Solar System and has the longest year – 165 Earth years. Vast white clouds move rapidly across its blue atmosphere.

Saturn's moons

Saturn has dozens of moons. Most are simply lumps of icy rock, but the largest of the moons, Titan, has a thick atmosphere and tar-like lakes.

Saturn

This planet is so light for its size that it would float in water – if there were an ocean large enough to contain it. Like the other giant planets, it has an atmosphere rich in hydrogen and, at its heart, a rocky centre.

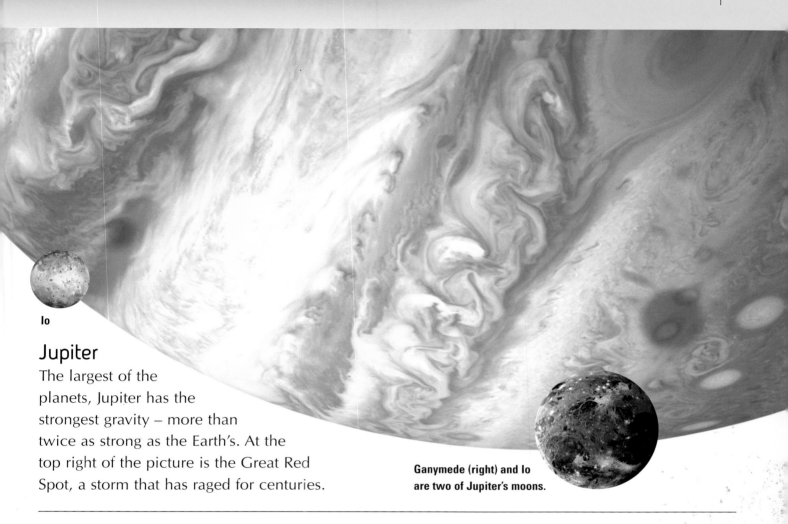

Io

Jupiter

The largest of the
planets, Jupiter has the
strongest gravity – more than
twice as strong as the Earth's. At the
top right of the picture is the Great Red
Spot, a storm that has raged for centuries.

**Ganymede (right) and Io
are two of Jupiter's moons.**

Uranus

Uranus has an atmosphere that
contains methane, which gives it
a blue-green colour. It spins on its
side, the result of a collision with
another planet millions of years ago.
Because of this, night on Uranus
can last more than 40 Earth years.

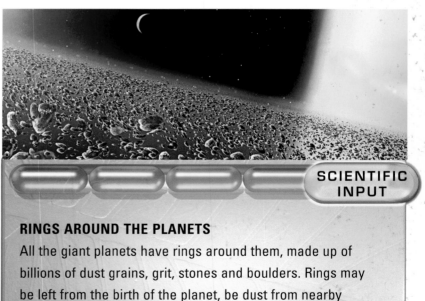

**SCIENTIFIC
INPUT**

RINGS AROUND THE PLANETS

All the giant planets have rings around them, made up of
billions of dust grains, grit, stones and boulders. Rings may
be left from the birth of the planet, be dust from nearby
moons, or the fragments of moons or comets that came
too close and were torn apart by the strong gravity.

SPACE RUBBLE

It is not only the planets that orbit the Sun. There are billions of other objects too, from tiny grains of dust to lumps of rock more than 2,000km across. Most of this material cannot be seen from Earth.

Sun

Mercury

Venus

Earth

Mars

Jupiter

Saturn

COMET

Comets are lumps of ice and grit that sweep towards the Sun on long orbits. As the sunlight warms them, twin tails of dust and gas form.

ASTEROID BELT

Asteroids are lumps of rock and metal left over after the planets formed. Some are 200km across. Most orbit between Mars and Jupiter.

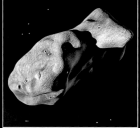

The Kuiper Belt contains lumps of ice and other frozen materials called KBOs (Kuiper Belt Objects). Many of these objects are more than 100km across.

The Oort Cloud is spherical, or rounded. The asteroid belt, the Kuiper Belt, and the orbits of the planets are all flat.

Neptune

Uranus

PLUTO AND CHARON

Pluto is a dwarf planet – a small, round world that orbits the Sun. Charon is the largest of its three known moons. The other two moons were first seen in 2005.

COMETARY NUCLEUS

Comets come from the outermost part of the Solar System. There, they make up the Oort Cloud. The cometary nucleus is the central part at the head of a comet.

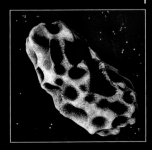

Satellites and space stations

Any object that orbits another in space is called a satellite. The Earth has one natural satellite, the Moon, and thousands of artificial ones.

The first artificial satellite, Sputnik 1, was launched from the USSR and went into orbit in 1957. Its radio beep was heard all over the world and marked the beginning of the space age.

Types of satellite

The satellite above is called Telstar, and was launched in 1962. It relayed TV and radio signals from one part of the Earth to another. Today, satellites are used for many different activities, including spying, weather monitoring, space research and navigation.

Space stations

A satellite which is designed to take people on board is called a space station. The first space station was the Soviet Salyut 1, launched in 1961. Another Soviet space station, Mir (below), was used by both US and Russian astronauts. The American space shuttles could dock with and transfer crew to and from Mir.

Orbits

A satellite – or any object – with the correct speed and direction will continue to orbit a planet or other large body in space without the need to use engines. Orbits can be either circular or elliptical (oval) in shape.

Astronauts at work on the International Space Station

International Space Station

The International Space Station (ISS) is being built by 16 countries, more than 300km above the Earth. It has had astronauts, including several space tourists, on board since 2000. When it is finished, it will be about the size of a football pitch.

Space exploration

Space travel is one of our greatest achievements. It has many practical benefits, but is driven by our urge to reach and study unknown worlds.

To escape Earth's gravity, survive in space and return safely home requires some of the most complex and powerful technology that people can build.

Rockets and spaceflight

To leave the Earth, all spacecraft use powerful rockets. Burning gases rush out of a rocket, pushing the spacecraft in the opposite direction. Smaller rockets are used to change course.

HISTORICAL DATA

THE FIRST HUMAN IN SPACE

Yuri Gagarin became the first cosmonaut (the Soviet term for an astronaut) on 12 April 1961. The first person to travel into space, he orbited the Earth once in Swallow, his Vostok 1 spaceship. He returned to Earth after 108 minutes in space.

Space shuttles

Space shuttles are American spacecraft designed to take off like rockets but land like planes. They have been used to launch satellites and to travel to the ISS. The first shuttle blasted into space in 1981, and the last shuttle mission was completed in July 2011, marking the end of the programme.

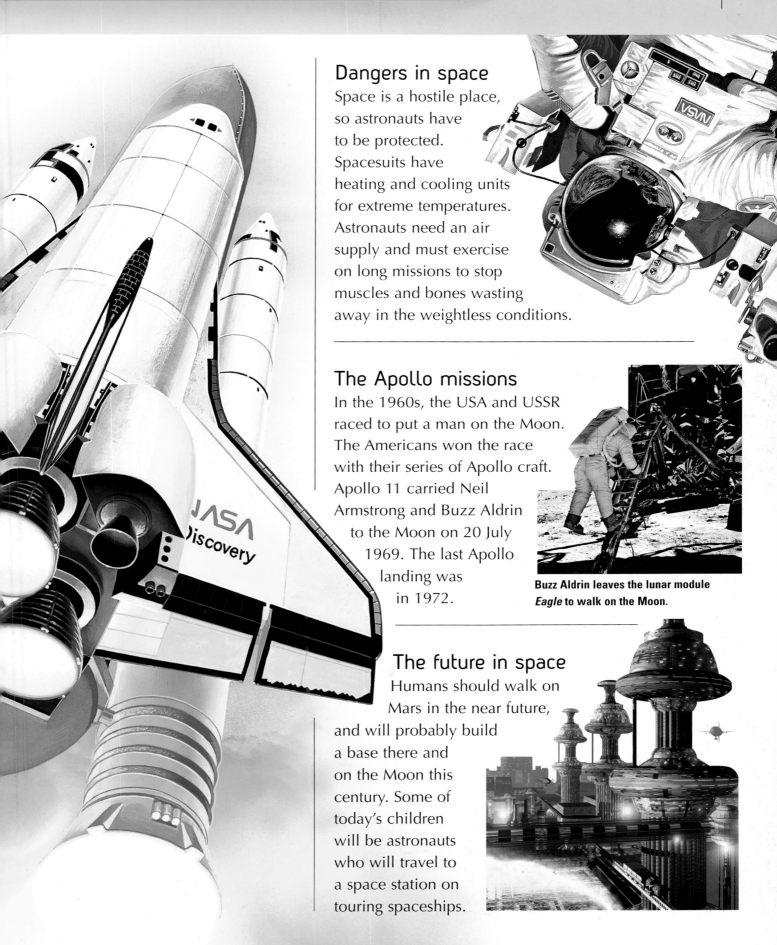

Dangers in space

Space is a hostile place, so astronauts have to be protected. Spacesuits have heating and cooling units for extreme temperatures. Astronauts need an air supply and must exercise on long missions to stop muscles and bones wasting away in the weightless conditions.

The Apollo missions

In the 1960s, the USA and USSR raced to put a man on the Moon. The Americans won the race with their series of Apollo craft. Apollo 11 carried Neil Armstrong and Buzz Aldrin to the Moon on 20 July 1969. The last Apollo landing was in 1972.

Buzz Aldrin leaves the lunar module *Eagle* **to walk on the Moon.**

The future in space

Humans should walk on Mars in the near future, and will probably build a base there and on the Moon this century. Some of today's children will be astronauts who will travel to a space station on touring spaceships.

Space robots

Humans have travelled only as far as the Moon. Robots have explored all of the Solar System's planets, and voyaged even deeper into space.

Some robots are probes that fly past or crash onto other worlds, but more advanced ones can land safely, and sometimes move around.

Mariner 10 travels towards Venus

Robot Moon probes

The Moon was the first destination for robot probes and it was in 1959 that an orbiting robot probe sent back the first images of the far side of the Moon.

Probes to Mercury and Venus

Mercury was visited by Mariner 10 in 1974–75, and is currently being studied by the Messenger probe. The hostile atmosphere of Venus has destroyed all the probes that have landed there, but a few have managed to send signals back to Earth first.

Robots on Mars

Many robots have been sent to Mars, mostly to search for signs of life or water. Advanced rovers such as this Exomars (left) have intelligence built in which allows them to make simple decisions for themselves.

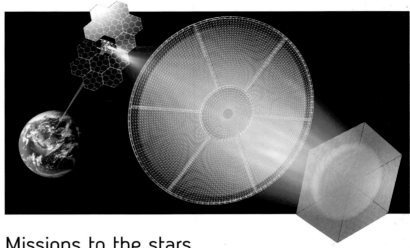

Probing asteroids and comets

Ten asteroids and four comets have been visited by probes. In 2004, a robot probe called Stardust collected samples from comet Wild 2, and returned them to Earth in 2006.

Missions to the stars

There are plans to use a powerful microwave beam to push a probe that weighs only a few grams. This would accelerate it to an enormous speed, and allow it to reach the nearest star in outer space in only a few decades.

Fly-by missions

These missions send space probes past planets to take photos and measurements. In the 1970s and 80s, the Pioneer and Voyager probes flew past the four 'gas giant' planets. The Voyager probes are now beyond the furthest planet and still going. Some fly-by probes use the gravity of the planets to increase their speed.

SCIENTIFIC INPUT

SPEED OF A SPACE PROBE

The Voyager probes are travelling at more than 12km a second, but even so they will not approach any stars for more than 40,000 years. Scientists are puzzled because the probes are not moving as predicted. This may be because of an unknown force. This artist's picture shows Voyager 2 approaching the planet Uranus on 24 January 1986.

Stars and star dust

Most of the points of light in the night sky are stars, which are vast balls of glowing gas. Many of them are bigger and brighter than the Sun.

LIFE CYCLE OF A STAR
Stages in the life of a star much more massive than the Sun.

1

A star is born in a huge, dark cloud.

2

The star shines for millions of years.

3

When out of fuel, it explodes as a supernova.

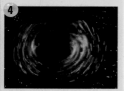

4

The dead core becomes a black hole.

Usually, the more massive a star is, the shorter its life. The most massive stars shine for only a few million years.

Red giants and white dwarfs

When stars like the Sun run out of fuel, they swell and redden, turning into red giants. The outer layers of red giants drift, spread and thin out, leaving behind them a hot core called a white dwarf. This is a group of white dwarfs.

Giants and supergiants

When stars approach the end of their lives, they swell into giants (10 to 100 times brighter than the Sun) or supergiants (10,000 to 100,000 times brighter). This is Betelgeuse, a supergiant in Orion.

Variable stars

Many stars are called variables because they change in brightness or colour, either gradually or suddenly. The variable star in the centre of this dust cloud gave off a sudden short flash of light only a few years ago.

Neutron stars and pulsars

A neutron star is a type of dead star that has been crushed by its own gravity. Some spinning neutron stars, called pulsars, send beams of radiation through space. When these beams sweep across the Earth, the beam can be detected as a pulse of radio waves.

Star dust

The space between stars (the interstellar medium or ISM) is not empty. The cloudy shapes in the image above are vast clouds of cosmic dust, thrown off by ageing stars. One per cent of the ISM in our galaxy is dust, the rest is gas.

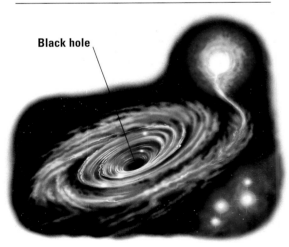

Black hole

Black holes

The more massive a star is, the more it shrinks when it dies, and the stronger its gravity becomes. The most massive stars become black holes, crushed so small that their gravity pulls in everything near them. Even light cannot escape.

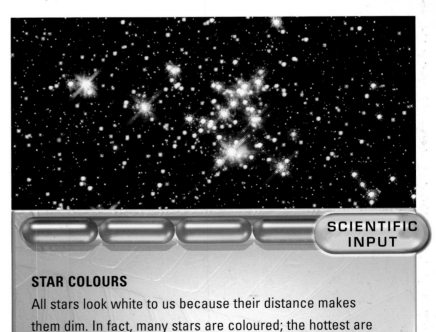

SCIENTIFIC INPUT

STAR COLOURS

All stars look white to us because their distance makes them dim. In fact, many stars are coloured; the hottest are blue-white. Stars a little cooler than the Sun are yellow and even cooler ones are orange or red. Some stars also look red because their light shines through dust clouds.

CONSTELLATIONS

On a clear, dark, moonless night it is possible to see about 2,000 stars in the sky. People have identified the patterns and shapes that they make and called them 'constellations'.

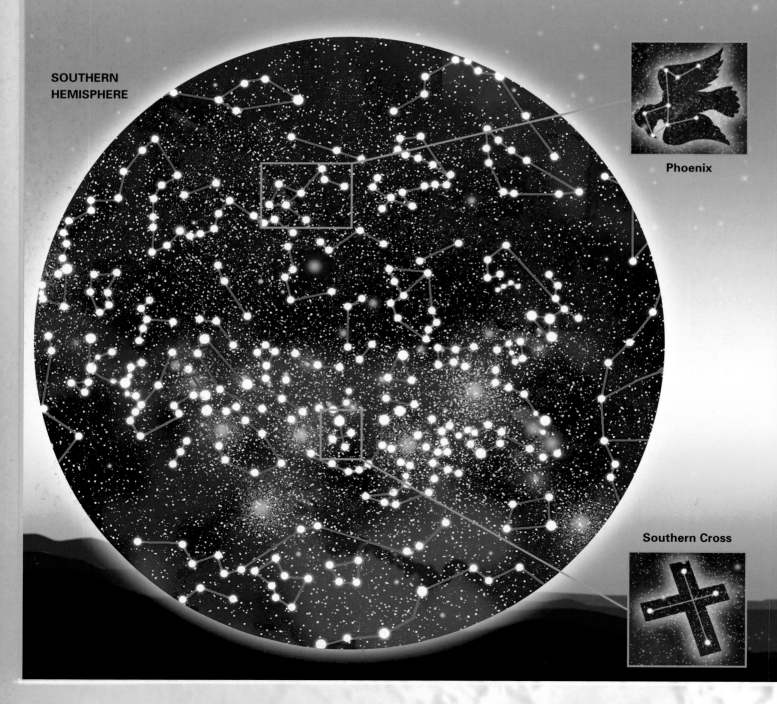

SOUTHERN
HEMISPHERE

Phoenix

Southern Cross

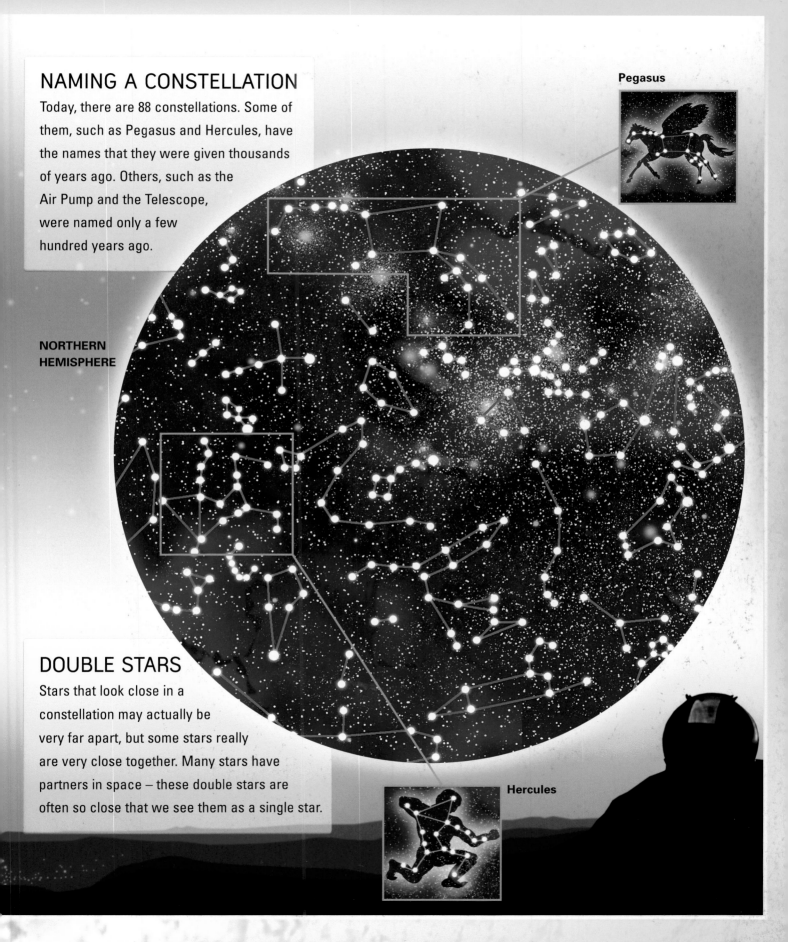

NAMING A CONSTELLATION

Today, there are 88 constellations. Some of them, such as Pegasus and Hercules, have the names that they were given thousands of years ago. Others, such as the Air Pump and the Telescope, were named only a few hundred years ago.

NORTHERN HEMISPHERE

Pegasus

DOUBLE STARS

Stars that look close in a constellation may actually be very far apart, but some stars really are very close together. Many stars have partners in space — these double stars are often so close that we see them as a single star.

Hercules

Space clouds

When people first used telescopes to look at the night sky, they saw many fuzzy shapes there. They called these shapes 'nebulae', which is Latin for 'clouds'.

TYPES OF GALAXY

Galaxies are classified by their shape. The Milky Way galaxy is a barred spiral galaxy.

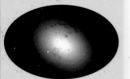

Elliptical galaxies are round or oval, and contain mostly old stars.

Spiral galaxies have arms where many new stars are born.

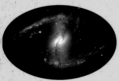

Barred spiral galaxies include a central bar shape made of stars.

Irregular galaxies are many different shapes and sizes.

There are many kinds of nebulae. Some are formed of billions of distant stars (these are usually called galaxies), while others – much closer to Earth – are glowing masses of gas, or dark sooty clouds.

The Milky Way galaxy

The Sun is grouped with at least 100 billion other stars to form a galaxy called the Milky Way. We see nearby stars as separate dots in the sky, but more distant stars in our galaxy merge together into a hazy band of light.

Other galaxies

Most stars in the Universe are gathered into galaxies, and there are more than 100 billion of these stretching through space. The largest of the galaxies contain millions of millions of stars.

Types of nebulae

Emission nebulae shine with light of their own, while reflection nebulae are lit up by nearby stars. Planetary nebulae are balls of hot gas from dying stars, and supernova remnants are glowing remains of dead stars.

The Orion nebula

This nebula is one of the easiest to see from Earth. It is a region of space where new stars are being born. In this part of the nebula, a young star called LL Orionis is causing ripples and waves in the gas clouds that swirl around it.

THE UNIVERSE

EVERYTHING THAT EXISTS — OR EVER HAS OR EVER WILL — IS PART OF THE UNIVERSE. THE UNIVERSE IS AN UNIMAGINABLY VAST, ENDLESS SPACE, BUT MOST OF THIS SPACE IS ACTUALLY EMPTY.

THE EXPANDING UNIVERSE

In the 1920s, astronomers were amazed to discover that the galaxies are all rushing away from each other. They also found out that the further apart the galaxies are, the faster they go. The astronomers realized that this meant that the whole Universe is expanding.

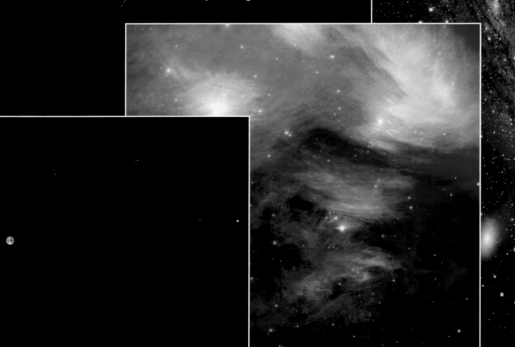

The Solar System
The 384,400km (1.2 light seconds) distance from the Earth (left) to the Moon (right) is tiny compared to the scale of the Universe in the next four images.

Local stars – the Pleiades
In our part of the Universe, most stars are a few light years (a few tens of thousands of billions of kilometres) apart.

Galaxies – Andomeda
Galaxies such as Andromeda contain around a million million stars and are a few hundreds of thousands of light years across.

THE BIG BANG

The expansion of the Universe has been going on since it began in a sudden burst of energy called the Big Bang, 13.7 billion years ago. The faint, remaining warmth of the Big Bang can still be measured.

THE END OF THE UNIVERSE

No one is certain how the Universe will end, but it is most likely that it will go on expanding and cooling forever. All the stars will slowly burn out, until the Universe is completely cold and dark.

Clusters – Capricorn
Galaxies form clusters like this small one in Capricorn. Our own Milky Way galaxy is part of a cluster called the Local Group.

Distant galaxies
These are some of the most distant galaxies we can see, using pictures taken by the Hubble space telescope. They are billions of light years away.

Life elsewhere

Are we alone in the Universe? Looking for an answer to this question is one of the biggest projects in astronomy today.

The search for life elsewhere is being carried out in many ways. While space robots search for life in the sands of Mars, powerful signals are on their way to the stars, and radio telescopes listen for messages from alien civilizations.

The original pattern has been coloured here to show the different parts of the message.

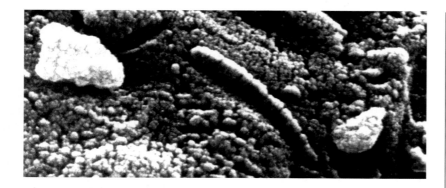

Is there life on Mars?
In 1984, a meteorite which came from Mars was found in Antarctica. In it, scientists found objects which look like bacteria, a very simple form of life. Many scientists now think that these structures were never alive.

Searching for life
This pattern was sent by radio into space in 1974, as a message to aliens. It includes the shape of a person and of the radio telescope that sent it, as well as a simple map of the Solar System.

Life near the giant planets
This is the frozen surface of Europa, one of the largest moons of Jupiter. Under these thick layers of ice, there is a sea 50km or more deep, that is warmed by the effects of Jupiter's gravity. It is thought that living creatures might exist there.

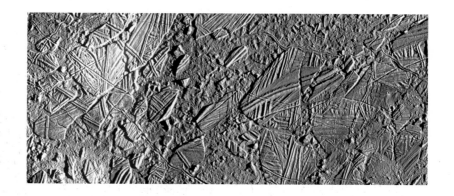

Signals from outer space

In 1977, a radio telescope in Ohio, USA, detected what is now known as the 'wow' signal. This signal was a sudden, powerful burst of radio waves from space that lasted for 72 seconds. It has not been detected again, and no natural cause for it has been discovered.

CULTURAL NOTE

SCIENCE-FICTION ALIENS

For many years, people have written books and made films about creatures from space – usually frightening and dangerous ones, unlike the friendly alien that appeared in the film *Men in Black* (above). The more unlike the Earth a planet is, the more different to us any intelligent creatures there are likely to be.

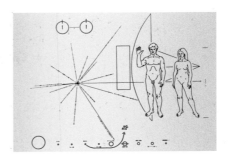

Postcard to an alien

This image was drawn on metal plates and sent into space on the Pioneer 10 and 11 space probes. It was intended to be a message that would be easy to interpret by any intelligent aliens who might find it.

Life at the extremes

Alien life might be like nothing we know on Earth. Floating creatures like these (below) may live in the clouds of giant planets, which are known to exist near many of the stars.

Astronomy

For thousands of years, people have gazed at the night sky. Their attempts to explain what they saw make astronomy a truly ancient science.

In 1609, Galileo made a telescope to study the stars. In 1687, Isaac Newton's mathematical laws of physics were published, explaining the motions of the Moon, planets and comets.

Telescopes

Optical telescopes gather light to make distant objects look both larger and brighter. Reflecting telescopes use a bowl-shaped mirror, while refractors use glass lenses.

Radio telescope

Many objects in space send out radio signals, and radio telescopes pick these up and make them stronger. The dish of a radio telescope reflects the signals to a concentrated point, like the mirror in a reflecting telescope.

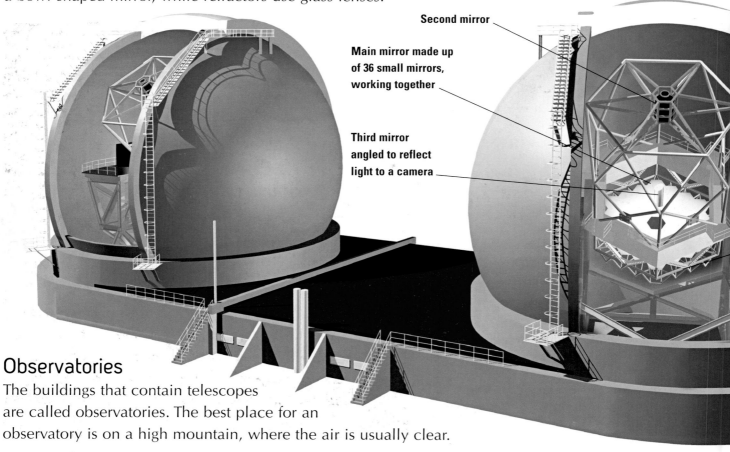

Second mirror

Main mirror made up of 36 small mirrors, working together

Third mirror angled to reflect light to a camera

Observatories

The buildings that contain telescopes are called observatories. The best place for an observatory is on a high mountain, where the air is usually clear.

Star gazing

Anyone can be an astronomer, and amateur astronomers do important work, such as finding new comets and studying variable stars. For all but the smallest telescopes, a tripod is essential to keep the image steady.

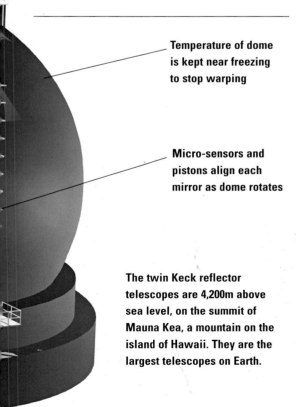

Temperature of dome is kept near freezing to stop warping

Micro-sensors and pistons align each mirror as dome rotates

The twin Keck reflector telescopes are 4,200m above sea level, on the summit of Mauna Kea, a mountain on the island of Hawaii. They are the largest telescopes on Earth.

Space telescopes

Several space telescopes orbit above the Earth. There is no air or weather there to interrupt their view of the stars. Also, some types of radiation from stars can only be measured above the Earth, because the radiation is 'soaked up' by the planet's atmosphere before it can reach the ground.

Stars from long ago

Stars are very far away, so their light takes years to reach Earth. If a star is described as 100 light years away, that means its light takes a century to reach us, and that we see that star as it used to be, a century ago.

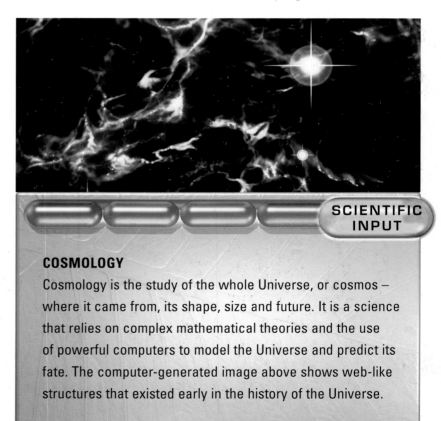

SCIENTIFIC INPUT

COSMOLOGY

Cosmology is the study of the whole Universe, or cosmos – where it came from, its shape, size and future. It is a science that relies on complex mathematical theories and the use of powerful computers to model the Universe and predict its fate. The computer-generated image above shows web-like structures that existed early in the history of the Universe.

Space facts

The distance between planets is given in astronomical units (AU), which are roughly equivalent to the distance from the Earth to the Sun. Light years are the distance travelled by light in one Earth year, or 9,460,730,472,580.8km.

PLANETS OF THE SOLAR SYSTEM
Mercury
Distance from Sun: 0.387 of Earth's
Radius: 0.382 of Earth's
Venus
Distance from Sun: 0.723 of Earth's
Radius: 0.949 of Earth's
Earth
Distance from Sun: 1 (149,597,871km)
Radius: 1 (6,371km)
Mars
Distance from Sun: 1.524 of Earth's
Radius: 0.532 of Earth's
Jupiter
Distance from Sun: 5.203 of Earth's
Radius: 11.19 of Earth's

Saturn
Distance from Sun: 9.555 of Earth's
Radius: 9.41 of Earth's
Uranus
Distance from Sun: 19.22 of Earth's
Radius: 3.98 of Earth's
Neptune
Distance from Sun: 30.11 of Earth's
Radius: 3.81 of Earth's

KEY SPACE MISSIONS
1957 Sputnik 1: first artificial satellite
1961 Vostok 1: Yuri Gagarin, first human in space and in orbit
1962 Mariner 2: first spaceship to Venus
1965 Mariner 4: first spaceship to Mars

1969 Apollo 11: Neil Armstrong and Buzz Aldrin, first humans on Moon
1971 Salyut 1: first space station
1973 Pioneer 10: first spaceship to Jupiter
1974 Mariner 10: first spaceship to Mercury
1979 Pioneer 11: first spaceship to Saturn
1981 Columbia shuttle: first re-usable spaceship
1986 Voyager 2: first spaceship to Uranus
1989 Voyager 2: first spaceship to Neptune
2000 First humans living in the International Space Station

Earthrise from the Moon

USEFUL WEBSITES

http://apod.nasa.gov/apod/ Discover the cosmos with the astronomy picture of the day.
www.kidsastronomy.com/ Astronomy and the Universe for kids of all ages.
www.bbc.co.uk/science/space/universe/exploration/ Past, present and future space exploration.
http://adc.gsfc.nasa.gov/adc/education/space_ex/index.html Space exploration website.

Natural World

Our planet is home to an incredible range of living things, from bacteria that can only be seen under a microscope to the enormous blue whale that is 33m long and can weigh more than 180 tonnes. More than 1.8 million species of plants and animals have been identified so far, but scientists estimate that up to 90 per cent more remain to be discovered.

Habitats and biomes

Plants and animals live in places, or habitats, that provide the food, water and protection they need to survive.

A biome is a large general habitat such as a rainforest or a hot desert. Each biome contains a number of different habitats that can support a variety of species.

Communities

Living things that exist in one habitat are a community. Many depend on each other. Plants in a pond habitat may add oxygen to the water which provides a place for insects and other creatures to lay their eggs. The plants and eggs provide food for fish and insects, which in turn may be food for birds.

Specialized habitats

Some living things require specific places to live. The giant panda's habitat is cool, wet, mountain forests in China where bamboo – which is 99 per cent of its diet – grows.

Biodiversity

Biodiversity describes the rich and varied forms of life on the planet. There are more than 1.8 million known species on Earth, but there may be millions more to discover.

In the sun

Some plants have evolved so they can obtain sunlight. Bladder wrack seaweed has air pockets that help it float on the surface.

Adaptation

Animals and plants have evolved to develop features that suit their habitat. This is called adaptation. Cactus plants in desert habitats have fleshy stems that swell so that they can store water. The elf owl, the smallest of all owls, uses this adaptation by making its nest in cacti in American deserts.

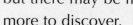

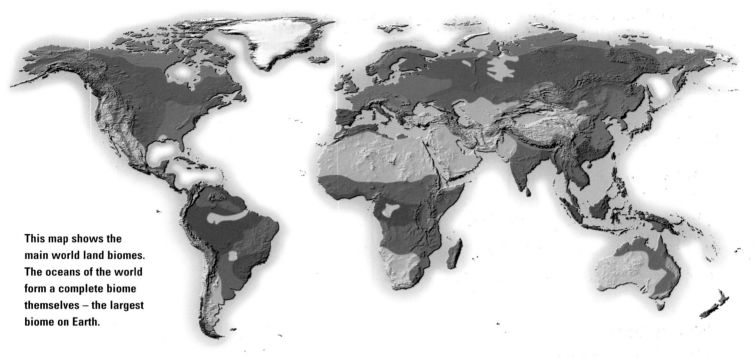

This map shows the main world land biomes. The oceans of the world form a complete biome themselves – the largest biome on Earth.

World biomes

Biomes are mostly shaped by climate because it influences what plants and animals can live in a region. Some creatures, such as human beings, have been able to adjust and adapt to thrive in many different biomes throughout the world.

Polar
Tundra
Coniferous forests
Desert
Tropical rainforest

Mediterranean scrub lands
Wetlands
Temperate woodland
Grassland and savannah
Mountains

Alpine biome

In the alpine or mountain biome, harsh winters and strong winds mean that only plants that lie close to the ground, such as mosses, lichens and purple saxifrage, can survive. Because of the cold climate, no reptiles live there, only warm-blooded vertebrates such as birds, mountain goats and the marmot (centre).

Two mountain ibex fight in their habitat in the alpine biome.

Ecosystems and cycles

An ecosystem is a complete community of living things together with their environment. It can be as large as a complete coral reef or as small as a single tree.

Nutrients and resources such as carbon, nitrogen and water help living things survive. They are used and re-used by nature in a continual exchange of the nutrients that is called a cycle.

A balanced system

No living thing exists on its own. Each is part of an ecosystem and has complicated relationships with other living things and with its habitat.

Herons eat fish.

Fish eat water beetles.

In a food chain, each level gets energy by feeding on the level below.

Water beetles eat tadpoles.

Tadpoles eat pondweed.

Pondweed uses energy from the Sun to grow.

Nitrogen cycle

Nitrogen is needed by all living things. It reaches the soil in rain, and in dead and rotting matter. Bacteria in the soil combines nitrogen with other substances to create nutrients which plants can absorb.

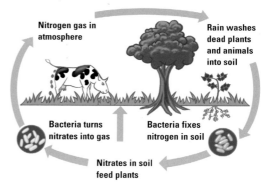

Nitrogen gas in atmosphere

Rain washes dead plants and animals into soil

Bacteria turns nitrates into gas

Bacteria fixes nitrogen in soil

Nitrates in soil feed plants

Food chains

A food chain is a way of showing how living things find food and then become food for others. The heron is the top predator in this simple food chain (left).

Epiphytic orchid

Symbiosis

Symbiosis is a relationship between two different species. This can benefit both – for example, the Egyptian plover bird gains food by cleaning the teeth of crocodiles.

Epiphytic plants, including some orchids, live on other plants in order to get greater access to sunlight.

Carbon cycle

Carbon is found in every living thing. Plants take in carbon dioxide from the atmosphere to help their growth. Animals eat plants, releasing carbon dioxide by breathing and also when they die and rot.

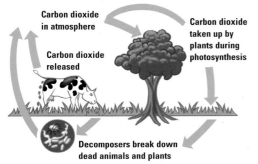

Carbon dioxide in atmosphere

Carbon dioxide taken up by plants during photosynthesis

Carbon dioxide released

Decomposers break down dead animals and plants

Producers and consumers

Plants are known as primary producers. They take sunlight and use it to help make food. Animals are consumers because they eat plants, other creatures or a mixture of plants and animals.

EARTH EVIDENCE

FUNGI

Fungi lack chlorophyll and do not make food by photosynthesis. Instead, they break down and digest the food outside their bodies before they absorb it. There are more than 70,000 known species of fungi including mushrooms, toadstools, yeasts and moulds. Fungi break down dead animals and plant matter, releasing chemicals and nutrients back into the soil.

CLIMATE ZONES

THE WEATHER PATTERN OF A REGION OVER A LONG PERIOD OF TIME IS CALLED ITS CLIMATE. CLIMATE ZONES ARE A WAY OF MAPPING THE VARYING MAJOR TYPES OF CLIMATES AROUND THE WORLD.

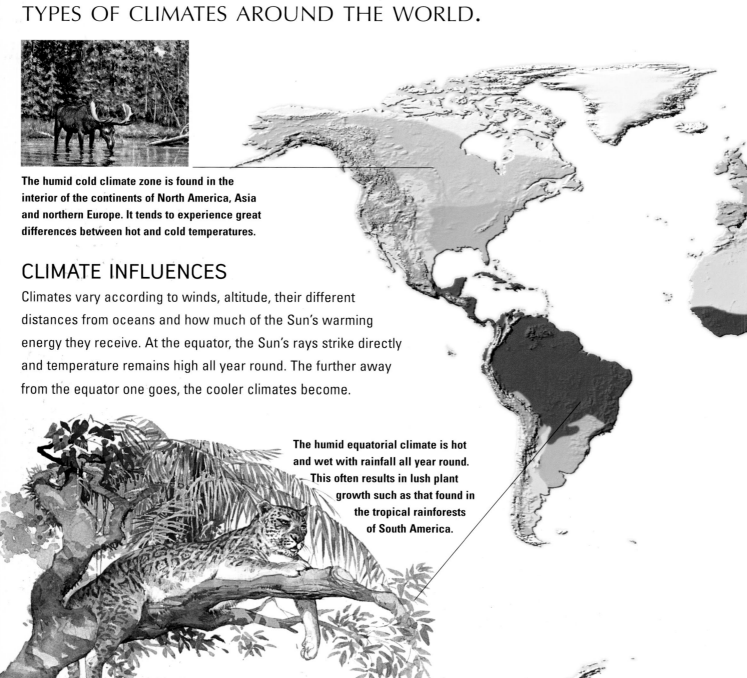

The humid cold climate zone is found in the interior of the continents of North America, Asia and northern Europe. It tends to experience great differences between hot and cold temperatures.

CLIMATE INFLUENCES

Climates vary according to winds, altitude, their different distances from oceans and how much of the Sun's warming energy they receive. At the equator, the Sun's rays strike directly and temperature remains high all year round. The further away from the equator one goes, the cooler climates become.

The humid equatorial climate is hot and wet with rainfall all year round. This often results in lush plant growth such as that found in the tropical rainforests of South America.

In a highland climate, it is colder on the mountains than on the lower ground surrounding them. The rain and snowfall levels are higher on the mountains.

KEY TO WORLD MAP

Polar

Highland

Arid and semi-arid

Humid equatorial

Temperate

Humid cold

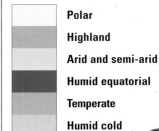

Arid and semi-arid climates have very little rainfall. They are dry and usually hot all year round, although some areas have cold winters. They often result in desert biomes. This frilly lizard lives in an arid climate zone in the desert interior of Australia.

Temperate climate zones can have rainfall all year round, for example in Europe. Or they can be warm and only have a short rainy season, as in the grasslands of the African savannah.

The polar climate around the northern and southernmost parts of the planet is very cold and dry. These penguins in Antarctica live in sub-zero temperatures for most of the year.

Weather

Weather describes the conditions in the atmosphere that affect an area, including temperature, rain, wind speed and the amount of sunshine.

The Sun heats the Earth's surface and also the atmosphere, creating winds and areas of high and low air pressure. These areas interact to form weather systems.

CLOUD TYPES
Clouds can be classified by their shape.

Cumulonimbus threaten thunderstorms.

Nimbostratus can bring rain or sleet.

Low-level cumulus can cover hilltops.

Cirrus are high-altitude wisps of cloud.

Cirrostratus are rippled and at a high altitude.

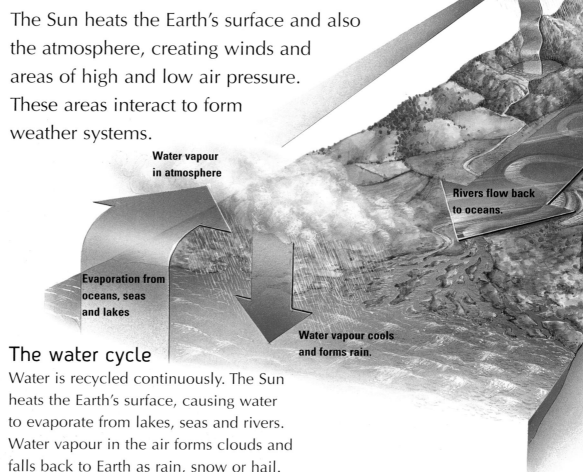

Transpiration from plants

Water vapour in atmosphere

Rivers flow back to oceans.

Evaporation from oceans, seas and lakes

Water vapour cools and forms rain.

The water cycle

Water is recycled continuously. The Sun heats the Earth's surface, causing water to evaporate from lakes, seas and rivers. Water vapour in the air forms clouds and falls back to Earth as rain, snow or hail.

Clouds and rainfall

Warm, moist air cools as it rises over high land or meets cooler air, forming clouds. When the cooled air can no longer support all the water it holds as vapour, rain falls. Sunlight shining on water droplets can form rainbows.

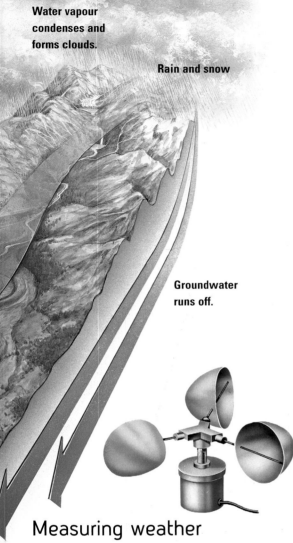

Water vapour condenses and forms clouds.

Rain and snow

Groundwater runs off.

Measuring weather

Weather details are measured and recorded using different instruments. These include thermometers and rain gauges. Anemometers (above) are used to measure wind speed.

Forecasting

Weather forecasting uses space satellites and computers to track the conditions in the atmosphere. Forecasters try to predict patterns of weather, although weather can be unpredictable and change quickly.

Snow and hail

Water droplets can freeze into ice crystals in clouds. The crystals join to form snowflakes, which fall in a snowstorm or are mixed with rain as sleet. Hailstones are balls of ice that fall mainly from storm clouds.

Humidity

The moisture in the air is called humidity. In general, the hotter the air, the more moisture it can hold. Humid conditions make animals feel sticky and hot, because sweat cannot evaporate quickly and easily.

EARTH EVIDENCE

GLOBAL WARMING

An increase in the average temperatures on Earth is called global warming. Many scientists believe that recent rises in temperature are due to deforestation (*see pp.30–31*) and the burning of fossil fuels. These release large quantities of gases such as carbon dioxide into the atmosphere, which trap more of the Sun's energy as heat and warm the planet.

WILD WEATHER

More than 1,500 thunderstorms happen around the world at any one time, and that is only one example of wild weather. Strong winds, lightning, heavy rain and snow can all cause havoc.

HURRICANES

Also known as typhoons or cyclones, hurricanes develop over tropical oceans. These giant windstorms often measure more than 600km in diameter and have winds of up to 200km/h. The middle of a hurricane is called the eye and is calm.

MONSOON RAINS

Monsoon is the name given to a wind which blows from one direction all winter and then another direction in summer. The most notable is the Asian monsoon which brings very heavy rains in the summer months (usually April to October). These often cause massive floods in Bangladesh, India and other parts of Asia.

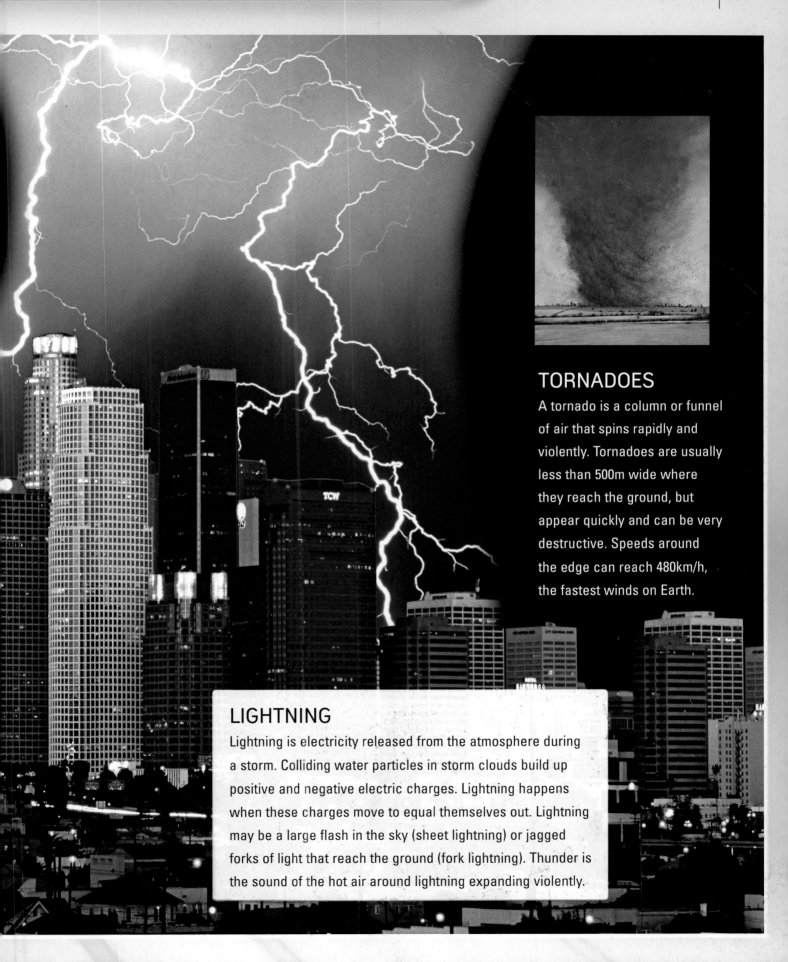

TORNADOES

A tornado is a column or funnel of air that spins rapidly and violently. Tornadoes are usually less than 500m wide where they reach the ground, but appear quickly and can be very destructive. Speeds around the edge can reach 480km/h, the fastest winds on Earth.

LIGHTNING

Lightning is electricity released from the atmosphere during a storm. Colliding water particles in storm clouds build up positive and negative electric charges. Lightning happens when these charges move to equal themselves out. Lightning may be a large flash in the sky (sheet lightning) or jagged forks of light that reach the ground (fork lightning). Thunder is the sound of the hot air around lightning expanding violently.

Plants

Apart from some bacteria and blue-green algae, plants are the only living things that can make their own food. There are more than 300,000 different species.

Plants are essential to other forms of life on Earth. They provide much of the planet's food and the oxygen found in the atmosphere.

Ferns are related to prehistoric vegetation that once covered the Earth.

Non-flowering plants

Non-flowering plants include mosses, liverworts, horsetails and over 10,000 species of ferns. Instead of roots, mosses and liverworts have thread-like anchors called rhizoids.

Roots

The roots of a plant are the part that is usually beneath the soil. Roots can collect water and nutrients from the soil through fine root hairs. They also help anchor the plant in place, and some plant roots can spread out a long distance underground.

The roots of this broad-leaved deciduous tree reach deep underground.

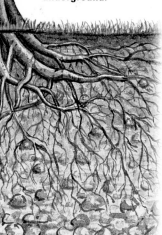

Photosynthesis

Plants make their food by a process called photosynthesis. A green pigment, chlorophyll, in the leaves absorbs energy from sunlight. This reacts with carbon dioxide gas (from the air) and water to create oxygen and carbohydrates such as glucose and starch. These are the plants' food.

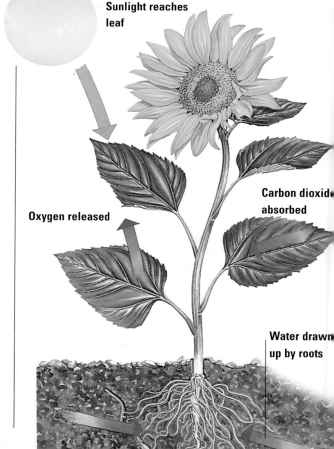

Sunlight reaches leaf

Oxygen released

Carbon dioxide absorbed

Water drawn up by roots

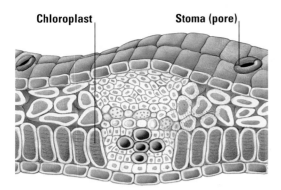

Chloroplast　　　**Stoma (pore)**

Anatomy of a leaf

Leaves vary in shape and size, but almost all have veins that carry water and food to and from the leaf. Leaves are packed with chloroplasts which contain chlorophyll. Gases pass in and out of tiny pores or holes in a leaf called stoma.

Stems

A stem supports the plant's leaves and flowers. They contain tubes called xylem and phloem. These transport water and food – nutrients – around the plant. In some plants, such as the cactus, food is made in the stem rather than the leaves.

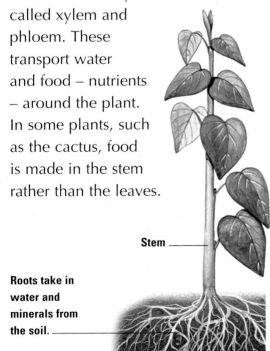

Stem

Roots take in water and minerals from the soil.

Storing nutrients

Some plants store nutrients such as starch in swollen growths for use during the growing season. They are usually underground, to protect them from plant-eating animals. Bulbs such as this onion have fleshy leaves wrapped together. Tubers such as the potato are solid.

AMAZING FACTS

FLESH-EATING PLANTS

Some plants that exist in areas with poor soil are carnivorous, gaining some or most of their nutrients from eating insects. Among the most famous is this Venus flytrap. A dragonfly, attracted to the plant, touches tiny trigger hairs on the leaf. In a tenth of a second, the leaf snaps shut around its prey. The spines stop it escaping as chemicals start to digest the insect.

PLANT REPRODUCTION

REPRODUCTION IS THE WAY NEW PLANTS ARE CREATED. MANY PLANTS HAVE FLOWERS THAT CONTAIN THEIR SEX CELLS AND ORGANS. THESE PRODUCE A SEED WHICH CAN GROW INTO A NEW PLANT.

NO SEEDS OR FLOWERS

Mosses and ferns reproduce with tiny spores instead of seeds. Ferns produce spores on the undersides of their fronds (feathery leaves). Sometimes a new plant is produced without either a seed or spore. The strawberry plant produces long stems called runners that can grow into the soil and form a new plant. However, strawberries also produce seeds, so they can reproduce in two different ways.

FLOWERING PLANTS

Most plants produce flowers containing separate male and female sex cells. Male sex cells are called pollen and the process of them joining with female sex cells is called pollination. Some plants pollinate themselves, but most rely on their pollen being carried to another plant before a new plant can be formed.

An Australian birdwing butterfly sips nectar from a flower. Its legs are coated in pollen. When it lands on a different plant, it may pollinate it.

The pollen sticking to this bee's body will rub off in the next flower the bee visits.

The poppy plant has bright red flowers. In the centre is the nectar that bees collect and use to make honey.

Pollen sac where bee stores pollen to take back to the hive for food.

POLLEN DISPERSAL

Flowering plants need outside help to move pollen. Wind disperses the pollen of plants such as grasses, while some aquatic plants rely on water to carry their pollen. Other plants have bright flowers and a sweet food, nectar, to attract insects or birds.

Pollen sticks to the feathers of this hummingbird as it uses its long bill to drink nectar.

Seeds and growing

Plants produce seeds that contain food stores and the makings of a new plant. Most seeds are inside fruits. The seeds of conifers are found on the surfaces of cones.

TYPES OF SEED
Fruits contain different numbers of seeds – from one to dozens.

Tomato

Fig

Melon

Avocado

Horse chestnut (conker)

Seeds need to move away from the parent plant to find their own space in the soil in order to grow. This movement is called dispersal.

Seeds

Seeds form after a plant is pollinated. They usually have a hard outer coating. Inside, there is a store of food that they use when they start to germinate or grow into a plant. The largest seed, of the coco de mer palm, weighs over 20kg.

Apple seed

Fruits

Fruits contain seeds. The fruits can be dry like pea pods, hard like acorns, or juicy like cherries and tomatoes. The seed inside these coffee berries (below) is the bean used to make coffee.

Coffee berry

Plant growth

Plants grow throughout their lives. Some grow rapidly – bamboo can grow 30cm in a single day. As plants develop, they grow from their root and shoot tips. The roots grow downwards towards moisture in the soil. Above ground, the plant usually grows upwards, although it will also bend its stems and grow towards sunlight – a process called phototropism.

Seed dispersal

Plants disperse their seeds in different ways. Some have fruits with hooks or burrs that catch on an animal's coat. Some seeds are eaten and carried away. Many seeds are carried by the wind. Others, such as this cucumber, explode, forcing out the seeds.

The squirting cucumber shoots out its seeds in a jet of liquid.

Germination

In soil, a seed germinates when the soil, water and temperature conditions are right. It splits and a root is formed that then drives downwards. A shoot heads upwards out of the soil and produces the first leaves.

1. Root grows down

2. Seed case splits

3. Seedling produces first leaves

Annuals and perennials

An annual plant germinates from seed, then grows, flowers, produces a seed and dies within a year. Perennial plants live longer. Their leaves and stem may die down but the roots survive. The plant will then flower again the following year.

Trees and forests

Trees are large plants which have solid, woody stems called trunks and can grow for many years. Forests of trees cover approximately 30 per cent of the land on Earth.

Trees are essential to the life of the planet because they release large amounts of oxygen into the air, create important habitats and help protect soil from erosion.

Tree anatomy
Trees have leaves, branches, roots and a stem. The outside of the woody stem is covered in bark. This tough, waterproof layer protects the living, growing sapwood inside.

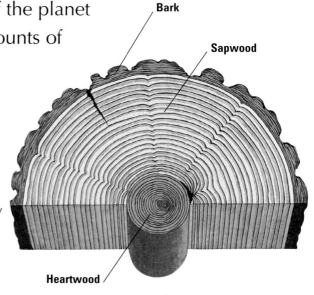

Bark

Sapwood

Heartwood

Deciduous trees
These trees include the oak, horse chestnut, elm and sycamore. They all bear flowers and have fruit which houses their seeds. In cooler climates, they shed their broad leaves in autumn to preserve food and water.

Coniferous trees
These trees have thin, needle-like leaves that they shed and re-grow all year round, so they are evergreen in winter. Their waxy leaves lose little water. This allows conifers such as pines to grow in cold regions.

Forest resources

Forests provide rich habitats. For humans, there is shelter, fuel, fruits and nuts to eat, and materials for building. Trunks of rubber trees can be tapped (above) to release a sticky liquid that forms natural rubber.

Temperate forests

Forests in temperate climates have mainly deciduous trees. In autumn, the leaves are drained of their chlorophyll, and turn different shades of red, yellow and brown.

AMAZING FACTS

RECORD-BREAKING TREE

The giant sequoia is a huge coniferous tree found in scattered clumps called groves in California, USA. The tallest grow up to 93m high, have trunks nearly 9m in diameter and can weigh over 6,000 tonnes. The oldest trees are about 3,200 years old, and a single mature tree disperses 300,000 seeds every year.

The taiga

The taiga or boreal forest is a broad band of coniferous forest that extends around the north below the tundra. Larger predators such as wolves hunt down moose and deer there.

RAINFOREST

RAINFORESTS ARE LUSH AREAS OF DENSELY PACKED TREES AND PLANTS FOUND IN WARM, WET REGIONS — TROPICAL RAINFORESTS — OR IN MILDER AREAS — TEMPERATE RAINFORESTS.

LIFE AT ALL LEVELS

Rainforests cover less than one-tenth of the Earth's land, but provide homes for millions of living things. Scientists estimate that between 60 and 90 per cent of all plant and animal species on Earth are found in rainforests. They exist at all levels — from the rodents, crabs, snakes and insects on the forest floor to the birds, bats, frogs, monkeys and other creatures high in the trees.

Tropical rainforests are found in warm areas that have very heavy rainfall (at least 200–1000cm per year). South and Central America are home to more than half of the world's tropical rainforests. Other major tropical rainforests are found in southeast Asia, parts of Africa and on islands in the Pacific Ocean.

Emergent trees poke out above the canopy.

The canopy is home to many birds, monkeys and other animals.

The understorey is made up of trees and vines able to grow in shady conditions.

The forest floor is damp and dark.

A rainforest has four layers: emergents, the canopy, the understorey and the forest floor. The canopy is formed by the tops of thousands of trees which interlock. They receive most of the forest's sunlight.

Hot and cold deserts

Deserts cover around a quarter of the world's land and are the driest places on the planet. They are regions of the world where rainfall is less than 250mm per year.

Deserts are not always hot and sandy – cold deserts exist as well. Whether they are hot or cold, deserts are tough places for the hardy animals and plants that live in them.

Finding water

For plants in hot deserts, getting and storing water is crucial for survival. Some have long roots that travel deep underground to seek out moisture. Others, such as cacti, have fleshy stems that swell to store water, or collect water from fog like the welwitschia plant.

Desert creatures

Insects, reptiles and some smaller animals obtain all their water from eating desert plants or seeking out waterholes or oases. In hot deserts, many live underground in burrows away from the searing heat. Many are nocturnal – sleeping during the day but active at night.

Barrel cactus

Pincushion cactus

Saguaro cactus

Welwitschia

Prickly pear

Barrel cactus

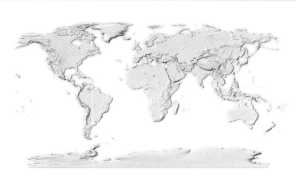

Desert regions

This map shows where the world's deserts are found. Hot deserts are on all continents except temperate Europe and frozen Antarctica. The largest desert is the Sahara, which covers much of North Africa. It is almost the size of the United States and is growing each year.

The Arctic

The area called the Arctic circles the North Pole and includes the Arctic Ocean. The ocean's high levels of fish provide food for Arctic peoples and some large mammals that include walruses and seals (above). Polar bears – the largest land meat-eaters on Earth – also live there.

Antarctica

Antarctica is a largely icy wasteland. Parts of the continent have less than 60mm of rain or snowfall each year. Average temperatures during the winter vary from –70°C to –20°C. Penguins survive due to the thick layers of fat and feathers that help insulate them from the extreme cold.

Tundra

The tundra makes up around 15 per cent of the planet's land. Only mosses, grasses and some small bushes and trees can survive its cold winter. In its short summer, plant life thrives, attracting millions of insects, birds and some plant-eating animals such as lemmings and caribou. The soil beneath the ground surface remains frozen all year.

OCEAN LIFE

THE PLANET'S SEAS AND OCEANS ARE FULL OF
AN EXTRAORDINARY VARIETY OF MARINE LIFE.
AROUND A QUARTER OF ALL THE KNOWN
SPECIES OF LIVING THINGS ON THE PLANET
ARE FOUND IN THE SEAS AND OCEANS.

OCEAN FOOD CHAINS

Microscopic ocean plants and animals known as plankton
provide food for millions of fish, molluscs such as clams, and
crustaceans including crabs and shrimp. These in turn provide
food for other fish and marine mammals such as seals and
walruses. Southern right whales (right) spend the summer
months feeding in the seas close to Antarctica.
They migrate north in winter to breed off
the coasts of South America, South
Africa and New Zealand.

SHALLOWS AND SEASHORES

While some creatures live in the ocean depths, most marine life exists much closer to the surface or in shallow water. Seashores, where a sea or ocean meets the land, provide homes in rock pools, beaches and cliff faces for many living things. Some animals have adapted to avoid being washed away by the tide. For example, clams dig deep in the sand and limpets attach themselves to rocks.

CORAL REEFS

Coral lives in warm, shallow waters and forms reefs that provide a rich habitat for many plants, fish and other creatures – it shelters more than a third of all marine life species. Coral is made up of animals called polyps. When they die, their hard skeletons help to form the reef. Australia's Great Barrier Reef is the world's largest coral reef and is 2,000km long.

Grasslands

Grasslands are biomes that feature gently rolling hills or flat land covered in grasses with some trees and bushes. These areas have distinct wet and dry seasons during the year.

Grasses and other plant life grows very quickly during the wet season. They provide plentiful food for rodents and birds, as well as large herds of grazing animals and their predators.

North American plains

The North American plains or prairies were once home to huge herds of bison. Today, much of the land has been cultivated. It supports large herds of cattle and sheep or is planted with cereal crops such as wheat and maize.

African savannah

Savannah grasslands in Africa are hot and dry, but the wet season prompts enough plant growth to support giant herds of antelopes, zebra, wildebeest and other grazing animals. The different animals graze in different ways and provide food for meat-eaters such as lions, cheetahs and hyenas. More than two million grazing animals follow the wet season, migrating every year in October into an area of Tanzania known as the Serengeti.

South American pampas

The pampas are large plains in South America that have rough grass or scrub and very few trees. They cover an area of 750,000km^2 – more than twice the size of Germany. They are home to many creatures including cavies (below), which are wild guinea pigs.

Australian grasslands

Australia's grasslands provide homes for vast numbers of insects, marsupials such as kangaroos, wallabies, koala and wombats, and birds such as the emu and kookaburra. The land is covered in tough grasses and clumps of trees that include wattle, eucalyptus and thorny acacia.

Antelopes on the Serengeti

Natural resources

The natural world has many useful resources. These include food, energy, materials and medicines used by people for thousands of years.

Natural resources vary from country to country. Saudi Arabia, for example, has a quarter of the world's known reserves of oil.

Food and farming

Farming is the rearing of livestock animals and growing of plant crops for food. Soil and climate help decide which crops are grown where. Maize (above) is the most common crop grown in North and South America.

Fishing

Around 200 million people work in the fishing industry. Most fish are caught in giant nets trailing from trawler ships. Fish and shellfish form a vital part of many people's diets.

Logging

Wood is one of the most useful and versatile of all the natural resources. The logging industry cuts down and transports trees. The wood is cut and processed to make many products. Wood fibres are used to make paper.

Materials for building

The natural world provides different materials for building. Many people live in huts made of bundled reeds (above), mud and grass, or clay bricks left to dry and harden.

Renewable resources

These can be restocked or renewed over time. Some living things, such as trees, are renewable, providing they are not used up at a faster rate than they can be replaced. Solar, wind and geothermal energy are also renewable resources.

Mining

Mining is the extraction of minerals from the Earth's crust. These include metals such as aluminium, copper and gold, gemstones and coal. Marble and limestone, used for building, are dug out in quarries (right).

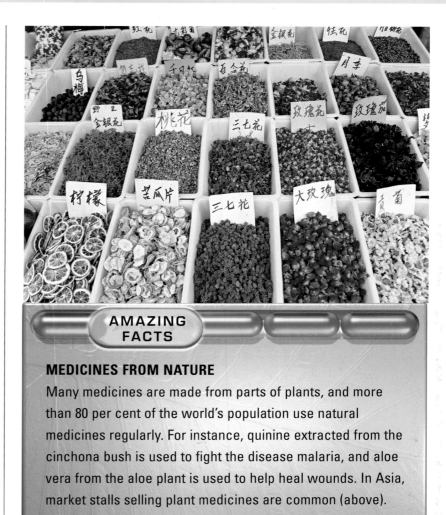

AMAZING FACTS

MEDICINES FROM NATURE

Many medicines are made from parts of plants, and more than 80 per cent of the world's population use natural medicines regularly. For instance, quinine extracted from the cinchona bush is used to fight the disease malaria, and aloe vera from the aloe plant is used to help heal wounds. In Asia, market stalls selling plant medicines are common (above).

Threats and conservation

Parts of the planet and many species of living things are under threat. This is mainly due to the growing numbers of people and high demand for the planet's natural resources.

Conservation is about protecting and looking after the natural world. Many schemes try to reduce threats to habitats and ecosystems, or look after threatened species.

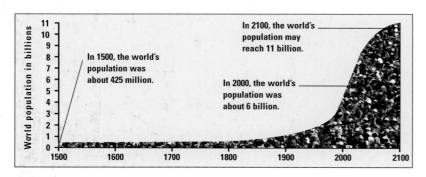

In 1500, the world's population was about 425 million.

In 2100, the world's population may reach 11 billion.

In 2000, the world's population was about 6 billion.

World population in billions

Population growth
The human population has boomed in the past 200 years. In just 40 years from 1950 to 1990 it doubled. Today, over 6.6 billion people live on Earth. And they all need food, water, shelter and many other goods and services.

Pollution
If harmful substances are released, they can pollute the environment. They sometimes damage habitats, kill living things, and can be very hard to clear up. Pollution includes litter on land, oil spills in water (above), or smoke from factories and car exhausts in the air.

Three Gorges Dam
The giant Three Gorges Dam in China generates electricity from running water. The 185m-high, 2.3km-long dam is controversial because a large area of land had to be flooded for the dam to work. The flooding destroyed wildlife habitats.

Land clearance

Thousands of square kilometres of forests and other open land are cleared every year. People do this for fuel or wood to sell, or to create farmland or space for settlements. This damages and destroys habitats for many animals and plants.

Endangered species

Over 4,000 different species of plants and animals including the tiger are now very rare and under threat of extinction. Hunting, the destruction of habitats and pollution are the main reasons for this.

National parks

Many countries have set aside protected areas of their land and water as national parks. The aim is to preserve the natural environment and the species that live there. Most national parks receive large numbers of visitors.

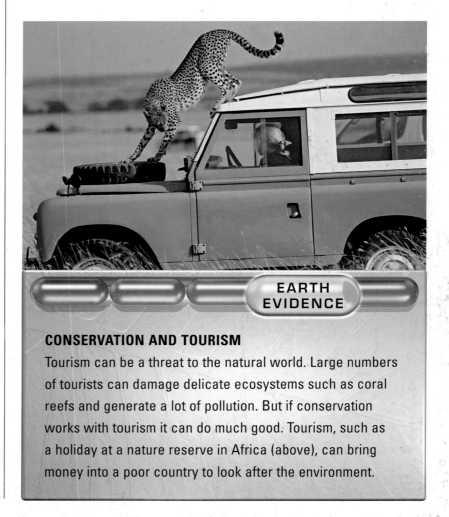

EARTH EVIDENCE

CONSERVATION AND TOURISM

Tourism can be a threat to the natural world. Large numbers of tourists can damage delicate ecosystems such as coral reefs and generate a lot of pollution. But if conservation works with tourism it can do much good. Tourism, such as a holiday at a nature reserve in Africa (above), can bring money into a poor country to look after the environment.

Natural world facts

Life on Earth varies enormously. The thousands of millions of living things live in a very large range of different habitats and conditions, from the hottest of deserts and rainforests, to warm seas, cold oceans and the frozen Antarctic.

LARGEST DESERTS
Sahara, northern Africa 9,100,000km²
Gobi, Mongolia/China 1,300,000km²
Patagonian, Argentina 670,000 km²
Rub' al Khali, Saudi Arabia/Yemen/
   Oman 650,000km²
Great Sandy, Australia 390,500km²
Great Victoria, Australia 390,500km²
Chihuahuan, Mexico/USA 360,000km²
Takla Makan, China 360,000km²
Sonoran, Mexico/USA 310,000km²
Kalahari, southern Africa 260,000km²

LARGEST FORESTED AREAS
Russian Federation 809 million hectares
Brazil 478 million hectares
Canada 310 million hectares

USA 303 million hectares
China 197 million hectares
Australia 164 million hectares
Democratic Republic of the Congo
   134 million hectares
Indonesia 88 million hectares
Peru 69 million hectares
India 68 million hectares

WEATHER RECORDS
Driest place on Earth: Calama,
   Atacama Desert, Chile, with zero
   annual average rainfall
Wettest place on Earth: La Réunion,
   Indian Ocean, 1,825mm in 24 hours
Coldest recorded temperature: Vostok
   Station, Antarctica, −89°C

Hottest recorded temperature: Al'
   Aziziyah, Libya, 58°C
Strongest wind (not a tornado): Mount
   Washington, New Hampshire, USA,
   372km/h

LARGEST PROTECTED AREAS
Northeast Greenland 972,000km²
Rub' al Khali, Saudi Arabia
   650,000km²
Great Barrier Reef, Australia 344,400km²
Papahanaumokuakea Marine National
   Monument, USA 341,362km²
Qiangtang, China 298,000 km²
Macquarie Island, Australia 162,060km²
Sanjiangyuan, China 152,300km²
Galápagos, Ecuador 133,000 km²

Sand dunes of the Sahara desert stretching to the horizon

USEFUL WEBSITES

www.mbgnet.net/ A good introduction to different biomes, plant life and reproduction.
www.cotf.edu/ete/modules/msese/earthsys.html A colourful website about planet Earth.
www.amnh.org/ology/?channel=biodiversity Describes biodiversity and its effects.
www.metoffice.gov.uk/education The UK Met Office site.

Animal Life

The range of animal life on our planet is amazing. There are animals big enough to crush us, and others too tiny to see without a microscope. All need to eat, and many spend much of their time trying not to be eaten. Human life is fairly new to this planet by comparison with many animals. But the biggest threat to many animals today comes from human activity.

What is an animal?

Animals are living things that eat plants and other creatures, and breathe oxygen. They can move and sense their surroundings.

Some animals spend most of their time alone, rarely seeing other creatures except to breed. Others live in social groups that can be huge – both humans and ants build settlements with millions of inhabitants.

Animal makeup

Animals have a lot in common with each other. Nearly all have brains, eyes, ears and legs. Animals are the only living things with muscles and nerves for movement and sensation.

Where animals live

The area where an animal lives is called its habitat. Habitats range from the top of a mountain to the ocean floor. Some animals, known as parasites, live on or inside other animals – for example, there are more than 1,000 types that can live inside humans. Animals are very adaptable and some can even survive being frozen solid or dried out.

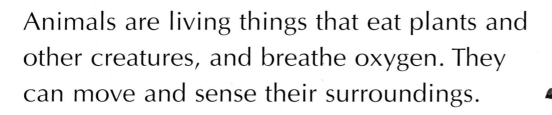

Orangutans live in the rainforests on the islands of Borneo and Sumatra.

Warm-blooded animals

Animals that are mammals are warm-blooded. They warm up or cool down to keep a constant body temperature. They may have fur to keep warm, or big ears to flap themselves cool. They may sweat to cool down and shiver to warm up.

Cold-blooded animals

Reptiles, amphibians and fish all control their temperature by moving between hot and cool places. They bask in the sun to warm up, for example, and are less active when it is cold. These animals are known as ectotherms, because their heat comes from outside the body. They all tend to move slowly until they begin to warm up.

Invertebrates

Today, 97 per cent of all animals are invertebrates. Like this sea anemone, invertebrates have no backbone and usually no bones at all. There are some, however, such as snails, that have a shell on the outside of their bodies, or a skeleton.

Vertebrates

These animals have a backbone, usually connecting to other bones to form an internal skeleton. Fish, amphibians, reptiles (below), birds and mammals are all in this group.

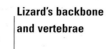

Lizard's backbone and vertebrae

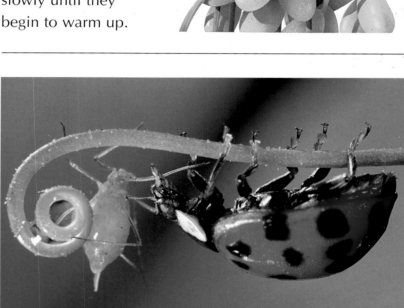

AMAZING FACTS

PREDATOR AND PREY

Animals that hunt other creatures for food are called predators. Some run faster than their prey, while others sneak up, lie in wait or make traps. They are equipped with weapons such as sharp teeth, claws or poison to kill or stun. Defensive animals have a range of avoidance methods such as speed, colour, spraying, hiding or stings. This ladybird (above) is advancing on its favourite food – a green aphid.

Evolution and extinction

Although about 30 million species are believed to live on Earth today, 4,500 million have existed since life began. So, nearly all are extinct – they have disappeared forever.

CHANGING OVER TIME
Horses changed greatly over 55 million years, as they adapted to different habitats, climates and roles.

Hyracotherium was dog-sized, with four toes.

Merychippus was twice as big, with three toes.

Equus, the modern horse, has only one toe.

Racehorses are bred for speed, not strength.

Each generation of living things can be slightly different from the last one. Over a long period, these small changes become big differences. This is evolution – animals constantly adapting.

Adapt or die
Often animals must adapt or die out. Many extinctions were the result of changes in sea level, temperature or climate, or the gradual movement of land masses.

The dodo was hunted to extinction in the 1600s.

Selective breeding
People have bred some animals to change their appearance, shape and nature. All dogs are descended from wolves but some have been bred to hunt, or to be sheepdogs or pets.

Natural selection
In his book *The Origin of Species* (1859), Charles Darwin showed how creatures have developed through 'natural selection'. They compete for resources such as food, shelter and mates. The weaker ones die, while the strong survivors slowly evolve over generations as they adjust to any changes in their environment.

Suiting new environments

Animals adapt to new environments. The brown bears who moved to the colder north became better hunters and fighters. They developed more fat layers for warmth, and paler fur for camouflage: they are now polar bears.

Convergent evolution

This is when entirely different species develop similar features. For example, anteaters, armadillos, aardvarks and echidnas all have sticky tongues to eat insects, but they are not closely related.

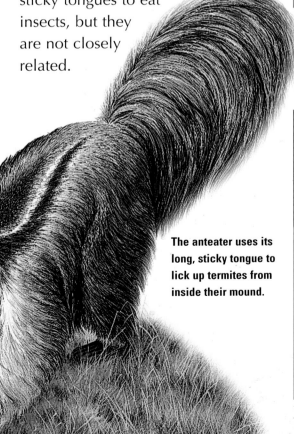

The anteater uses its long, sticky tongue to lick up termites from inside their mound.

Fossil evidence

We know about animals from millions of years ago because of fossils – animal remains stored in rock. A sea animal such as an ammonite (1), sinks when it dies. Sediment covers it (2), and it gradually hardens into rock (3). The fossilized shell can be preserved for millions of years (4).

EARTH EVIDENCE

END OF THE DINOSAURS

Dinosaurs died out 65 million years ago, having ruled the Earth for 160 million years. No one knows exactly why, but it seems the planet became much colder at this time. One idea is that a huge asteroid hit the Earth, raising so much dust it blocked out the Sun for months. This killed the plants dinosaurs fed on, which meant the carnivores had nothing to eat. The 'global winter' could also have been caused by volcanic eruptions.

CLASSIFYING NATURE

EVERYTHING THAT HAS EVER LIVED CAN BE GROUPED BY ITS CHARACTERISTICS, USING THE CLASSIFICATION SYSTEM DEVISED BY SWEDISH BOTANIST CAROLUS LINNAEUS IN THE 18TH CENTURY. THIS USES LATIN SO THAT EVERYONE USES THE SAME TERMS.

THE FOUR ERAS

The Precambrian era of life on Earth (purple) began 3.5 million years ago. The Palaeozoic (blue) saw a huge rise in creatures and the beginning of plants. It was followed by the Mesozoic period (green) – the age of reptiles. The Cenozoic (orange) is the age of mammals.

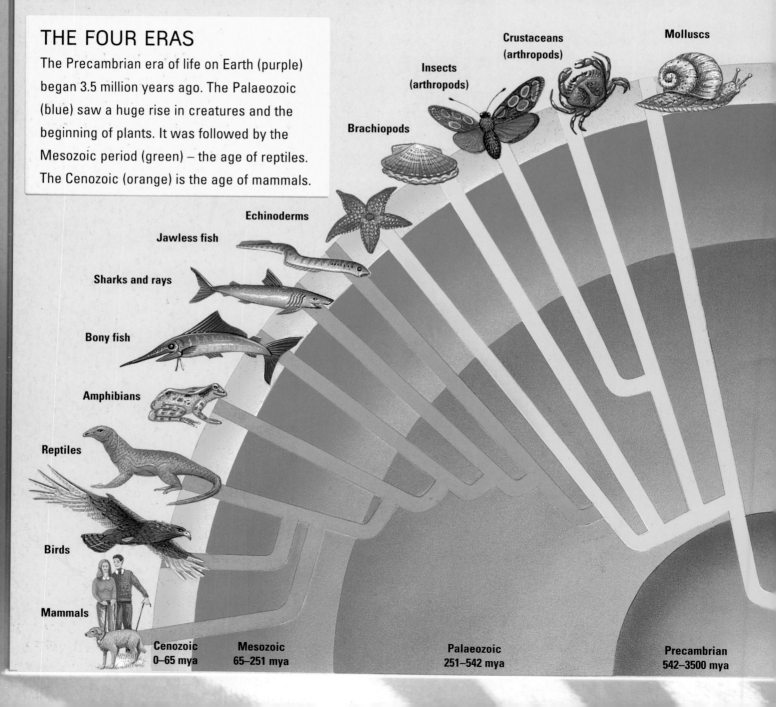

Molluscs

Crustaceans (arthropods)

Insects (arthropods)

Brachiopods

Echinoderms

Jawless fish

Sharks and rays

Bony fish

Amphibians

Reptiles

Birds

Mammals

| Cenozoic 0–65 mya | Mesozoic 65–251 mya | Palaeozoic 251–542 mya | Precambrian 542–3500 mya |

KINGDOMS

Living and once-living organisms are divided into groups called kingdoms, the largest of which are animals and plants. These are then divided into smaller groups, called phyla (*sing*. phylum). There are more than 20 phyla in the animal kingdom.

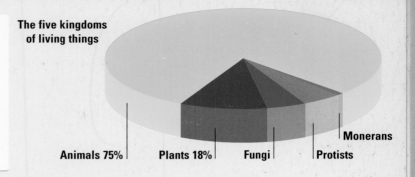

The five kingdoms of living things

Animals 75% | Plants 18% | Fungi | Protists | Monerans

CLASS, FAMILY AND SPECIES

Each phylum is divided by class, order, family, genus and species. For example, humans are in the phylum Chordata (with backbones), class Mammalia (animals with hair that produce milk), order Primates (refined hands and feet, and a large brain), family Hominidae (great apes), genus *Homo* (humans), and species *Sapiens* (thinking man).

Worms

Coelenterates

Single-celled organisms, sponges

Single-celled organisms

Bacteria

Fungi

Algae

Mosses

Ferns

Cycads

Conifers

Flowering plants

Precambrian
3500–542 mya

Palaeozoic
542–251 mya

Mesozoic
251–65 mya

Cenozoic
65–0 mya

How animal life developed

Life on Earth developed over billions of years, and began as tiny, single-celled creatures. All these early animals were invertebrates, with no bones, and lived in the sea.

Scientists believe that life began 3.5 billion years ago when chemicals containing carbon were mixed by chance. They combined to become living things.

First life

The first single-celled organisms were bacteria and amoeba. They floated in the warm, nutrient-rich sea, surviving either by eating tiny particles, or making their own food from sunlight. They still exist all over the world today.

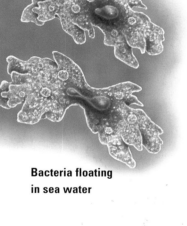

Bacteria floating in sea water

Sponges collect food by pumping water through their bodies.

Worms

The first worms were flat and small, and many lived inside other animals as parasites. Slowly, they developed thin, round bodies that were like a protective tube. The next stage of evolution was a segmented body that made burrowing into mud easier.

Worms are invertebrates.

Multi-celled creatures

About a billion years ago, more complex, multi-celled creatures evolved. Early ones, such as sponges, are groups of cells that can live separately or together, can become very large, but cannot move themselves about. Later ones, such as jellyfish and sea anemones, are far more complicated. For instance, they can hunt or protect themselves by stinging other creatures.

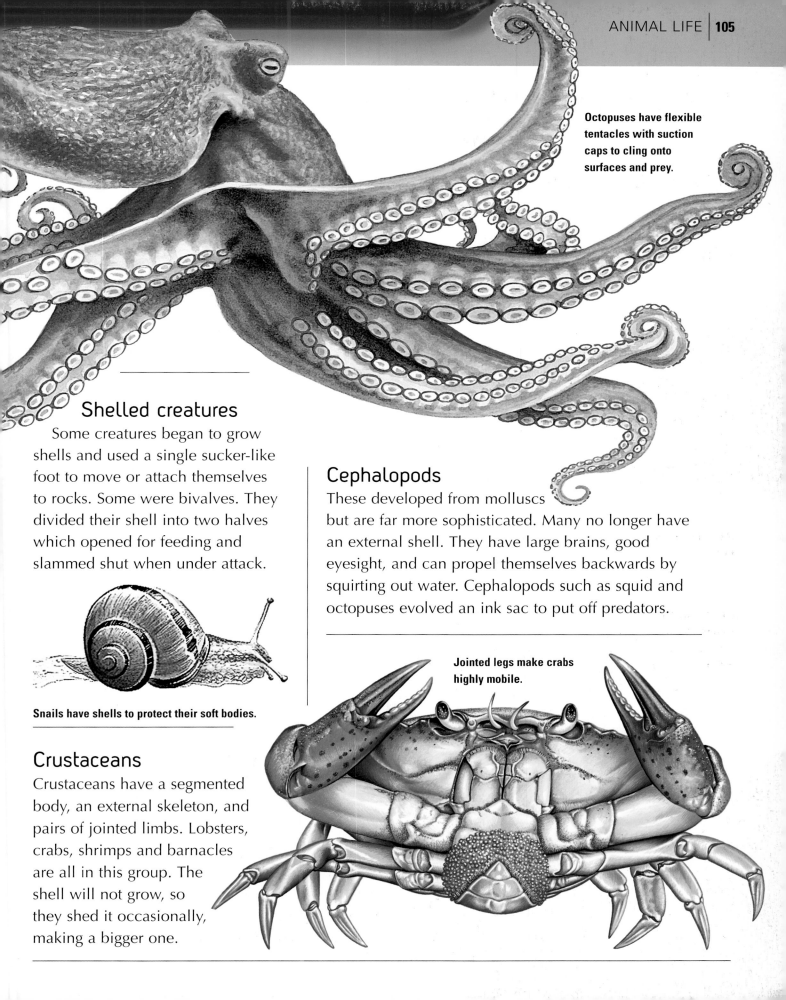

Octopuses have flexible tentacles with suction caps to cling onto surfaces and prey.

Shelled creatures

Some creatures began to grow shells and used a single sucker-like foot to move or attach themselves to rocks. Some were bivalves. They divided their shell into two halves which opened for feeding and slammed shut when under attack.

Snails have shells to protect their soft bodies.

Cephalopods

These developed from molluscs but are far more sophisticated. Many no longer have an external shell. They have large brains, good eyesight, and can propel themselves backwards by squirting out water. Cephalopods such as squid and octopuses evolved an ink sac to put off predators.

Jointed legs make crabs highly mobile.

Crustaceans

Crustaceans have a segmented body, an external skeleton, and pairs of jointed limbs. Lobsters, crabs, shrimps and barnacles are all in this group. The shell will not grow, so they shed it occasionally, making a bigger one.

Primates

The 180 primate species have long limbs with flexible fingers and toes, and forward-facing eyes. Most have nails rather than claws. The most advanced primates (including humans) are intelligent and live in social groups.

Most primates are suited to living in forests and survive mainly on fruit and vegetation, although some eat meat as well. Many are under threat either because they are being hunted or their habitat is destroyed.

Gorillas can grow to 175kg in the wild, but are often bigger when kept in captivity.

Monkeys

With their grasping hands and a long tail to help them balance, monkeys such as these howlers are excellent at climbing, swinging and running from tree to tree. They have tough pads to protect their bottoms when sitting, and big stomachs to help them digest their main diet of leaves.

Humans

Like apes, humans have no external tail. Unlike apes, they do not have body hair all over, so need clothes for warmth. Humans walk upright on two long, straight legs with large feet. They take a long time to grow, have the biggest and most complex brains on Earth, and are the only animals to use spoken and written languages.

Lemurs

Only found on the island of Madagascar, off east Africa, lemurs have flourished because there are no rival primates. Ring-tailed lemurs like these have long, stripey tails so they can see each other as they forage for food on the ground.

Apes

Unlike monkeys, apes have no tail. The largest apes are gorillas. The most intelligent are chimpanzees, which use sticks and stones as tools and pass this knowledge on to their young. Apes walk on all fours, supporting their weight on their knuckles. They live socially in large groups of up to 40.

Other mammals

Mammals replaced the ancient reptiles as the dominant animals on Earth. They can adapt to many different habitats on land and in the sea. There are even some that fly.

There are around 4,500 species of mammal. All have bones, teeth, some hair or fur, breathe through lungs and give their young milk – even the dolphin, one of the few sea mammals.

Warm-blooded animals

All mammals, including humans, keep a constant body temperature of just under 37°C, unlike cold-blooded animals. This means they can stay active all the time. In most mammals, hair or fur helps keep heat in.

Flying mammals

Bats are the only flying mammals. Their wings are flaps of skin joining their fingers together. Most bats have poor eyesight. Instead – like dolphins – they use echolocation. They send out bursts of high-pitched sound to get a picture of their surroundings from how fast the sound bounces back.

MARSUPIAL GROWTH
Kangaroos and koalas give birth to live young that then grow in a body pouch.

1 A newborn kangaroo (joey) crawls up into the pouch.

2 The pouch has teats from which the joey gets milk.

3 The joey stays in the pouch for several months while it grows.

Biggest mammal

The blue whale grows up to 33m long and weighs up to 180 tonnes. Its heart is the size of a small car. It has no teeth, so to feed, it opens its massive mouth wide to take in water. It then filters out its food – tiny sea creatures called krill. The blue whale may swallow 3.6 tonnes of krill a day.

Monotremes

These are the only egg-laying mammals. These primitive animals include the platypus (below), and are found in Australia and New Guinea. The mother lays eggs, but provides the young with milk.

Large cats

The lion is one of the five big cats, the others being the tiger, jaguar, leopard and snow leopard. This male lion can rest in the open because lions have no natural predators. He protects the group, or pride, while the females cooperate to hunt down their diet of fresh meat. Most other cats hunt alone.

Smallest land mammal

An adult pygmy shrew only weighs 2g. It needs to eat all the time to stay alive, consuming its own weight in bugs and insects every day. Its heart beats 750 times a minute, but this almost doubles when it is frightened. It releases a foul-tasting liquid to deter predators.

THE ELEPHANT

Elephants are the largest land mammal, weighing up to 6 tonnes. Both the African and the smaller-eared Asian elephants are highly intelligent animals that learn and pass on skills.

FAMILY HERDS

Elephants live in herds of 8–12, always led by a female. Pregnancies last for about 20 months and the whole group welcomes and takes care of babies, who are born weighing roughly 100kg. Males come and go, leaving the herd at the age of about 14 years, and sometimes forming herds of their own.

ELEPHANTS' TRUNKS

The trunk is the elephant's nose. But as well as smelling, it is used to breathe, wash and hold sticks to scratch or beat off flies. Elephants also use their trunks to eat up to 260kg of grass, vegetation and fruit, and drink 100 litres of water a day, grip trees, communicate with other elephants and even to sense ground vibrations.

AFRICAN ELEPHANTS

There are two species in Africa, depending on the habitat: forest and savannah elephants. These creatures have been hunted for their ivory tusks (their teeth), and are often unpopular with farmers because they destroy large areas of vegetation as they search for food. Their numbers have dropped from millions to about 500,000 and they are now an endangered species.

Birds

Birds fly by flapping their wings or gliding. They are the only vertebrates that can. They are also the only animal with feathers.

Bald eagles scoop up fish to eat.

There are about 9,600 species of bird. Their flying ability allows them to live in places other animals cannot easily reach, such as cliffs and crags.

WATERBIRDS

Waterfowl such as ducks and geese are good swimmers, with webbed feet.

Ducks are strong swimmers and fliers.

Geese live together in large flocks

Herons are wading birds with long, thin legs.

Swans are the largest of the waterfowl.

Seabirds

The sea and the shoreline are rich sources of food and attract many seabirds. Some only come to land to breed and raise their young. Black frigate birds (above) attack tropicbirds and steal their prey.

Birds of prey

These hunting birds only eat fresh meat. They can see four times better than humans, and spot prey from high above. They have sharp claws called talons for grabbing and hooked beaks for killing their victims.

Flightless birds

Some birds such as rhea, emus and cassowaries are flightless. Instead they are fast runners. Ostriches are quickest, at 72km/h. Others, such as the emperor penguins of Antarctica (below), are expert swimmers.

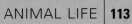

Tropical birds

Exotic birds live in tropical rainforests and other warm habitats, where they live off the plentiful fruit. They include parrots (above) – the only bird that holds food with its feet – and are brightly coloured to ward off predators.

Wading birds

These have long legs or bills to feed in the shallows and at water edges. Flamingoes (above) use their bills to filter out the mud from the small plants and animals that they eat.

SCIENTIFIC INPUT

NESTS AND YOUNG

Birds lay eggs that hatch into young. They often build nests in trees and other inaccessible places to protect them from predators. The females lay up to 20 eggs, depending on species, and most sit on the eggs to keep them warm until they hatch. The chicks eat the food in the egg before pecking their way out through the shell. Often, both parents help to feed the chicks until they can fend for themselves.

Snakes

Snakes are reptiles with no legs, eyelids or external ears. Their skin is covered with smooth, dry scales. They live anywhere that is warm.

Of the 2,700 species of snake, about 700 are venomous. These have fangs through which they inject prey with poison that paralyses, stuns or kills.

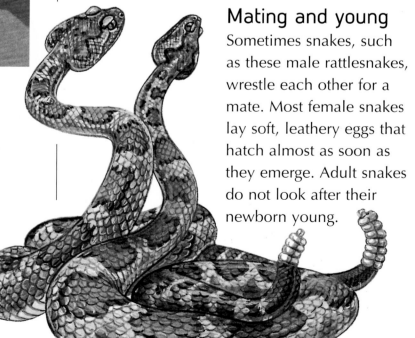

An anaconda prepares to swallow a capybara whole.

Diet and prey

Snakes are carnivorous, eating only meat or eggs. They either grab, stun or constrict – squeeze and suffocate – their prey. The prey is always whole when the snake squeezes it past its elastic jaws.

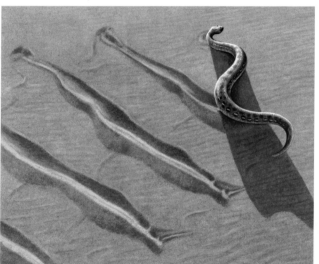

Movement

Snakes have different ways of moving. Some wriggle side to side, some thrust the front of their body forwards, while others raise and flatten scales on their belly. The sidewinder (above) throws its body sideways across the sand. Some snakes can reach 20km/h in short bursts, which is fast enough to catch a running animal.

Mating and young

Sometimes snakes, such as these male rattlesnakes, wrestle each other for a mate. Most female snakes lay soft, leathery eggs that hatch almost as soon as they emerge. Adult snakes do not look after their newborn young.

Pit organ

The green pit viper is coloured to blend in with the trees and shrubs it inhabits. It has heat sensors on the side of its head to detect the body heat coming off its varied diet of birds, rats, frogs and lizards.

Snake senses

Snakes have poor vision and they can only hear low sounds. Their most important sense is smell. They use their constantly flicking forked tongues to tell from what direction a scent comes. Many can sense infrared radiation coming from prey through their pit organs. They also sense vibration through their contact with the ground.

Other reptiles

Reptiles were the first animals with backbones that were able to survive on land. They now live on every continent except Antarctica.

Reptile skin is tough because it is covered with scales made of tough keratin. It does not grow, so it must be shed every so often.

TURTLE BIRTH
Most reptiles lay eggs. Sea turtles return to land to lay eggs in the sand.

1
The female hauls herself onto the beach.

2
She lays her eggs and returns to the sea.

3
The hatchlings use their snouts to break out.

4
They crawl towards the safety of the sea.

Tortoises and turtles

These are the only reptiles with hard shells, into which they can pull their heads, legs and tails for protection. Turtles (left) live in water, while tortoises (above) stay on land.

Chameleons

These animals can change colour to match their surroundings. They use this camouflage to hide in trees during the day, coming out mostly at night to catch insect prey.

Lizards

Lizards usually have a long tail and four legs that stick out sideways, so they sway from side to side as they move. Many can shed their tails to flee predators. Most live on the ground but some are good climbers.

Komodo dragons are the largest lizards, and are capable of attacking big animals such as deer. They live in Indonesia.

Lizard defence

When threatened, the frilled lizard makes itself look big and frightening by unfurling its yellow and red frill like an umbrella, showing its teeth, and hissing and waving its tail. If that fails, it scuttles up the nearest tree.

Alligators live in the USA and China.

Crocodiles live in Africa, Asia, the Americas and Australia.

Gharials live in Asia.

Crocodiles and alligators

These reptiles lie low in the water with just their eyes and nostrils above the surface. Gharials have narrow snouts for catching fish. The crocodile's lower front teeth stick out when the mouth closes.

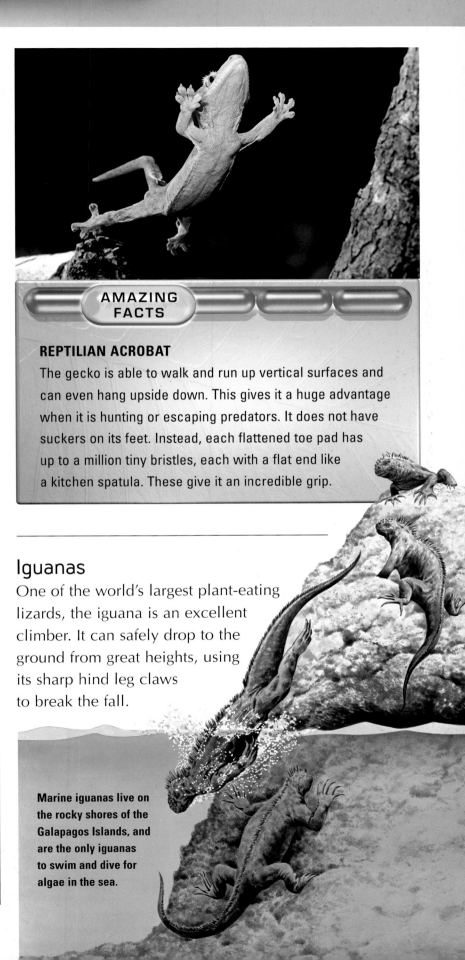

AMAZING FACTS

REPTILIAN ACROBAT

The gecko is able to walk and run up vertical surfaces and can even hang upside down. This gives it a huge advantage when it is hunting or escaping predators. It does not have suckers on its feet. Instead, each flattened toe pad has up to a million tiny bristles, each with a flat end like a kitchen spatula. These give it an incredible grip.

Iguanas

One of the world's largest plant-eating lizards, the iguana is an excellent climber. It can safely drop to the ground from great heights, using its sharp hind leg claws to break the fall.

Marine iguanas live on the rocky shores of the Galapagos Islands, and are the only iguanas to swim and dive for algae in the sea.

Amphibians

Amphibians can live both in and out of water. They thrive in many different habitats – deserts, mountains, rainforests – if there is freshwater. They are cold-blooded.

Toads have warty skin.

Amphibians breathe through gills (like fish) or lungs (like mammals), or sometimes both. Most adult amphibians can also breathe through their smooth, hairless skin.

Self-protection

As they have no fur, feathers or claws, amphibians are tempting snacks. They protect themselves with poison glands that irritate the mouth and eyes of attackers. Some have brightly coloured skin to warn off predators.

Metamorphosis

The young of amphibians grow by metamorphosis – they change form as they develop. They start in a clump of eggs called spawn, become larvae or tadpoles with gills, and finally develop lungs and legs.

Frogs and toads

Both frogs and toads have bulgy eyes, sticky-tipped tongues and short, fat bodies with webbed feet. Frogs usually wait for their prey to pass by, while toads stalk their victims.

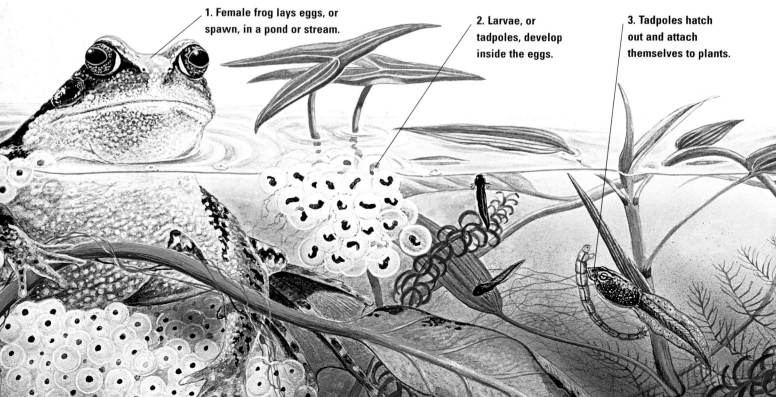

1. Female frog lays eggs, or spawn, in a pond or stream.

2. Larvae, or tadpoles, develop inside the eggs.

3. Tadpoles hatch out and attach themselves to plants.

**Fire
salamander**

Salamanders

These amphibians live near or in water, have a long tail and short legs. They can grow these again if one is cut off. The fire salamander (above) has distinctive yellow and black markings and hunts prey at night.

Communication

Frogs and toads use sound to communicate. The loudest fill up pouches of stretchy skin in their throats with air, releasing it to make a distinctive croak.

**5. Fully grown
frogs leave the water.**

**4. Tadpoles slowly
turn into frogs.**

Newts

**Crested
newt**

This amphibian has no grooves on its body. Most newts are aquatic or semi-aquatic, but some have adapted to live on land, returning to water only to breed. They swallow their fish and insect prey whole.

Cave-dweller

Cave salamanders are thin enough to wriggle between rocks and cave walls as they hunt for insects and worms. The blind cave salamander (right) has scarlet gill tufts for breathing on either side of its head.

**Cave
salamander**

AMAZING FACTS

LIFE IN THE TREETOPS

Tree frogs have extra-thick skin to survive their dry habitat in the treetops. They are small and lightweight, but they are exceptional climbers because they have sticky pads on the ends of their curled fingers and toes. These are filled with a glue-like mucus that allows them to rest on the most slippery leaf. Some tree frogs can leap through the air, spreading their toes like a parachute to glide safely onto a branch.

MIGRATION

Some animals follow a pattern of movement during the year, travelling huge distances to find food, to escape the cold, or to breed. Some seem to remember where to go, others use landmarks or even navigate by the stars. Strangely, birds often fly past suitable habitats on their globetrotting journeys, possibly following ancient instincts.

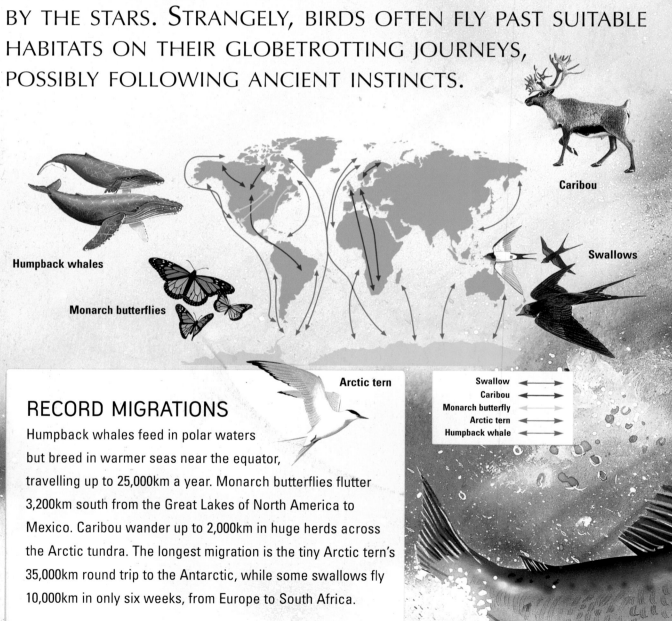

Caribou

Humpback whales

Monarch butterflies

Swallows

Arctic tern

Swallow	◄──►
Caribou	◄──►
Monarch butterfly	◄──►
Arctic tern	◄──►
Humpback whale	◄──►

RECORD MIGRATIONS

Humpback whales feed in polar waters but breed in warmer seas near the equator, travelling up to 25,000km a year. Monarch butterflies flutter 3,200km south from the Great Lakes of North America to Mexico. Caribou wander up to 2,000km in huge herds across the Arctic tundra. The longest migration is the tiny Arctic tern's 35,000km round trip to the Antarctic, while some swallows fly 10,000km in only six weeks, from Europe to South Africa.

A SALMON'S JOURNEY

Salmon are born in rivers, and swim down to the sea to find food. After 1–4 years, they return to breed, travelling enormous distances across oceans. They do not eat during the journey and can lose half their body weight. They sometimes have to leap out of the water to climb waterfalls, as here, and the long swim upstream against the current leaves them so exhausted that many die. Others make this epic journey several times.

Life in the water

Most of the Earth is covered by water, where the main life form is fish. They breathe through gills, extracting oxygen from the water.

There are three types of fish: jawless, cartilaginous and bony. Bony fish make up about 95 per cent of all fish species.

Freshwater fish

Some fish live in the freshwater of rivers and lakes. Some, such as trout, prefer fast-flowing streams, while others, such as carp, like slow-moving water.

Archer fish spit water at their insect prey, toppling it into the water.

EARTH EVIDENCE

POND LIFE

Ponds are often rich in nutrients, so they support many different animals and insects. People have kept fish in ponds for thousands of years, either for food or as pets. Common pond fish include koi carp (above) and goldfish, which are often an easy target for predators such as the heron.

Jawless fish

These primitive creatures suck up food from the seabed or clamp themselves to a victim and tear at its flesh with their rough tongues. They were the first vertebrates. Only a few, such as this lamprey and the deep sea hagfish, have survived.

Deep-sea fish

A few hundred metres below the waves, the sea is dark and cold, with little food. Deep-sea fish tend to have big eyes or rely on long feelers to detect prey there and attract mates. They are slower and less agile than other fish.

The deep-sea angler has a long spine like a fishing rod which it lights up to attract other fish for its food. Other deep-sea fish can also make light. This is called bioluminescence.

Self-defence

Some fish use bright colours or poison to deter predators. Some have much more dramatic means of protection. When threatened, the porcupine fish (above) swallows lots of water. This causes it to swell and makes its spines stick out. It becomes impossible for predators to bite it.

Ocean predator

The shark is an extremely efficient killing machine that hunts its prey by smell. It has powerful jaws with an array of biting and crushing teeth that are continuously replaced by rows growing behind. Instead of bones, its skeleton is made of cartilage. Sharks have to keep swimming or they sink.

A blue shark eating its squid prey

On the reef

Coral is alive. It is made up of millions of tiny animals called polyps, which produce a protective shell that over a long period creates a reef. This environment offers shelter and food to many animals, acting like a rainforest in the warm, clear water.
Fish that are immune to polyp stings hide in the cracks and crevices of the coral, where octopuses, moray eels, starfish, clams and other marine creatures also hunt and rest.

Camouflage

Some animals that need to hide from prey or predators use camouflage as a way to conceal their presence. The simplest disguise is the worm's brown skin against brown earth.

Camouflage is especially important to animals that are active during the day, when they can be easily seen. Some stay still so they do not give themselves away, while others mimic the call of fiercer creatures.

Colour and camouflage

Colour allows an animal to blend in with its surroundings. For example, shrimps match their background because they are transparent. The fur of the sloth (right) often has a green tinge. This is because it houses bacteria that reacts to the moist conditions of the South American rainforest in which the sloth lives, providing effective camouflage.

Imitation

Animals can have shapes that mimic their environment. The stick insect's thin body and legs look like branches, and it is the colour of the wood. If it is disturbed it drops to the ground like a dead twig, and if that does not work, it flies off. Other insects mimic the veins of leaves.

Distraction

Another technique is to distract with stripes, spots or speckles that look like the animal's surroundings. The zebra's stripes look like tree shadows and also merge in the heat haze, making it hard for hunting lions to pick out individuals.

Insects and spiders

There are six insects for every other creature on Earth. They have been around for 500 million years, and are found almost everywhere on the planet except in the sea.

Insects are the recyclers of the planet because they eat dead animals, fallen trees and other rubbish. However, some transmit disease. Others, such as bees, are vital to plant reproduction (*see pp.78–79*).

Insect anatomy

Insects have six legs and three body parts: the head, thorax (chest) and abdomen (belly). Their bodies are held together by an outer shell called the exoskeleton. They have no lungs and breathe through holes in their sides.

Most winged insects have two pairs of wings.

Insect legs are jointed.

Insects use their antennae to 'smell'.

Winged insects

The rapid beating of an insect's wings creates a humming or buzzing sound. Bee or wasp wings beat 200 times a second, while mosquitoes' reach 500 times a second and hoverflies' twice that.

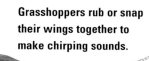

Grasshoppers rub or snap their wings together to make chirping sounds.

Ants

There are many kinds of ant, all living in colonies where each one has a job to do. These leaf cutter ants bite off leaves and carry them to their nest. The leaves are used to grow the ants' food, a fungus.

The process of changing from caterpillar to butterfly is called metamorphosis.

1. Tiny larva hatches and starts to eat.

2. The fully grown caterpillar attaches itself to a twig.

3. It sheds its skin, revealing a green pupa (chrysalis).

4. Inside the pupa a butterfly forms.

5. The skin splits and the adult butterfly emerges.

Stag beetles fighting

Beetles

Beetles make up the largest group of insects, and are the most heavily armoured with their thick shells. Many beetles are pests and eat crops or trees, but some, such as ladybirds, feed on plant-eating creatures.

Dragonflies

The dragonfly has two pairs of wings, which work separately. This means it can change direction instantly when it spots danger or food with its massive eyes. The dragonfly is one of the fastest of the flying insects.

Insect life cycle

Some insects such as butterflies grow in four stages. From the egg hatches a caterpillar larva or grub that eats leaves. Later, it sheds its skin and creates a hard shell called a pupa. It emerges from the pupa as an adult. Other insects, such as grasshoppers, have only a three-stage cycle in which they progress from egg to wingless nymph to adult.

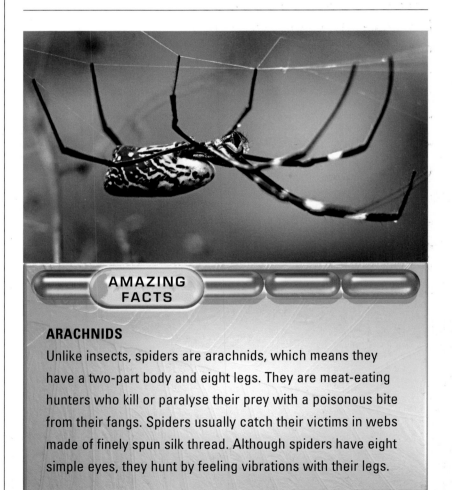

AMAZING FACTS

ARACHNIDS

Unlike insects, spiders are arachnids, which means they have a two-part body and eight legs. They are meat-eating hunters who kill or paralyse their prey with a poisonous bite from their fangs. Spiders usually catch their victims in webs made of finely spun silk thread. Although spiders have eight simple eyes, they hunt by feeling vibrations with their legs.

Animal facts

Humans are in a minority. For every person on Earth, there are about 200 million insects, 1 million of which are ants. We are not just outnumbered by bugs. There are two dolphins and – probably – one rat for every human on Earth.

AVERAGE LIFESPANS
Dragonfly 24 hours
Mouse 2–3 years
Rabbit 5 years
Kangaroo 9 years
Chicken 15 years
Lion 25 years
Hippopotamus 40 years
Dolphin 65 years
Elephant 70 years
Rhinoceros 70 years
Parrot 80 years
Tortoise 100 years
Deep sea tubeworm 170–250 years
The longest living animal recorded
is an ocean quahog clam 405 years

FASTEST...
In the air: peregrine falcon 322km/h
Attacking: the jaws of the trap-jaw
   ant snapping shut 233km/h
On land: cheetah 112km/h
In the water: sailfish 109km/h
Racehorse 80 km/h
Racing dog: greyhound 72km/h
Over long distances: pronghorn
   antelope 72km/h
Non-flying bird: ostrich 69km/h
Insect: dragonfly 58km/h
Of the whales: killer whale 56km/h
Human 45km/h
Reptile: spiny-tailed iguana 34km/h
Running insect: cockroach 5km/h

PREGNANCY, AVERAGE LENGTH
Hamster 16 days
House mouse 19 days
Rabbit 32 days
Cat 62 days
Dog 65 days
Lion 108 days
Sheep 148 days
Chimpanzee 237 days
Human 260–290 days
Dolphin 276 days
Whale 365 days
Giraffe 395–425 days
Camel 406 days
Rhinoceros 560 days
Indian elephant 624 days

A tawny owl preparing to land

USEFUL WEBSITES

www.nhm.ac.uk/   Information on the natural world from the Natural History Museum.
www.g-kexoticfarms.com/funanimalfacts.html   A wealth of animal facts and statistics.
www.kidscom.com/cgi-bin/Animalgame/animal.pl   Animal facts and games.
http://kids.nationalgeographic.com/Animals/CreatureFeature/   Fact files on animals.

Body Science

Humans dominate other animal species through intelligence, not physical strength. Our bodies have mouths that can speak, and hands that can build, rather than fangs and claws. Unlike other animals, the human body needs the protection of clothes, healthcare and prepared foods. However, it is highly adaptable, and outlasts the bodies of most other animals.

Bones and skeletons

The skeleton is the body's support structure. The muscles attached to the skeleton allow us to move.

From the six tiny bones inside the ears to the six long bones in the legs, every part of the skeleton is constantly renewing itself.

Bone structure

Every bone is coated with a thin membrane that covers a hard, dense outer layer. There is lighter, sponge-like material underneath this layer. In the core of each bone is a fatty substance called marrow. Bones also contain networks of nerves and blood vessels.

Pivot – first vertebra of backbone rotates around second

Hinge – one knee bone fits into curved end of another

Ball-and-socket – at shoulder, ball shape fits into cup shape

Saddle – base of thumb bone fits into u-shape of wrist bone

Ellipsoidal – egg shape of arm bone fits in cup of wrist

Plane – giding joint between heel bones in each foot

Joints

A joint is the meeting-point of two or more bones, and most of them allow free motion in one or more directions. Ligaments encase joints to protect them. Only a few joints are not mobile

Teeth are made of enamel, the hardest material in the body.

The ribs protect the soft organs of the body, such as the heart.

Bones keep the amount of calcium in the bloodstream in balance, absorbing and releasing it as required.

The femur is a long bone and is adapted to withstand stress.

Bone types

There are five main types of bone: long bones, such as the main bones in the limbs; short bones such as the heel; flat bones, such as those in the dome of the skull; sesamoids such as the kneecaps, which are small and round; and irregular bones such as the vertebrae of the spine

Cartilage

This strong but flexible material is connected to some bones. It has a smooth surface that allows joints to move easily, and lets our ears and noses be flexible while keeping their shape.

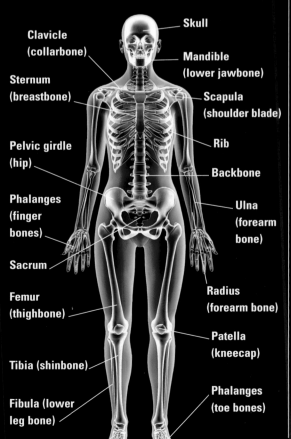

Cartilage

Parts of the skeleton

The skeleton is made up of 206 bones. They allow motion and give shape to the body, as well as giving protection to internal organs. Most blood cells are made inside bones.

Clavicle (collarbone)

Sternum (breastbone)

Pelvic girdle (hip)

Phalanges (finger bones)

Sacrum

Femur (thighbone)

Tibia (shinbone)

Fibula (lower leg bone)

Skull

Mandible (lower jawbone)

Scapula (shoulder blade)

Rib

Backbone

Ulna (forearm bone)

Radius (forearm bone)

Patella (kneecap)

Phalanges (toe bones)

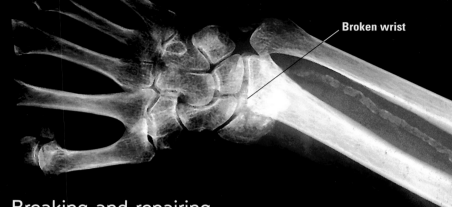

Broken wrist

Breaking and repairing

When a bone is broken it usually repairs itself, as long as the ends are held together. This can be done by the surrounding tissues, as with broken ribs, or by plaster casts, as with broken limbs. First, a blood clot forms to stop bleeding. Fibres grow across the break, and soft bone forms on them. Gradually, hard bone replaces soft bone.

AMAZING FACTS

THE SKULL

The skull protects the brain as well as the eyes and nasal passages. The bones that form the skulls of babies and children have some flexibility to allow for growth. Those of adults are locked solidly together, except for the jawbone. Inside the skull, six tiny bones in the ears magnify vibrations of the eardrum so that these can be heard as sounds.

Muscles and movement

Muscles allow us to move, hold us upright, and keep many of our internal organs working.

Muscles make up about half of the weight of an average person. They grow stronger or weaker depending on how much they are used.

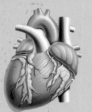
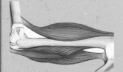
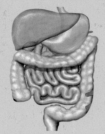

How muscles work

Muscles are made of fibres that shorten when they receive a signal from the nerves. Because muscles can only pull, not push, they often work in pairs. The biceps, for example, bends the arm, and the triceps straightens it again.

Tendons and ligaments

The ends of a skeletal muscle (see left) are usually attached to the bones they move by cords of very strong tissue called tendons. Where tendons move across bones – such as in the hands and feet – they are often covered in a lubricating layer, called a synovial sheath, to reduce friction.

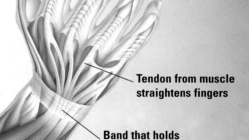

Tendon from muscle straightens fingers

Band that holds tendons in place

Using muscles

The more muscles are used, the stronger they become. By exercising muscles, you increase the strength and size of the individual muscle fibres. The process also 'teaches' muscles how to work effectively, by ensuring that fibres contract together. Muscles usually use oxygen to contract, but can work without it.

Some very fit footballers are able to use their muscles to execute extraordinary manoeuvres in order to reach the ball.

Muscle fibres

Every skeletal muscle is made of two types of fibre, in roughly equal numbers. Fast twitch fibres contract quickly and powerfully, but tire rapidly. They allow people to sprint and to lift heavy weights. Slow twitch fibres contract more slowly, but can work for longer. They are used for cycling and long-distance running.

BLOOD AND CIRCULATION

BLOOD TRANSPORTS BOTH NUTRIENTS AND OXYGEN AROUND THE BODY. THE OXYGEN BREAKS DOWN THE NUTRIENTS, SO THAT THE ENERGY THEY CARRY CAN BE USED.

CIRCULATION

The heart continuously pumps blood through the lungs to receive oxygen from them, turning it bright red. This fresh blood is then pumped through the body. The oxygen is used up and replaced by the waste gas carbon dioxide, which darkens the blood. This blood then flows back through the heart to the lungs, where the carbon dioxide is removed and exhaled.

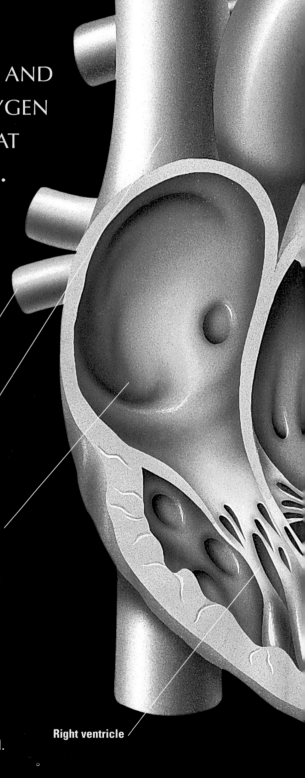

Pulmonary veins, carry oxygen-rich blood from lungs to heart

Superior vena cava, a vein that carries stale blood to the heart

Right atrium

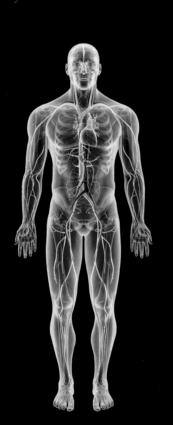

BLOOD

The heart pumps about five litres of blood round the body every minute, and beats more than three billion times in a lifetime. Blood consists of different types of cell suspended in a fluid called plasma. Red cells carry oxygen, white cells fight infection, and platelets help blood to clot so that wounds can be closed and healed.

Right ventricle

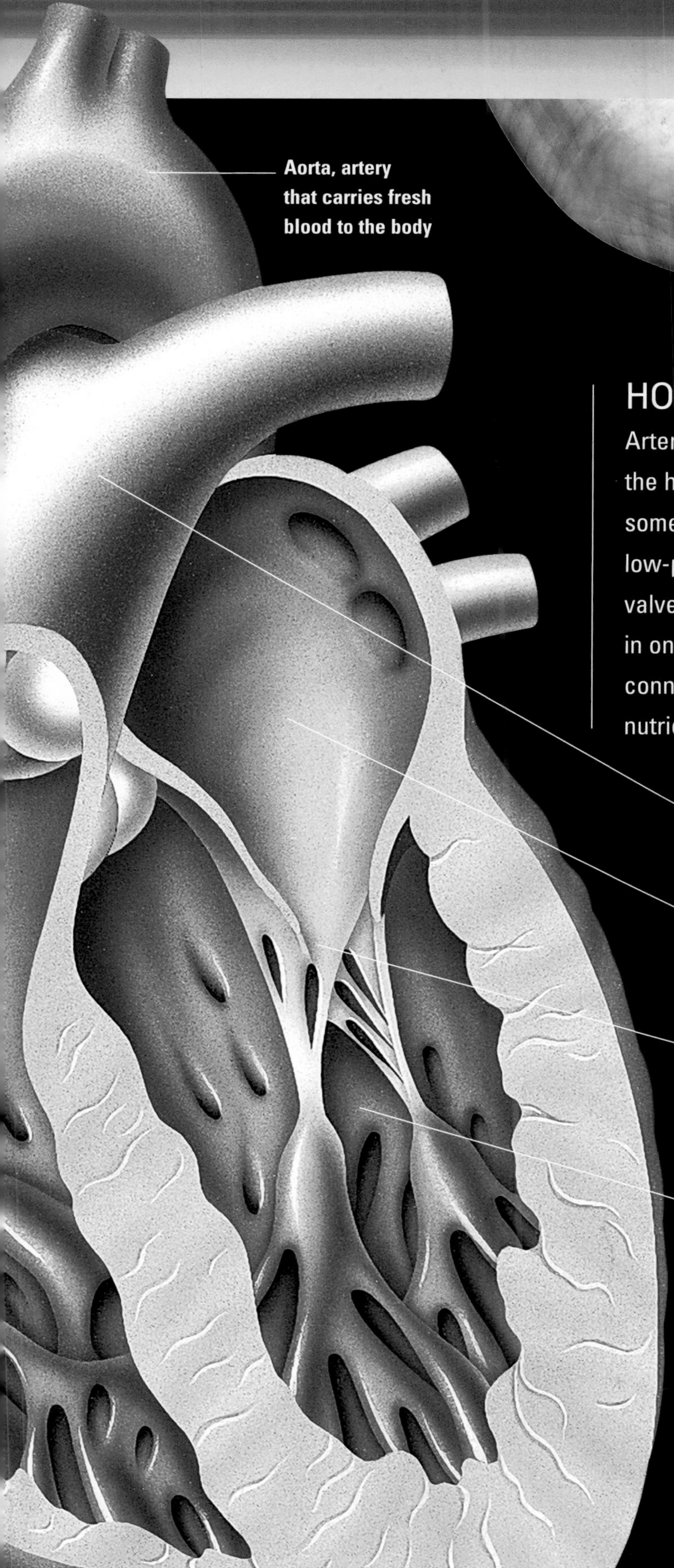

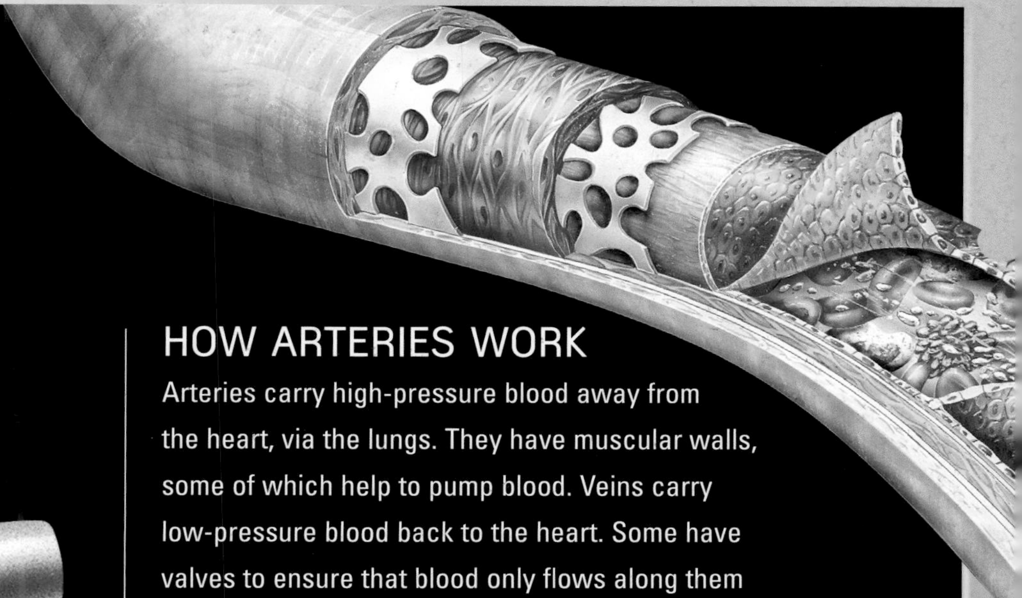

Aorta, artery that carries fresh blood to the body

HOW ARTERIES WORK

Arteries carry high-pressure blood away from the heart, via the lungs. They have muscular walls, some of which help to pump blood. Veins carry low-pressure blood back to the heart. Some have valves to ensure that blood only flows along them in one direction. A network of narrow capillaries connects veins and arteries, with thin walls so that nutrients and waste can leave and enter them.

Pulmonary artery, carries stale blood to the lungs

Left atrium

Heart valve between left atrium and left ventricle

Left ventricle

THE HEART

The heart beats automatically, with no need for instructions from the brain. It speeds up during exercise, to supply the cells with the extra nutrients and oxygen that they need. The 'lub-dub' sound of the heart's beat is made by the valves inside it closing.

Brain and nerves

All your thoughts, ideas and emotions, and your sense of who you are, exist in your brain. How exactly the mind is linked to the brain is a mystery.

The brain sends a constant stream of control signals to the body. However, we are conscious of only a few of them.

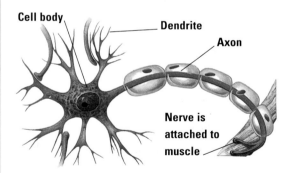

Skilled movement

Touch

Consciousness

Speech

Sight

Hearing, smell and taste

Cerebellum

The nervous system

The brain and spinal cord make up the central nervous system, which controls the body. The peripheral nervous system is a complex network of nerves all over the body. It carries messages to and from the central nervous system.

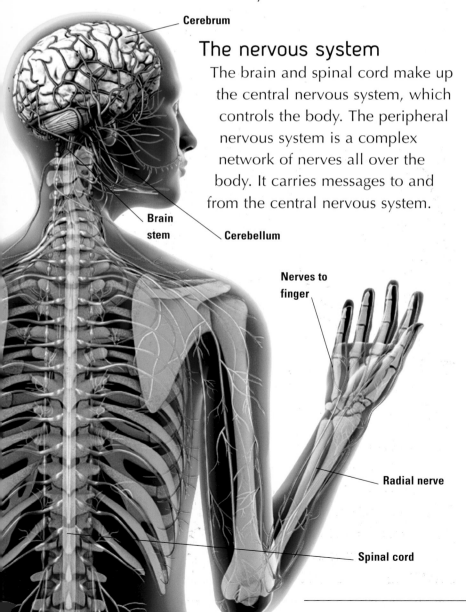

Cerebrum

Brain stem

Cerebellum

Nerves to finger

Radial nerve

Spinal cord

The brain

The brain is composed of three main parts: the cerebrum, where thought occurs, the cerebellum, which coordinates the muscles, and the brain stem, which controls breathing and heart rate. Different areas of the brain control different body functions.

Cell body

Dendrite

Axon

Nerve is attached to muscle

How nerves work

Electrical nerve signals travel along nerve cells (neurons, above). Chemical messengers, neurotransmitters, control the way the signals travel across the gaps (synapses) between neurons.

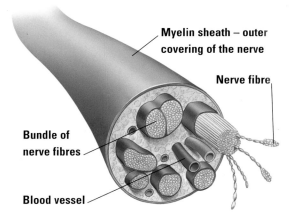

Myelin sheath – outer covering of the nerve

Nerve fibre

Bundle of nerve fibres

Blood vessel

Sensory and motor nerves

Sensory nerves send signals from receptor cells (such as those in the skin that detect heat, cold, pressure and pain) to the brain. Motor cells transmit signals from the brain to the muscles, which contract in response.

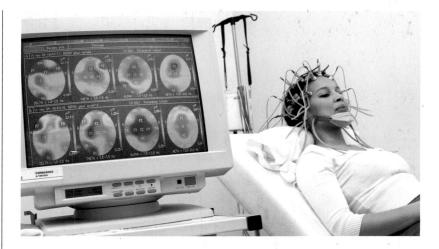

Brainwaves

The many tiny electrical signals in the brain change depending on what we see and hear. Some can be measured on the scalp and displayed on the screen of an electroencephalograph (above). The pattern of activity also shows whether we are awake, asleep or dreaming.

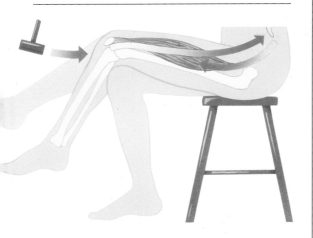

Reflexes

The brain is not involved in responding to every nerve signal. When a knee is tapped with a hammer, the spinal cord reacts to the signals from the skin receptors. It sends a signal down a motor nerve to contract the muscles, causing the leg to kick out in a reflex action.

SCIENTIFIC INPUT

AUTONOMIC NERVOUS SYSTEM (ANS)
The ANS adjusts our bodies to cope in different conditions. 'Sympathetic' responses are triggered by either mental or physical stress (above). The reactions can include increased heart and breathing rates. Calmer periods bring 'parasympathetic' responses, the opposite effect.

Thinking and dreaming

The mind is mysterious. No one knows exactly how emotions or memories work, nor how we make mental 'models' of the world around us.

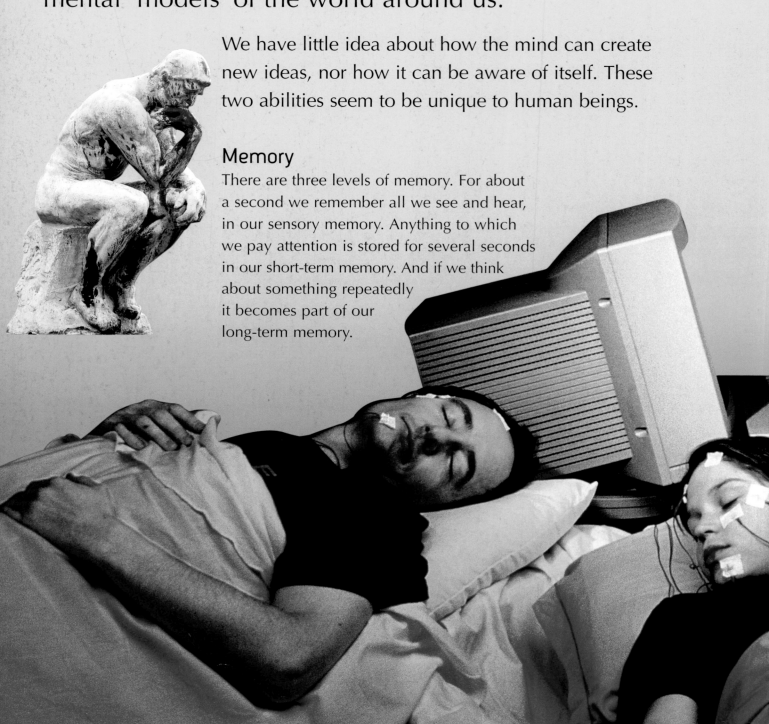

We have little idea about how the mind can create new ideas, nor how it can be aware of itself. These two abilities seem to be unique to human beings.

Memory

There are three levels of memory. For about a second we remember all we see and hear, in our sensory memory. Anything to which we pay attention is stored for several seconds in our short-term memory. And if we think about something repeatedly it becomes part of our long-term memory.

Sleep

We spend about one-third of our lives asleep, though the amount of sleep we need lessens as we grow older. There are two types of sleep. During rapid eye movement (REM) sleep we dream. Non-rapid eye movement (NREM) sleep, by contrast, is deep and dreamless. Every night, we have about five alternating periods of each type.

Brainwaves can be monitored to study what happens when we are asleep.

Dreaming

Each night our brains organize the experiences of the day. We 'relive' some of these experiences – though with many details changed – as our dreams. This painting by René Magritte captures the strange and yet familiar qualities of a dream.

Senses

All our information about the world comes through our five senses. These are sight, hearing, touch, smell and taste.

The brain organizes signals it receives from our sense organs. It uses them to put together a mental 'model' of the world.

Touch

Touch tells us about the temperature, weight, texture and shape of objects. Touch receptors are concentrated where they are needed, so there are more in the skin of our fingers than in the same area on our backs.

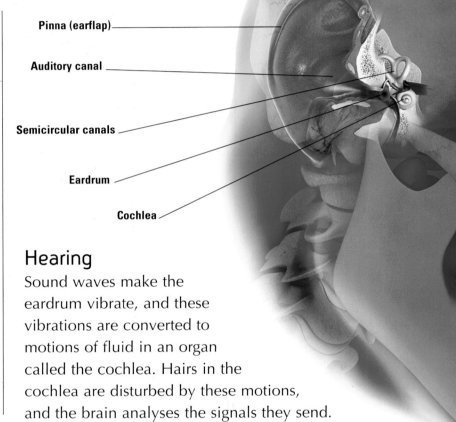

Pinna (earflap)

Auditory canal

Semicircular canals

Eardrum

Cochlea

Hearing

Sound waves make the eardrum vibrate, and these vibrations are converted to motions of fluid in an organ called the cochlea. Hairs in the cochlea are disturbed by these motions, and the brain analyses the signals they send.

Taste

Chemical receptors called tastebuds tell us how salty, sweet, sour or bitter things are, but we need to use our sense of smell to identify different foods. It is difficult to distinguish chocolate, tea and coffee with the sense of taste alone.

Balance

Our inner ears allow us to stand and walk without falling. They also allow us to hear. In each ear there are three fluid-filled tubes called semicircular canals. The motion of the fluid sends signals to the brain, so it can stabilize our movements.

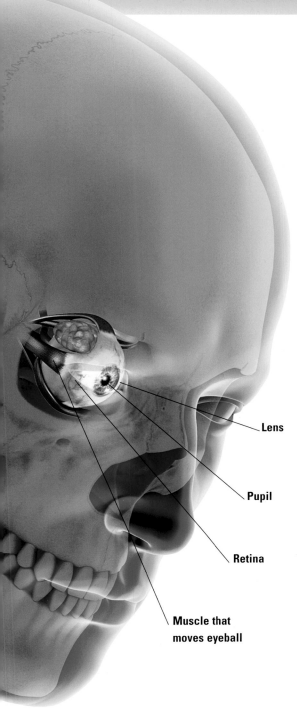

Lens

Pupil

Retina

Muscle that
moves eyeball

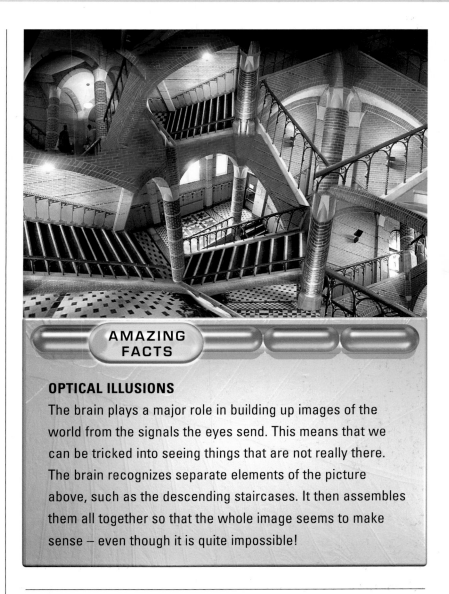

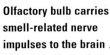

AMAZING FACTS

OPTICAL ILLUSIONS

The brain plays a major role in building up images of the world from the signals the eyes send. This means that we can be tricked into seeing things that are not really there. The brain recognizes separate elements of the picture above, such as the descending staircases. It then assembles them all together so that the whole image seems to make sense – even though it is quite impossible!

Sight

Light entering the eyes is focussed by flexible lenses onto the light-sensitive retinas. There, different colours and brightnesses are changed to electrical signals and sent to the brain. The brain adds extra information to the signals to generate a complete picture.

Smell

We have hundreds of different smell receptors, each able to identify a different airborne chemical. By combining the responses from groups of these receptors, we can identify thousands of different smells. Taste and smell are linked senses. Together they allow us to enjoy many different flavours.

Olfactory bulb carries
smell-related nerve
impulses to the brain

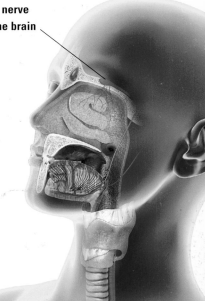

Skin, hair and teeth

Except for the eyes, every part of a person that you can see is dead! The outer layers of skin, nails, hair and teeth are made up entirely of dead cells. They form a protective barrier against the environment.

Throughout our lives, these layers wear away and are replaced. The teeth are replaced just once, but skin, hair and nails grow continuously to renew themselves.

Girl with the longest hair in the world

Hair

Hair on the head protects it from hot sun and cold air. Eyebrows and eyelashes keep sweat and grit out of the eyes. Our distant ancestors had thick body hair that stood up in the cold, providing a warm layer. We still get goosepimples, but no longer have enough body hair to keep us warm.

Skin

The skin protects us in many ways. It is a barrier against disease and rough surfaces, and it senses damaging heat or cold. The amount of blood flowing through it varies to regulate the amount of heat we lose, preventing overheating or chilling.

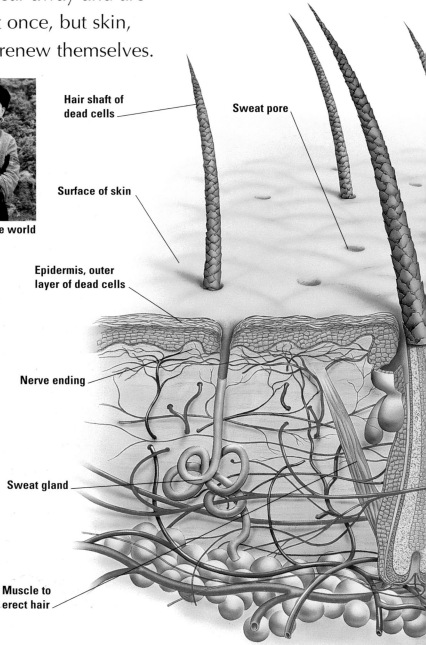

Hair shaft of dead cells

Sweat pore

Surface of skin

Epidermis, outer layer of dead cells

Nerve ending

Sweat gland

Muscle to erect hair

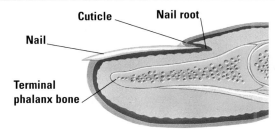

Cuticle
Nail root
Nail
Terminal phalanx bone

Nails

Our fingertips come into contact with hard and rough surfaces throughout the day, but the skin on them has to be quite thin to allow us to feel things. Nails have evolved to allow the fingers and toes to be both tough and sensitive.

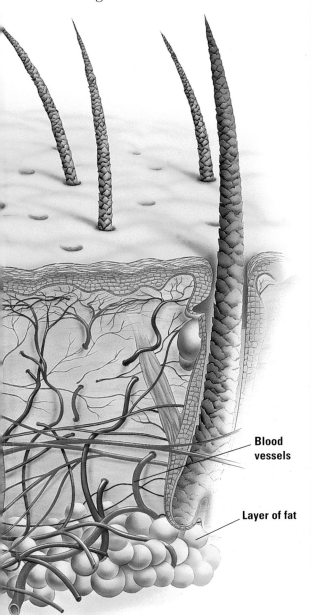

Blood vessels

Layer of fat

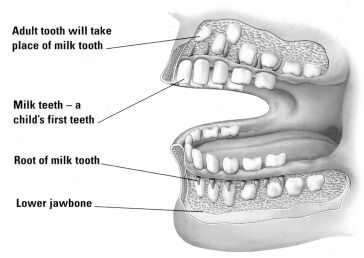

Adult tooth will take place of milk tooth

Milk teeth – a child's first teeth

Root of milk tooth

Lower jawbone

Teeth

The shapes of teeth have evolved for different functions. The incisors cut off pieces of food, canines are for tearing, and premolars and molars are used for grinding. Teeth are covered in a layer of protective enamel, which is the hardest substance in the human body.

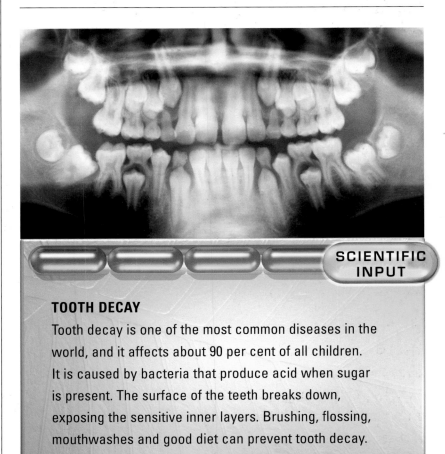

SCIENTIFIC INPUT

TOOTH DECAY

Tooth decay is one of the most common diseases in the world, and it affects about 90 per cent of all children. It is caused by bacteria that produce acid when sugar is present. The surface of the teeth breaks down, exposing the sensitive inner layers. Brushing, flossing, mouthwashes and good diet can prevent tooth decay.

Lungs and breathing

Every minute, about 5 to 6 litres of air passes into and out of the lungs. The air drawn into the lungs is about one-fifth oxygen, and some of this oxygen is absorbed by the blood.

When we exercise, the body needs more oxygen and produces more carbon dioxide, so we breathe faster and more deeply.

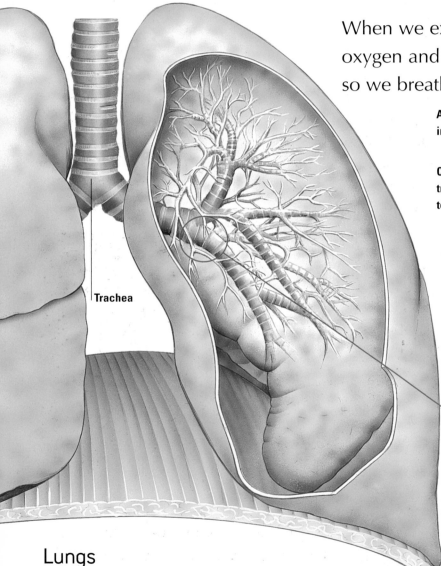

Trachea

Alveolus in lung

Blood vessel

Carbon dioxide travelling back to lungs

Oxygen

Body cell

Gas exchange

The heart pumps the oxygen-rich blood round the body, where it is transferred through the capillary walls to the cells. Carbon dioxide is transported by the blood from the cells to the lungs to be exhaled.

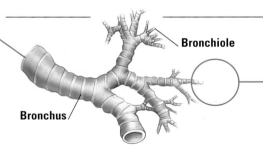

Bronchiole

Bronchus

Lungs

The lungs are delicate, but are protected by the ribs and a lubricating membrane called the pleura. The windpipe, or trachea, connects the throat to the lungs. A flap of skin called the epiglottis stops food and liquids from entering the lungs.

Bronchi and bronchioles

The trachea divides into two bronchi, each one going to a lung, where it is divided further into bronchioles. The bronchioles change diameter to control the flow of air in the lungs.

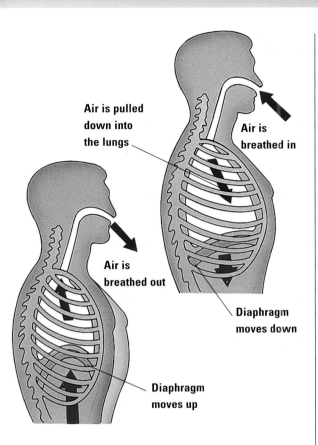

Air is pulled down into the lungs

Air is breathed in

Air is breathed out

Diaphragm moves down

Diaphragm moves up

Breathing

When we breathe, many muscles work together to draw in air. The diaphragm under the lungs flattens, and the intercostal muscles spread the ribs. The lungs expand, drawing in air. To exhale, the muscles relax again.

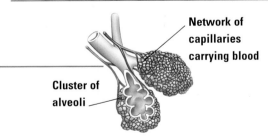

Network of capillaries carrying blood

Cluster of alveoli

Alveoli

The bronchioles end in bunches of tiny, round alveoli. The lining of each alveolus is damp and very thin, allowing gases to pass easily into and out of the blood.

Vocal cords

Humans are unique in being able to speak – even advanced animals such as chimpanzees can produce only a few simple sounds. When we speak, two folds of tissue in the throat called vocal cords are pulled close together. They vibrate as air from the lungs passes between them. The tongue, teeth, lips, nose and the 'roof' of the mouth all modify the vibrations to form word-sounds.

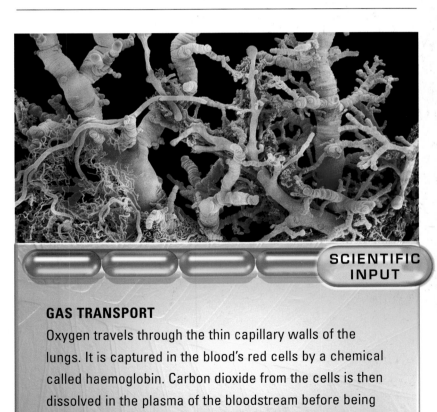

SCIENTIFIC INPUT

GAS TRANSPORT

Oxygen travels through the thin capillary walls of the lungs. It is captured in the blood's red cells by a chemical called haemoglobin. Carbon dioxide from the cells is then dissolved in the plasma of the bloodstream before being passed out through the capillary walls. This model shows capillaries in a lung and has been magnified many times.

EATING AND DIGESTION

LIKE ANY MACHINE, THE BODY HAS TO HAVE FUEL TO SUPPLY IT WITH THE ENERGY IT NEEDS. BECAUSE THE BODY CONSTANTLY RENEWS ITSELF, CHEMICALS FROM FOOD ARE NEEDED TO BUILD CELLS AS WELL.

FOOD FOR LIFE

Carbohydrates supply us with readily available energy, fats provide stored energy for later use, and proteins give us bulk-building material. Small amounts of vitamins and minerals are needed for the body to function. Water makes up 70 per cent of the body and needs to be topped up constantly. It is important to eat the right amount of each of the foodstuffs (right) to be healthy.

Cakes and sweets contain a lot of sugar and unhealthy types of fat, and should be eaten sparingly.

Milk, cheese and yoghurt supply calcium and protein, but some contain unhealthy types of fats.

Vegetables contain vitamins, minerals and also fibre, which help in the process of digestion.

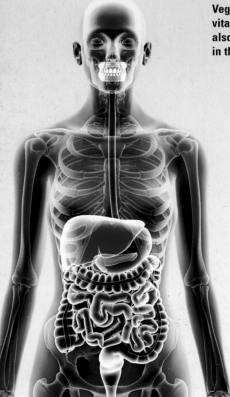

DIGESTION

Once swallowed, food is mixed with acids in the stomach and then moves on to the intestines. Here, the chemicals that the body needs are absorbed from it into the body. The chemicals used to break down food are produced in the pancreas and liver, as well as in the walls of the intestines.

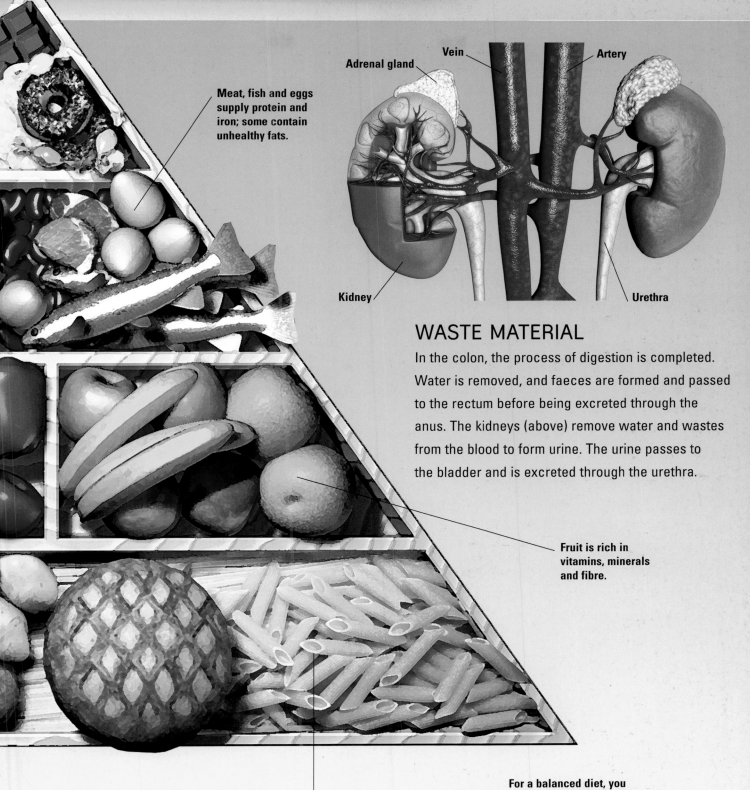

Meat, fish and eggs
supply protein and
iron; some contain
unhealthy fats.

Adrenal gland

Vein

Artery

Kidney

Urethra

WASTE MATERIAL

In the colon, the process of digestion is completed.
Water is removed, and faeces are formed and passed
to the rectum before being excreted through the
anus. The kidneys (above) remove water and wastes
from the blood to form urine. The urine passes to
the bladder and is excreted through the urethra.

Fruit is rich in
vitamins, minerals
and fibre.

Bread, pasta and rice
are the main sources
of carbohydrates.

For a balanced diet, you
should eat some of all the food
groups in the pyramid. However,
the higher up the pyramid a food
is, the less you should eat of it.

Hormones and metabolism

The body is not only controlled by electrical signals sent through the nervous system. It also uses chemicals called hormones to regulate the processes of life.

Hormones are produced in organs called glands, and released into the bloodstream to be transported to the areas they control.

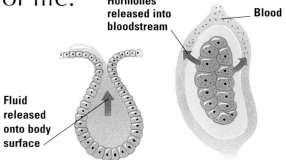

EXOCRINE GLAND   **ENDOCRINE GLAND**

The endocrine system

Not all glands produce hormones. Those that do make up the endocrine system. This system controls growth and metabolism, and affects feelings and emotions.

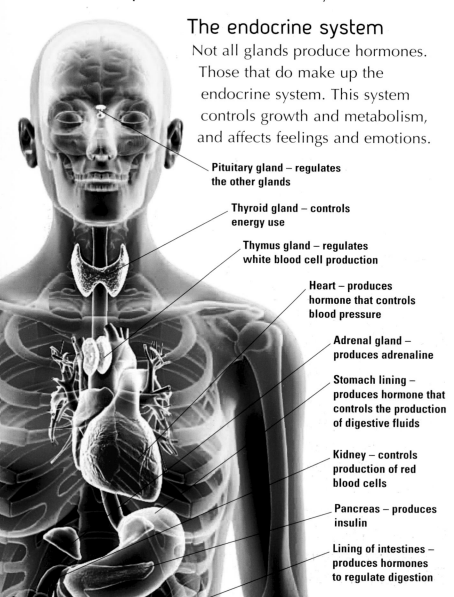

Pituitary gland – regulates the other glands

Thyroid gland – controls energy use

Thymus gland – regulates white blood cell production

Heart – produces hormone that controls blood pressure

Adrenal gland – produces adrenaline

Stomach lining – produces hormone that controls the production of digestive fluids

Kidney – controls production of red blood cells

Pancreas – produces insulin

Lining of intestines – produces hormones to regulate digestion

Glands

Glands that produce fluids – such as milk, tears, saliva, mucus or sweat – secrete them through tubes called ducts. Endocrine glands do not have ducts. The hormones they produce are secreted from their surfaces.

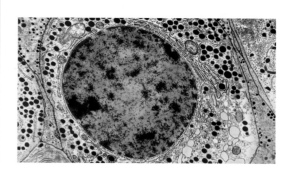

Pituitary gland

This controls all the others. It also produces hormones that control growth and trigger the production of eggs in women each month. This is a hormone-producing cell (pink, above) inside the pituitary gland.

Daily rhythms

The levels of some hormones vary through the day, and our behaviour changes as a result. Most people are most alert in the mornings, are physically strongest in the afternoon, feel tired in the late evening and are most deeply asleep at around 2am. Blood pressure and temperature are lowest in the early morning, and highest in the early evening.

A balanced diet provides the chemicals that the metabolism needs.

Adrenaline

When we are frightened or startled, a hormone called adrenaline is released, which prepares our bodies to fight or to run away. Extra blood flows to the muscles and less to the digestive system and skin, our pupils widen and the heart speeds up. The amount of energy-producing glucose in the blood increases.

SCIENTIFIC INPUT

INSULIN AND THE PANCREAS

The pancreas produces a number of hormones. These include insulin, crystals of which are shown above. Insulin controls the way in which a type of sugar called glucose is transferred from the blood to the tissues, where it is used to produce energy. A disease called diabetes reduces insulin production, resulting in too much glucose in the blood.

Metabolism

The many chemical reactions that take place in the body together make up the metabolism. Metabolism does two things. Firstly, metabolic reactions build up chemicals to make tissues. Secondly, they break them down, often to release energy.

Genes and chromosomes

Our bodies are made up of organs, and organs are made of tissues, and tissues of cells. Inside each cell are complex chemicals that control the body's shape and functions.

CELL DIVISION
Everyone begins life as a single cell, which divides many times.

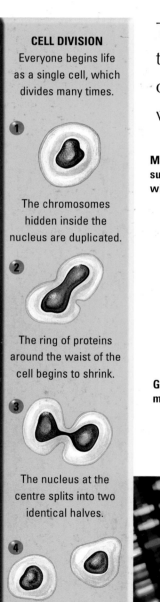

1 The chromosomes hidden inside the nucleus are duplicated.

2 The ring of proteins around the waist of the cell begins to shrink.

3 The nucleus at the centre splits into two identical halves.

4 The two 'daughter' cells separate from one another.

The structures of these chemicals are passed down through the generations, which is why we are similar to our parents. But they merge and change in the process, which is why we are not identical to our parents.

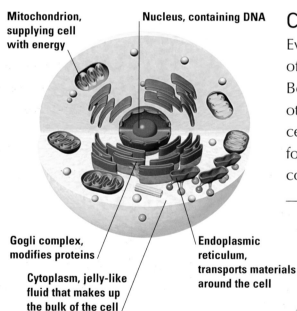

Mitochondrion, supplying cell with energy

Nucleus, containing DNA

Gogli complex, modifies proteins

Cytoplasm, jelly-like fluid that makes up the bulk of the cell

Endoplasmic reticulum, transports materials around the cell

Cells and nuclei

Every part of the body is made up of cells, each too small to see. Bones, nerves, muscles and other tissues are each built from cells of a particular type. Except for red blood cells, every cell is controlled by a central nucleus.

Genes

Cell nuclei contain a set of chemical instructions called genes, which tell the cell how to grow. Characteristics – such as eye colour – are passed on from parents to children through genes. The image on the left is a computer representation of the genome – the human genetic code.

DNA and chromosomes

A gene is made up of a sequence of structures, each of which look like the rungs of a twisted ladder. The ladder is a molecule of a chemical called deoxyribonucleic acid (DNA). The DNA molecules are coiled up tightly to form chromosomes (far right).

The DNA strands wind round each other to form a double helix.

Each 'rung' of the DNA ladder is a pair of chemical units called bases.

Strips made of sugar and other molecules hold the DNA together.

Mutations

When cells divide, the DNA is not copied perfectly. It can also be altered by chemicals or by radiation. These changes in DNA are called mutations. They can result in offspring who are very different to their parents.

Inheritance

When an egg is fertilized by a sperm cell, the chromosomes (above) from one parent exchange some DNA with the chromosomes of the other. A new set of chromosomes forms with the mixed DNA. These chromosomes are those of the child that grows from the egg. So the child will inherit some of the characteristics of each parent.

Evolution

Over many generations, animal species develop to suit where they live through the process of evolution. When resources are limited, animals fight. Those with differences that give them an advantage survive to breed and pass on their DNA. For example, these finches (above) have evolved beaks that are best suited to the types of food available in their different habitats.

Sex and reproduction

Human beings are able to have children because of their reproductive systems. A man's and woman's genes mix, producing a child who has characteristics of both parents.

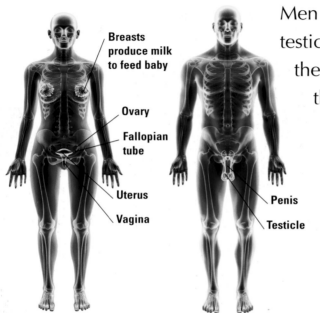

Breasts produce milk to feed baby

Ovary

Fallopian tube

Uterus

Vagina

Penis

Testicle

Men produce moving cells called sperm in their testicles, and women produce cells called eggs in their ovaries. A sperm can fertilize an egg, which then develops into a new human being.

Male and female

The type of chromosomes (genetic material) carried by the sperm determine whether a person is male or female. From puberty until the menopause, women produce eggs on a monthly cycle. Men produce sperm from puberty until old age.

Conception

To conceive a child, a man inserts his penis into a woman's vagina. He releases a fluid called semen, which contains millions of sperm. The sperm swim through the woman's uterus. On the way, one of them may fertilize an egg in one of the two fallopian tubes.

Early stages of life

The instant a sperm has penetrated the egg, no other sperm may enter. The fertilized egg travels down the fallopian tube to the uterus. The egg cell divides many times, developing into an embryo and then a foetus. Within three months, the foetus has a face and a beating heart.

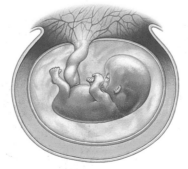

Fertilized egg cell

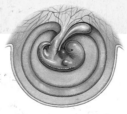

4 weeks

8 weeks

28 weeks

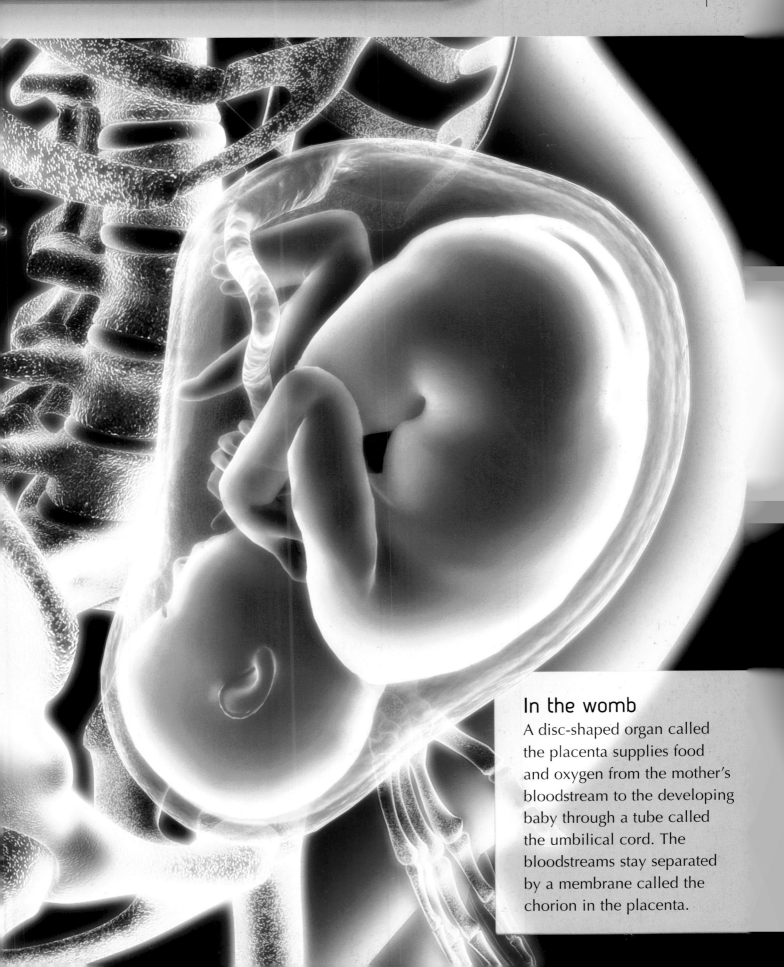

In the womb
A disc-shaped organ called the placenta supplies food and oxygen from the mother's bloodstream to the developing baby through a tube called the umbilical cord. The bloodstreams stay separated by a membrane called the chorion in the placenta.

Growth and ageing

Human beings take around 20 years to complete their physical growth and become adults. The processes of physical decline and ageing begin soon afterwards.

Alongside the physical changes through life, there are emotional changes too, especially during puberty. The development of the brain and intelligence can be continuous all through a person's life.

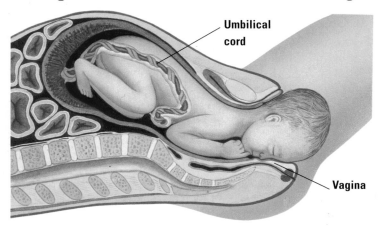

Umbilical cord

Vagina

Giving birth

About nine months after conception, the uterus begins to contract powerfully and rhythmically. It pushes the baby out of the uterus through the vagina – usually head first. After the baby has emerged, the umbilical cord is cut.

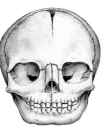

When young, children's skulls are rounded.

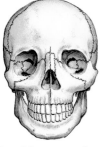

In adolescence, the face becomes longer.

Early years

Compared to many other animals, newborn babies are vulnerable – to begin with, they cannot even control their body temperature. But development is very rapid, and within three years most children can walk, talk and have well-developed personalities.

Bone development

Bones develop at different rates, which means that the shapes of the body and face change. At around ages 12 to 14, both boys and girls experience a 'spurt' in height, due to an increase in the growth rate of their long bones. Bones become less flexible and more brittle with age.

Puberty

Puberty usually takes place between the ages of about 9 to 14 for girls, and 10 to 17 for boys. It is when the hormones oestrogen (in girls) and testosterone (in boys) cause many changes. The production of eggs (girls) and sperm (boys) begins, body hair appears and voices get lower.

Ageing

When someone ages, their muscles get weaker, their sight and hearing deteriorate, and some of their mental skills, such as memory, decline. Egg production ceases in women around the age of 50, during the menopause.

AMAZING FACTS

TWINS

Identical twins result from an egg which splits in two after it has been fertilized. Because their DNA is the same, identical twins are the same gender and look very similar to each other. Most twins are non-identical, or 'fraternal'. They are conceived from two separate eggs, and each may be male or female.

The family unit

Humans are social, preferring to live in groups. Often, the most important group is the family. Families often protect and support both their children and their older members. The roles and sizes of families vary greatly in different countries and cultures.

DEFENCE SYSTEMS

THE BODY FACES MANY DANGERS, FROM PHYSICAL DAMAGE, EXTREME ENVIRONMENTS AND INFECTIOUS DISEASES. TO DEFEND ITSELF, IT HAS MANY DIFFERENT SYSTEMS AND BARRIERS.

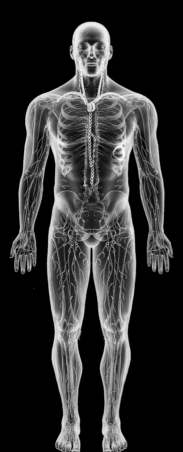

A RANGE OF DEFENCES

Shivering and sweating defend against cold and heat, and the skin tans as a protection against sunburn. A network of vessels called the lymphatic system extends throughout the body (left). Lymph fluid moves between blood, tissues and lymph vessels. Lymph nodes in the groin, armpit and neck filter out and destroy harmful organisms.

THE IMMUNE SYSTEM

The immune system consists of the lymphatic system and white blood cells. It produces special proteins called antibodies to destroy bacteria. The system can 'remember' many of the organisms that infect it, so that it can respond very rapidly and effectively if it meets them a second time.

Bacillus anthracis (orange) are the rod-shaped bacteria that cause the disease anthrax.

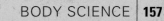

SURFACE DEFENCES

The skin, and mucous membranes such as those in the nose and lungs, act as barriers to infection. They have disease-fighting bacteria and fungi living on them. If the lungs are punctured, their damaged tissues produce chemicals that attract white blood cells to them. The walls of blood vessels in the area also change to allow white cells to pass through them easily.

A neutrophil white blood cell engulfs *Bacillus anthracis* bacteria to protect the body.

WHITE CELL DEFENCES

There are five types of white cell. Basophils release chemicals that trigger tissue defences. Eosinophils help fight viruses. Lymphocytes attack cancer cells and viruses. And monocytes and neutrophils physically engulf dangerous micro-organisms. White cells live in both the bloodstream and the lymphatic system, and are manufactured in the marrow of the larger bones.

Health and fitness

Keeping fit and healthy can add decades to a person's life and make it more enjoyable. Public services, such as clean water and vaccinations, are vital for this too.

Health and fitness depend on getting enough sleep, taking exercise and having regular health checks.

HOW A VIRUS ATTACKS

1. The virus attacks a cell.

2. The virus injects its genetic material into the cell.

3. The genetic material establishes itself in the cell.

4. The cell is forced to make new viruses.

5. The new viruses leave the dying cell.

Daily portions of fruit and vegetables are essential for health.

Body defence systems

The body can defend itself from infections, but if it responds too slowly it may not survive. Vaccination involves injecting a weakened version of a virus such as measles. This triggers the immune system to develop a defence against the full-strength virus.

A balanced diet

A balanced diet includes plenty of fresh fruit and vegetables, and wholemeal bread or healthy cereal, which all provide dietary fibre. It also includes lots of water, and only small amounts of sweet or fatty foods. Eating either too much or too little leads quickly to poor health.

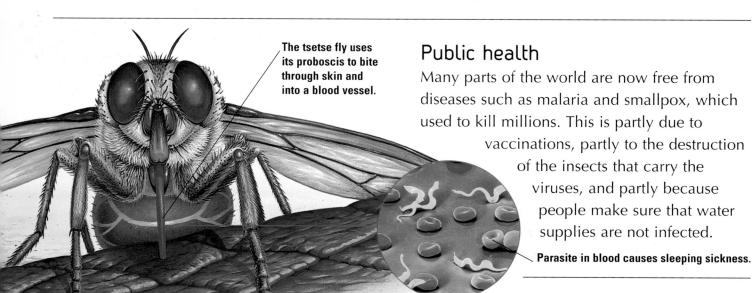

The tsetse fly uses its proboscis to bite through skin and into a blood vessel.

Public health

Many parts of the world are now free from diseases such as malaria and smallpox, which used to kill millions. This is partly due to vaccinations, partly to the destruction of the insects that carry the viruses, and partly because people make sure that water supplies are not infected.

Parasite in blood causes sleeping sickness.

Keeping fit

The best way to keep fit is to spend at least 30 minutes a day on activities that will raise the heart rate. This can include running or swimming, or taking part in sports such as football, netball, tennis or basketball. It may involve visiting a gym or simply walking briskly. Being fit extends the lifespan of a person, increases their resistance to disease, and is also very enjoyable.

Training

The body adapts to cope with the way it is used. Muscles strengthen and grow if they are exercised. Speed, coordination and stamina also improve with regular training. The right clothes – including footwear – are important to reduce the risk of injury, allow free movement, and avoid overheating or chilling.

Stretching

If an exercise session is started or stopped too quickly, especially in cold conditions, strained ('pulled') muscles and other problems result. Stretching before and after exercise avoids these problems. Regular stretching also helps to reduce the stiffness that affects the joints of older people.

Body facts

All the body systems must support each other in order to survive, and they need the right materials to do this. As well as large amounts of water, protein, fat, carbohydrate and fibre, small quantities of many other chemicals are essential.

BODY SYSTEMS

Circulatory: transports nutrients and oxygen to the cells and wastes (including carbon dioxide) from them.

Digestive: breaks down food into nutrients.

Endocrine: controls the body through hormones.

Immune: defends against disease (the lymphatic system is part of the immune system).

Integumentary (skin, hair and nails): provides a protective barrier.

Muscular: provides movement and structure.

Nervous: allows thinking, control and sensation.

Respiratory: supplies the blood with oxygen and returns carbon dioxide to the air.

Reproductive: produces children.

Skeletal: gives shape and protection and is moved by the muscular system.

Urinary: removes wastes.

VITAL VITAMINS AND MINERALS

Vitamins

A: Retinol
B1: Thiamine
B2: Riboflavin
B3: Niacin
B5: Pantothenic acid
B6: Pyridoxine
B7: Biotin
B9: Folic acid
B12: Cyanocobalamin
C: Ascorbic acid
D: Ergocalciferol and Cholecalciferol
E: Tocopherol
K: Naphthoquinone

Minerals

Calcium	Manganese
Chlorine	Molybdenum
Chromium	Phosphorus
Cobalt	Potassium
Copper	Selenium
Fluorine	Sodium
Iodine	Sulphur
Iron	Zinc
Magnesium	

Skateboarders have balance, agility and muscular strength

USEFUL WEBSITES

www.rigb.org The website contains a comprehensive tour of the human anatomy.

www.apples4theteacher.com/elibrary/bodybook.html Interactive website about the body.

www.kidskonnect.com/component/content/article/31-health/337-human-body.html Fast facts for kids on the human body.

www.bbc.co.uk/science/humanbody/ BBC website about the human body and mind.

Story of the Past

Throughout history, there have been many changes, from the early farmers who grew crops rather than roaming for food, to the growth of cities with very large populations. These constant changes can create conflict as people try to preserve their way of life or impose it on others. Many empires have grown before disappearing forever, and this cycle continues in today's world.

Early civilizations

Humans evolved over thousands of years. They were always on the move, searching for food and hunting wild creatures. Later they learned to grow crops and breed animals.

They built permanent settlements and organized societies. This was the beginning of civilization.

Australopithecus 'southern man'   **Homo habilis** 'handy man'   **Homo erectus** 'upright man'   **Homo sapiens** 'thinking man'

Development of humans

Nearly five million years ago, humans evolved from hominids (great apes). They were bipedal, walking on two legs. Scientists have called them *Homo sapiens*, which is Latin for 'thinking man'.

Prehistory

The word 'prehistory' describes the many thousands of years when modern humans lived but before written records began. People hunted animals and gathered foods such as nuts, seeds, fruits and roots. Some illustrated their everyday lives in cave paintings.

The Stone Ages

The Stone Ages lasted from about 700,000 to 3000BCE. Over this period, humans began to use sophisticated tools such as axes, spears and grindstones to hunt, cut and process food.

From around 8000BCE great centres, such as the Neolithic settlement of Çatal Hüyük in Turkey (below), were built. Here, many mud houses were crammed together, and entered via ladders and holes in the roofs.

The Bronze Age

Metals came into use during the Bronze Age. The hardest was bronze, an alloy of tin and copper that could be cast into any shape. Bronze was in use right across Europe and into India by 1500BCE. The Assyrians used bronze to make weapons, but later tipped their arrows with iron.

Development of writing

The earliest examples of writing were at the beginning of the Bronze Age. The cuneiform writing of Sumer (in today's Iraq) used wedge-shaped marks cut into soft clay tablets (right). The Egyptians used hieroglyphs.

The Iron Age

The first people to heat iron ore, hammer out its impurities and dip it in cold water to set it were the northern Asian Hittites in the 14th century BCE. Iron tools encouraged the spread of farming and the material was also used to make items such as weapons, cooking pots and statues.

AMAZING FACTS

INVENTION OF THE WHEEL

Early wheels were simple solid wooden discs with a hole for the axle, possibly inspired by the use of turntables to make pottery. The first wheels for transport were made by the Sumerians sometime before 3000BCE, the date they first appear in drawings. The invention of the wheel allowed people to move heavy loads over long distances, and this had a huge influence on farming, trade and war.

The ancient Egyptians

The Egyptians created a highly organized civilization that lasted from about 3100 to 30BCE. Their powerful nation had a rich culture based around a belief in an afterlife.

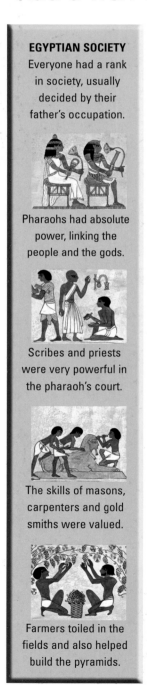

EGYPTIAN SOCIETY
Everyone had a rank in society, usually decided by their father's occupation.

Pharaohs had absolute power, linking the people and the gods.

Scribes and priests were very powerful in the pharaoh's court.

The skills of masons, carpenters and gold smiths were valued.

Farmers toiled in the fields and also helped build the pyramids.

The kingdom developed from desert peoples who settled along the banks of the River Nile in northeastern Africa.

Farming

Every summer, the Nile flooded and washed dark, fertile mud onto the land. Canals and ditches were dug to irrigate the fields. Typical crops were wheat and barley, used to make bread and beer, and the flax needed to produce linen cloth.

Khufu 2558–32BCE

Hatshepsut 1473–58BCE

Ramesses II 1279–13BCE

Cleopatra 51–30BCE

Godlike rulers

In total, more than 300 pharaohs ruled Egypt. They were nearly all men who passed power from father to son. Pharaohs were both political and religious leaders for their people. A pharaoh made laws and decided when to go to war. He or she also represented the gods on Earth.

The Great Pyramid

The largest ancient Egyptian structure was the Great Pyramid at Giza. The tomb of King Khufu, it took 20 years to build, and was completed in 2528 BCE. At 146.5m high, it is the largest of three pyramids at Giza.

Hieroglyphs

Egyptian writing was based on a 700-strong alphabet of picture symbols called hieroglyphs. Scribes wrote on paper made from the dried reeds of papyrus that grew by the Nile, or the writing was carved into the stone of temples and tombs. It took years to learn to write it.

Egyptian gods

The Egyptians had many gods, each with specific roles. Everything about the gods was symbolic. So Osiris (right), as god of the dead, wears mummy bandages. He has a green face and holds a farmer's crook and flail to show he is also the god of new life.

Building a pyramid

Huge blocks of stone were floated along the Nile and fitted tightly together by thousands of workers. The completed structure was covered in creamy white limestone and capped with gold, so that it glistened across the red desert. Later pharaohs were buried in hidden tombs in an attempt to stop tomb-raiding.

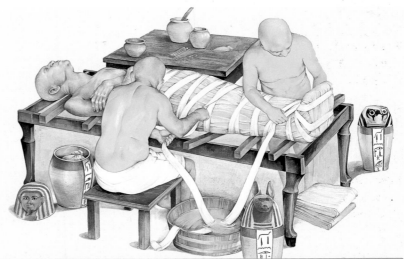

CULTURAL NOTE

MUMMIFICATION

To preserve a pharaoh for the afterlife, the dead body was mummified. Priests removed the vital organs and stored all of them except the brain (which was considered worthless) in canopic jars. The corpse was dried out using natron salt, and then stuffed, wrapped in bandages and placed in a set of richly decorated coffins. The body was buried with shabtis – slave statues who would serve their master.

THE QIN DYNASTY

THIS CHINESE DYNASTY, LED BY THE RUTHLESS SHI HUANGDI (LEFT), UNIFIED CHINA FROM 221BCE. HE STANDARDIZED THE WRITTEN LANGUAGE, THE COINAGE, AND WEIGHTS AND MEASURES.

The first wall was built of rammed earth. In the 15th century CE, during the Ming dynasty, large parts of the wall were rebuilt using bricks and stone.

THE GREAT WALL

At this time, the fortifications that protected northern China from attacking tribes were improved with the building of large sections of a Great Wall. It was up to 9m high, and wide enough for five galloping horses. Thousands of Chinese died building it. Rebuilt many times since, at 6,400km, it is the longest and largest construction in the world.

Every soldier's face
is different.

A TERRACOTTA ARMY

Shi Huangdi was buried in 206BCE inside
a city-sized mausoleum. There, his body
was guarded by more than 8,000 life-size
terracotta figures of warriors and horses,
lined up in precise military order. The project is
thought to have occupied 700,000 workers over 38 years. The
clay army was unearthed in 1974, and is still being excavated.

TRADE ALONG THE SILK ROAD

After Shi Huangdi's death, the Han dynasty ruled China
for four centuries. A major factor in its success was an
increase of traffic along the Silk Road, a series of trade
routes connecting Asia and the Mediterranean. This
was the channel for exporting Chinese goods
such as silk, pottery and tea to the
Roman empire and beyond.

The ancient Greeks

The sophisticated ancient Greek civilization left lasting legacies in politics, medicine, science, the arts and architecture.

The Greek empire was a loosely linked set of city-states on the mainland and islands near Athens. The period 500–350BCE is known as the Greek Classical Age.

Greek warfare

Wars were common between Greek city-states as well as with neighbouring countries. In sea battles, the Greeks sailed triremes (ships with three rows of oars) at full speed to ram into enemy boats. They were also well organized on land. For example, Spartan soldiers fought in close formation, overlapping their shields for protection.

A painted 'all-seeing eye' to help and guide the Greeks at sea

The Olympics

The first Olympic Games were held in 776BCE and then at four-year intervals afterwards. They grew out of military training, and included discus and javelin throwing, the long jump, wrestling and sprinting.

City-states

The Greek empire was made up of about 300 city-states, some of them tiny. Greece was frequently torn by rivalry, especially between Athens and Sparta. Athens introduced democracy, while Sparta was run like a military camp. Most city-states were prosperous and relied on slaves to do much of the hard work.

Doctors and scholars

The Greeks valued education, using observation and reasoning to find out about the world around them. Doctors such as Hippocrates studied the body and illnesses. Scholars such as the mathematician Archimedes and the philosopher Aristotle laid the groundwork for modern science.

Greek architecture

The Greeks loved public buildings and left a huge legacy of architectural ideas. Best known is the Parthenon, a beautifully proportioned temple set on the sacred hill of the Acropolis in Athens. Completed in the 5th century BCE, it is still standing. Other major buildings included huge open-air theatres that could seat audiences of 10,000.

Alexander the Great

In 336 BCE, aged only 20, Alexander became king of Macedonia. This well-educated and accomplished soldier took over the Greek empire before ruthlessly conquering vast areas from Greece to northern India.

CULTURAL NOTE

THE GODS OF ANCIENT GREECE

The ancient Greeks believed that their gods lived on Mount Olympus. There were many gods, and they used their powers to help or hinder ordinary people. The head god was Zeus (3), with his wife Hera (4) by his side. His brother Hades (6) ruled the underworld, Demeter (5) was goddess of the Earth, and Aphrodite (2) goddess of beauty. Hermes (1) was the gods' messenger.

The Roman empire

At its peak, the Roman empire covered much of Europe and reached into Africa and Asia.

The Romans had a sophisticated way of life, with planned cities and organized government, but their society relied on slavery.

Jupiter   Juno   Neptune   Diana
Mars
Venus   Apollo

CULTURAL NOTE

GODS OF ANCIENT ROME
Many Roman gods were borrowed from the Greeks, but given different names. For example, the chief Roman god was Jupiter, not Zeus. Every home had a shrine or room dedicated to a god and there were public temples across the empire, the largest being the domed Pantheon in Rome.

Efficient army

The army was organized into groups called legions, cohorts and centuries. Most fighting was on foot and the well-equipped soldiers could link their shields into an impenetrable barrier called the tortoise formation.

Roman games

Amphitheatres, where bloodthirsty games and fights, sea battles and animal hunts were held, were very popular. Rome's Colosseum (right), opened in 80BCE, and could seat 50,000 spectators on three levels to cheer on the gladiators fighting to the death in the arena. Losers were spared or killed on a thumbs-up or thumbs-down signal from the emperor.

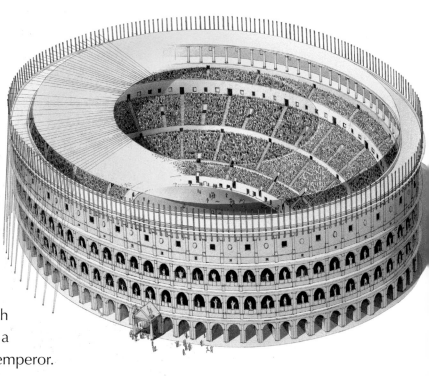

The Roman baths

Every major Roman town had public baths, heated by an underfloor hot-air system called a hypocaust. All baths had a cold room, a warmer area where dirt could be scraped from the skin, and a pool for a refreshing dip.

Theatre

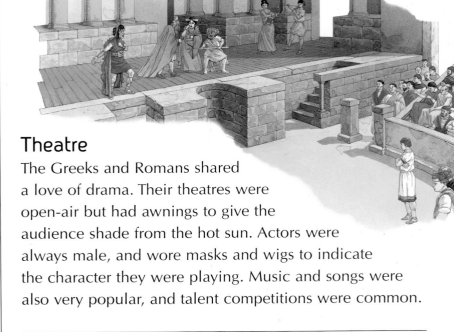

The Greeks and Romans shared a love of drama. Their theatres were open-air but had awnings to give the audience shade from the hot sun. Actors were always male, and wore masks and wigs to indicate the character they were playing. Music and songs were also very popular, and talent competitions were common.

Feats of engineering

The Romans were great builders and engineers. Cities were planned on a grid pattern and public fountains supplied with fresh water through a system of aqueducts. The channels and pipes of the aqueducts would usually travel underground, but they were built on high arches to cross valleys.

Emperors and the empire

Rome became an empire when Augustus was appointed emperor in 27BCE. Known as 'First Citizen', an emperor was all-powerful and his word was law. Many of the Roman emperors were plotted against, and several, including Julius Caesar, were assassinated.

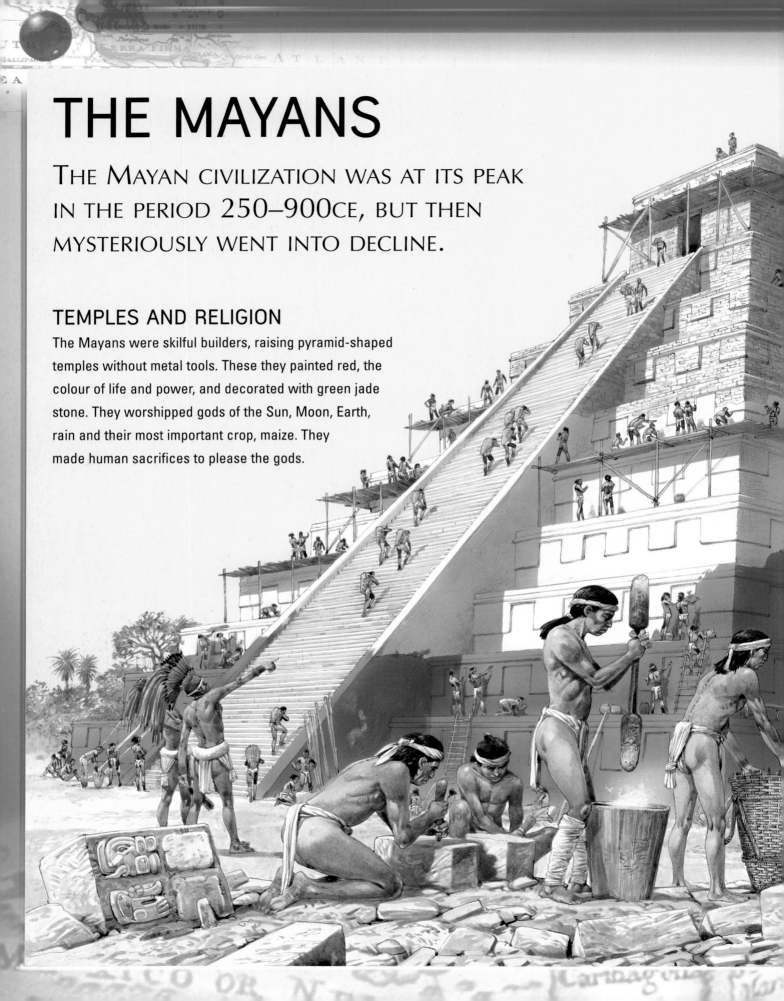

THE MAYANS

THE MAYAN CIVILIZATION WAS AT ITS PEAK IN THE PERIOD 250–900CE, BUT THEN MYSTERIOUSLY WENT INTO DECLINE.

TEMPLES AND RELIGION

The Mayans were skilful builders, raising pyramid-shaped temples without metal tools. These they painted red, the colour of life and power, and decorated with green jade stone. They worshipped gods of the Sun, Moon, Earth, rain and their most important crop, maize. They made human sacrifices to please the gods.

CITIES AND VILLAGES

The Mayan civilization was made up of a number of city-states, each ruled by a king claiming to be descended from the gods. Although most Mayans lived in farm villages, they built huge cities with vast populations, such as Copán, which was 13km long and 3km wide and featured temples, palaces and squares. Many of its monuments were carved with images of astronomy and astrology.

The Castillo, the main pyramid in the city of Chichén Itzá, was built around 800CE. Its base is 55m square.

The four staircases each had 91 steps and there was a platform on top, making a total of 365 – the number of days in the Mayan year.

MAKING WAR

Mayan kingdoms fought each other regularly, for trade and power, and to capture prisoners for religious sacrifices. Soldiers wielded short spears and wooden axes with stone blades, plus throwing weapons such as sticks and javelins. For armour, they wore cotton jackets stuffed with salt.

Medieval Europe

The Medieval period, or Middle Ages, lasted from the 6th to the 15th centuries. It was a time of hardship, with many wars, famines and plagues.

Religion was more important than nation. Great cathedrals were built to praise God and the Church influenced everyday and political life.

Castles and fortifications

Built to protect land and survive the frequent wars, castles became gradually more fortified. Narrow, slit windows meant arrows could be fired at attackers from a safe place. Most castles could withstand sieges.

The Crusades

A series of crusades were mounted between 1096 and 1291. Christian armies from Europe tried, and failed, to drive the Muslim Turks from the Holy Lands of the Bible. Knights took part to win lands and fortune.

Joan of Arc was captured and burned at the stake by the English in 1431.

The Hundred Years War

From 1337 to 1453, there was a series of conflicts between England and France, largely over English claims on French land. Despite setbacks, the French won, due to the leadership of Joan of Arc and their superior resources.

WEAPONS OF WAR

Methods of war changed when the stirrup made horse-riding easier, and knights on horseback became an essential part of armies.

Archers fired a barrage of deadly arrows – and the English longbow was much feared.

Crossbows shot a bolt with great power. They were easier to use than bows, so less practice was needed.

Knights carried shields and wore chainmail – small, linked iron rings that protected them from most weapons.

Feudal life

For much of this period, the social order was unchanged. The king, at the top, offered land in return for support from the nobles. They in turn allowed peasants to farm the land in exchange for goods or their service when required.

The Black Death

In the 14th century, this plague killed 25 million, about a third of the people of Europe. The Black Death was carried by fleas travelling on rats. It quickly spread through countries weakened by famine. No treatment was possible, and villages and towns were left deserted as the inhabitants died or fled.

AMAZING FACTS

THE VIKINGS

These fighters sailed their fast, strong boats across the sea from Scandinavia and up rivers to raid rich settlements such as monasteries. They were keen traders, fierce warriors and eventually settlers, giving their name to the Normans (Norsemen) of France, and the English city of York (Jorvic).

Tournaments

These were a popular way of practising fighting skills and providing entertainment. Knights fought each other on foot, or sometimes in a joust on horseback, toppling opponents with long lances. Those who were defeated paid a ransom of money or equipment.

Explorers

From the 15th century onwards, European explorers sought new lands, gold, silver and precious spices. Some of them also wanted to spread the Christian faith.

Improved navigation and map-making, and the manufacture of caravels (small, fast ships that could sail against the wind) made longer journeys possible.

Henry the Navigator discusses the building of a new ship.

Conquering the Aztecs

The Aztec civilization of Mexico was among the first casualties of European exploration. It was destroyed by a mix of Western diseases and Spanish firepower. The Aztecs had a strong religious culture based around sacrifice.

Henry the Navigator

Between 1424 and 1434, the son of the king of Portugal, Prince Henry, paid sailors to explore the coast of Africa. This opened up new trading routes down the east coast of Africa. Henry had ships built and even founded a school of navigation in Portugal to train future explorers. Later Portuguese sailors reached India and the Far East.

The New World

Between 1492 and 1502, the Italian sailor Christopher Columbus sailed his fleet west from Spain four times. He hoped to find a new route to Asia. However, he did not realize that the islands and mainland where he landed were part of a new world, the then unknown continent of North America.

Eastern trade route

In 1497–98, Portuguese explorer Vasco da Gama led the first European expedition to sail round Africa straight to India. This new route allowed Portugal to be the first to take over lands and colonize parts of east Africa. It increased opportunities for the Europeans to trade in valuable Indian spices and jewels.

Round the world

In 1519–22, Ferdinand Magellan sailed round the tip of South America, across the Pacific and back round Africa to Spain, completing the first round-the-world journey. He died on the way, as did most of his 270-strong crew – only 18 survived.

Magellan was killed on Mactan, in the Philippines.

AMAZING FACTS

INCA GOLD

The Inca civilization of about 12 million people, based in and around the Andes mountains in South America, was known by the Spanish to have much gold. In 1532, adventurer Francisco Pizarro held the Inca king for a ransom of a room filled with 11 tonnes of the precious metal. Then he killed the king anyway.

Cook and Australia

It took centuries for European explorers to reach the southern Pacific. It was not until 1768–79 that James Cook mapped many of its islands. He found some communities that had been established by local seafarers 1,500 years before.

AGE OF REVOLUTION

ACROSS EUROPE AND NORTH AMERICA, A PERIOD
OF REVOLUTION HELPED TO SHAPE THE MODERN AGE.
IN MANY COUNTRIES, DEMOCRATIC GOVERNMENT
REPLACED THE RULE OF KINGS AND QUEENS.

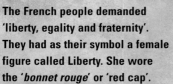

The French people demanded
'liberty, egality and fraternity'.
They had as their symbol a female
figure called Liberty. She wore
the '*bonnet rouge*' or 'red cap'.

FRENCH REVOLUTION

From 1789, poor government and a huge gulf between rich and poor
fuelled a revolution in France. This marked the end for the unpopular
king, Louis XVI, and his wife Marie Antoinette. She was one of at least
18,000 nobles and their allies who were
sent to the guillotine during the Reign
of Terror, 1793–94. It was also the
start of a ten-year upheaval as a
new republic was established.

During the French Revolution, on 14 July 1789, the Bastille prison in Paris was stormed by the revolutionaries. The prison was a symbol of royal power and a place where ammunition and weapons were stored.

THE RISE OF NAPOLEON

A brilliant general called Napoleon used his position as a war hero to become military dictator of France, electing himself emperor from 1804. He reformed the way France was governed. Banished to the Italian island of Elba, he briefly regained power, but was finally defeated at the Battle of Waterloo in 1815. In 1821, he died in exile on the island of St Helena.

THE AMERICAN REVOLUTION

The 13 colonies of North America resented the taxes and laws imposed by Britain. Partly funded by France, and fuelled by ideas of independence, they fought against the British from 1775. The British could not sustain the far-away conflict. The war was won by 1781, and American sovereignty recognized from 1783.

The Industrial Revolution

During the 18th century, the introduction of new technology and new sources of power led to the beginning of mass production.

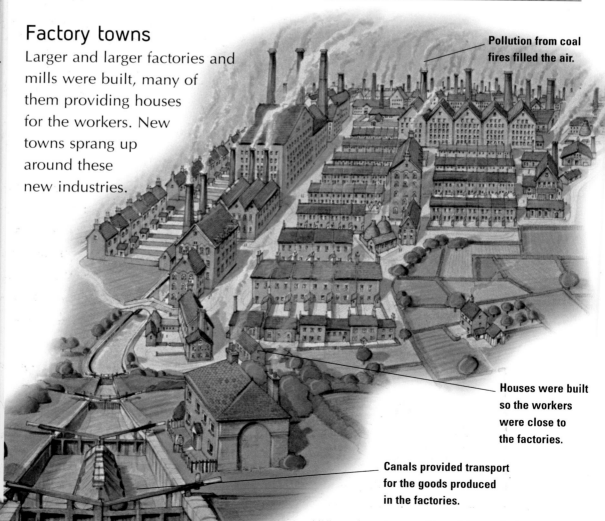

TEXTILE REVOLUTION

Machines allowing one person to do the work of many transformed the economy.

The Spinning Jenny spun yarn at the turn of a handle.

Arkwright's water frame made thread at speed.

The cotton gin separated cotton fibre and seeds.

The Jacquard loom used punch cards to make cloth.

There was social change right across Europe. People who had typically farmed and lived in small villages moved to factories or office work in smoky towns.

Water wheels

Water power began to take the place of horse power. The energy taken from moving water powered the new machines, which were grouped together to create the first factories.

Factory towns

Larger and larger factories and mills were built, many of them providing houses for the workers. New towns sprang up around these new industries.

Pollution from coal fires filled the air.

Houses were built so the workers were close to the factories.

Canals provided transport for the goods produced in the factories.

Iron construction

A new, cheap material, cast iron, allowed engineers to develop new techniques for building large structures such as bridges. This is the first iron bridge, built in England in 1779. From 1784, the even stronger wrought iron was also available.

Child labour

Factories and coal mines needed cheap labour, and children were the solution. They were small enough to crawl along tunnels and under machinery, and were forced to work long hours in return for poor pay.

Steam power

Steam began to replace water and wind power. The need for rapid transport prompted the development of steam locomotives and railroad systems.

HISTORICAL DATA

SLAVERY

The Industrial Revolution boosted the use of slavery as a source of labour. Packed slave ships carried chained-up human cargo from Africa to America in terrible conditions. The slaves were then put to work on plantations to produce cotton, sugar and tobacco. In 1780, Pennsylvania was the first US state to abolish slavery, and other states and countries gradually followed.

The Saint Pierre, or Number 33, built in France in 1844

Colonies and migration

From 1800, western countries created huge empires in Africa and Asia. Powerful navies protected ships that ferried slaves and raw materials around the globe.

North America and Australia attracted many migrants from Europe. The first settlers were sometimes exiled criminals, but many followed in search of work, and then stayed on and sent money back home.

The Irish potato famine

Food shortages and economic problems were major causes of migration. One example is the Great Irish Famine of 1845–51, when the failure of the potato crop starved a million people and led at least half that number to board ships travelling to the USA.

Gold rushes

The discovery of gold deposits started gold rushes in North America, Canada, New Zealand and Australia during the 19th century. People travelled across the world to mine and pan for the precious nuggets, and they established many new settlements.

Miners pan for gold in California, USA.

MIGRATION TO THE USA

For many years, packed boatloads of immigrants arrived in the USA. This led to the creation of an entry point on Ellis Island, in New York harbour. Between 1892 and 1954, more than 20 million immigrants arrived there for registration and medical checks before dispersing all over the country.

WORLD WAR I

THE GREAT WAR WAS THE WORST CONFLICT THE
WORLD HAD EVER SEEN. AN ENTIRE GENERATION
OF YOUNG MEN DIED: 8.5 MILLION SOLDIERS AND
MORE THAN TWICE THAT NUMBER OF CIVILIANS.

A trench on the Western front with Allied soldiers and tanks firing on the German enemy.

THE START OF THE WAR

On 28 June 1914, Archduke Ferdinand of Austria
was assassinated by an enemy Serb. Allies of both
Austria and Serbia were drawn in and Europe was
at war within six weeks. This was the first 'total
war', fought on a scale never known before.

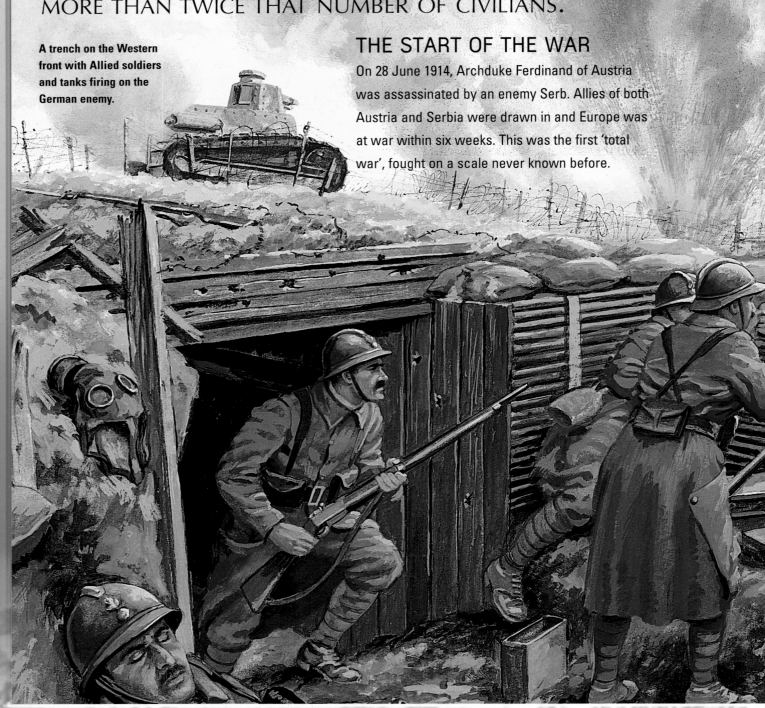

TRENCH WARFARE

The 'Western front' of trenches and fortifications stretched for more than 600km from the French coast to Switzerland. A similar 'Eastern front' separated Austria and Russia. The trenches were cramped, waterlogged and rife with rats and disease. Lines of troops were ordered 'over the top', often to be mown down by machine guns.

German soldiers defended their position on the Western front with machine guns and poison gas.

AFTER THE SLAUGHTER

The turning point in the war came when the USA entered the fray in April 1917, following the sinking of some of their merchant ships. American supplies and reinforcements, combined with a naval blockade to starve Germany, brought an end to the war on 11 November 1918.

World War II

This war was fought on land, sea and air around the globe. Some people estimate that the total number of dead, from fighting, famine and disease, was as high as 72 million.

WEAPONS OF WAR

Key weapons were battleships and submarines at sea, fighters in the air, and tanks on land.

The Spitfire fighter was a single-seater used by the British and their allies.

Tiger 1 was the common name given to the German heavy tanks.

The USS Gearing DD710 was the ultimate World War II destroyer.

German U-boats enforced naval blockades against Allied shipping.

The war pitched Britain, the USA and the Soviet Union against Germany, Italy and Japan. It was fought across Europe, Asia, Africa and in the Pacific. A major turning point was the German failure to conquer the Soviet Union in 1943.

Adolf Hitler

Adolf Hitler gained power in Germany in 1933. He occupied neighbouring territories without opposition until the invasion of Poland prompted Britain and France to declare war.

War in the air

With Germany in control of most of Europe, it needed to win the war in the air to be able to invade Britain. But the British were developing new, faster planes, and these won the Battle of Britain in the summer of 1940.

Beginning of the end

On 30 April 1945, realizing that he had lost the war, Adolf Hitler killed himself in a bunker in Berlin. On 7 May 1945, the German high command signed unconditional surrender documents (below) – the war was over in Europe and Africa.

Pearl Harbor

In December 1941, the Japanese attacked the US fleet at Pearl Harbor in Hawaii. Expecting the Americans to join the war anyway, they hoped to destroy their navy first. This led to years of sea battles in the Pacific.

HISTORICAL DATA

THE HOLOCAUST

Hitler blamed many of Germany's problems on the Jews, and began to persecute them soon after he came to power. During the war, about six million Jews died. Many were taken by train to extermination camps where they were killed by poison gas, or were worked or starved to death. Tens of thousands of Roma people, the mentally ill, the physically disabled and homosexuals were killed in the same way.

Hiroshima and Nagasaki

The Japanese refused to surrender, so in August 1945, the USA dropped atom bombs on two Japanese cities. About 150,000 people died instantly, and World War II was finally over.

Independence

Many former Asian and African colonies gained their independence after the war. These included India in 1947 after a long campaign led by Mohandas Gandhi (above). One of the first acts of the United Nations was to divide Palestine into two, creating the new state of Israel.

The Cold War

This was a period of international tension that lasted from 1945 until the 1990s. It was between two great superpowers, the USA and the Soviet Union, supported by their own allies.

This was a clash of beliefs. The USA believed in capitalism – an economic system of free trade and private profit. The Soviet Union championed communism – state-controlled, common ownership.

The Soviet leader Nikita Khrushchev (left) and the US president John F. Kennedy (right) in a cartoon about the 1962 Cuban crisis.

Superpower struggle

The USA and the Soviet Union each tried to get the upper hand using technology and spies. They also sent troops or aid to opposite sides in wars in Korea, Vietnam and Afghanistan. In 1962, disagreement over the placing of nuclear missiles in Cuba threatened to cause a third world war.

Space race

There was also great competition between the superpowers in space exploration. The Soviet Union was first into orbit, launching the Sputnik satellite in 1957. The Americans landed the first astronauts on the Moon in 1969 with the Apollo 11 mission.

The fall of the Berlin Wall

On 13 August 1961, the Soviet Union began to build a large wall to separate West Berlin from East Berlin. The wall symbolized the division of Europe and, over the years, many people were killed trying to cross from East to West. Here, young people are celebrating shortly before the wall was pulled down in 1989. Germany was formally unified in 1990. The Soviet Union collapsed into a set of republics in 1991.

Chairman Mao

From 1949–76, communist China was led by the strong military and political leader, Mao Zedong. He isolated China from the rest of the world, controlling everything. Everyone had to work on collective farms, and the people were made to read his political ideas in the Little Red Book (left). Many opponents were executed.

The modern world

The late 20th and early 21st centuries have seen the growth of the Asian economies, climate change and increased terrorist activities.

Among the biggest developments has been the growth of international trade and communication. Brands and technologies have become global. It is now possible to buy identical goods in many different countries across the world.

End of apartheid

In South Africa, the apartheid system separated people by their colour or race. It ended in 1990, when activist Nelson Mandela was released from 28 years in jail, then elected president.

Peacekeeping forces

In troubled parts of the world, the blue-helmeted soldiers of the United Nations peacekeeping force try to maintain order. They ensure the rule of law and help with economic development. The force received the Nobel Prize for Peace in 1988.

Middle East unrest

Israeli–Palestinian conflict over Gaza and the West Bank (above) has led to unrest. Iraq has suffered terribly since the 2003 fall of Saddam Hussein in the Iraq War. And there is tension between Iran and the West over the development of nuclear technology.

Living in space

Since 2000, astronauts from many nations have visited the International Space Station (ISS), orbiting 340km above the Earth. The ISS is used for research, but has also welcomed five paying tourists. Space has now become a holiday destination!

Financial markets

Around the world, people buy and sell goods, stocks and bonds in huge numbers. For example, a decision taken in a stock exchange in Chicago (above) could have results in Hong Kong or Zurich. This 'globalization' is changing the world in which we live.

Terrorism

The 9/11 terrorist attack on the World Trade Center in New York in 2001 showed that global terrorism has arrived. Extremists are prepared to kill themselves to publicize their views.

1961   1991   2004

EARTH EVIDENCE

GLOBAL WARMING

Average temperatures on the Earth are rising because of the gases released by factories, cars and planes among other things. This is changing the climate, making both floods and droughts more likely. Whole environments are affected – Arctic ice is melting and mountains have less snow. In Switzerland (above), twice as much ice melted in Alpine glaciers between 1991 and 2004 than in the 30 years before.

History facts

The world has a population of about 7 billion, living in around 200 countries. It is estimated that, in total, more than 100 billion people have lived on Earth. Lifespans were short at first – only 20–35 years. Now they average 67 years.

WORLD POPULATION

25000BCE	3 million
10000BCE	4 million
1BCE	200 million
1000	275 million
1500	450 million
1650	500 million
1750	700 million
1850	1.2 billion
1900	1.6 billion
1950	2.55 billion
1975	4 billion
1990	5.3 billion
2000	6.1 billion
2010	6.9 billion predicted
2020	7.7 billion predicted
2050	9.3 billion predicted

SEVEN ANCIENT WONDERS

Great Pyramid of Giza, Egypt
Hanging Gardens of Babylon
Temple of Artemis, Ephesus
Statue of Zeus, Olympia
Mausoleum at Halicarnassus
Colossus of Rhodes
Pharos of Alexandria

SEVEN MODERN WONDERS

Empire State Building, New York, USA
Itaipú Dam, Brazil/Paraguay
CN Tower, Toronto, Canada
Panama Canal, Central America
Channel Tunnel, France/UK
Delta Works, the Netherlands
Golden Gate Bridge, San Francisco, USA

PEOPLE KILLED IN WARS (mi = million)

Second Congo War, 1998–2007 5.4 mi
Vietnam War, 1959–73 2.1 mi
Korean War, 1950–3 2.5–3.5 mi
World War II 1939–45 60–72 mi
Second Sino-Japanese War, 1931–45 20 mi
Russian Civil War, 1917–21 5–9 mi
World War I, 1914–18, 20 mi
Taiping Rebellion, China, 1851–64 20 mi
Napoleonic Wars, 1804–15 3.5–6 mi
Thirty Years' War, 1618–48 3–11.5 mi
Conquests of Tamerlane, 1360–1405 7–20 mi
Mongol conquests, 13th c. 30–60 mi
Manchu conquest of Ming China, 1616–62 25 mi

Oilfields ablaze, Kuwait, Persian Gulf War, 1990

USEFUL WEBSITES

www.bbc.co.uk/history/   A wide range of historical facts, fun and games for kids.

www.channel4.com/programmes/tags/history/   Many different topics, including children in history.

http://teacher.scholastic.com/histmyst/index.asp Information on many aspects of world history.

www.un.org/Pubs/CyberSchoolBus/   Covers current global issues.

People and Society

People are social creatures. They live and work in groups to solve major tasks that they cannot perform on their own. Over many centuries, people have occupied lands that have become countries with their own leaders and laws. They often have a similar culture founded on shared beliefs. Food, language, customs, clothing, art and music are all part of their society.

The human population

The first human beings probably lived in Africa. Today, there are about 7 billion people all over the planet.

No two people are totally alike in looks, beliefs and personality. They belong to different cultural or religious groups, and vary in the way they live and behave.

Population and growth

The world population passed 3 billion for the first time in 1960. By 2000, it had doubled. Many of these people live in large cities. As its population boomed, Tokyo (below) began to form a large urban area with the city of Yokohama. Together, these cities are home to over 34 million people.

Family

The family is the basic social unit of most people on the planet. A family that is made up of just parents and their children is called a nuclear family. Extended families are where grandparents and other relatives live under the same roof.

Living in a community

Some groups of families live closely together. The Yanomamo tribes (above) live in South America's rainforests, in a giant communal house called a *shabono* or *yano*.

Life expectancies

Advances in health and medicine mean that people live longer lives than in the past. In wealthy nations, people have a life expectancy of more than 80 years, but it is less than 50 years in the poorest countries.

Ethnic groups

The common ties of language, history, culture and religion link people in ethnic groups. In a busy city, there are dozens of different ethnic groups, and this can sometimes cause problems when the different cultures clash.

Growing up

Many cultures have some form of coming-of-age ceremony to signal a child's passage into adulthood. Boys from the Shan people of Myanmar and northern Thailand take part in the Poy Sang Long ceremony. This is a three-day event in which boys dressed as princes are carried to a monastery, where they become novice monks for a period of time.

CULTURAL NOTE

WEDDINGS

Marriage is a decision made by two people to join together, usually to build and care for a family. Marriages often begin with a joyful ceremony called a wedding where the two pledge themselves to each other. More rarely, there are much larger weddings. Here, 25,000 couples take part in a massed wedding held by the Unification Church in 1995.

HOMES AND SETTLEMENT

SHELTER IS ONE OF THE MOST BASIC HUMAN
NEEDS. PEOPLE FIRST TOOK SHELTER IN
TREES AND CAVES. OVER TIME, THEY
BEGAN TO BUILD PERMANENT
HOMES THAT WERE GROUPED
TOGETHER IN A SETTLEMENT.

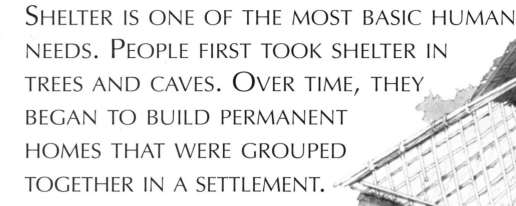

CITY LIFE

Cities contain thousands, sometimes millions,
of people who live very closely together. Many
have homes in tall blocks of flats or apartments.
Sometimes, very poor people are forced to live in
home-made shacks and shelters in shanty towns that grow up
around the edges of a city such as São Paolo, Brazil (above).

BUILT TO SUIT

Homes are built using whatever materials are available and to suit the local environment. This longhouse in Borneo, Indonesia, is built on giant stilts to avoid the regular flooding there and to let cool air circulate underneath. People live in private spaces on one side of the building, while there is a large public shared area on the other side.

The longhouse has ladders into each of the private dwellings. The space underneath can be used to prepare crops or shelter livestock.

TEMPORARY HOMES

In some parts of the world, people do not live in one place. They move around to find food for themselves or for their herds of animals. These people are known as nomads and often live in tents. Other people are forced to live in temporary homes because of natural disasters, a lack of food or war.

Health and education

Public services work to improve the health of people, and provide a system of education for everyone.

In some countries, the education is poor and hospitals few and far between. Sometimes charity organizations provide treatment.

Disease

Some diseases, such as this salmonella bacteria (right), are caused by eating bad food. Others are carried by insects, or transmitted from one person to another. Drugs have been developed to fight many diseases.

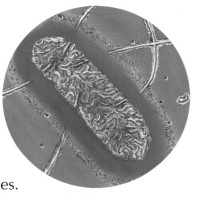

Health organizations

These organizations help to improve health by showing people safer ways of behaving, such as keeping wounds clean. They also help fight disease. Here, a medic gives a young child a vaccination that will protect him.

Literacy

Literacy is the ability to read and write. In wealthy countries, most children learn at a young age and there are plenty of books, schools and teachers. In poorer countries, there are not as many resources.

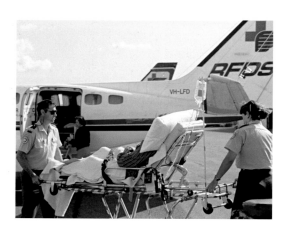

Flying doctors

In places such as Australia, there are many people who live far away from towns. They rely on education by radio. When they are seriously ill, they call on the flying doctor (above) to bring medical help to them, or if necessary, airlift them to a hospital.

Education

Education is concerned with gathering information about the world. Most education is carried out in schools – these schoolchildren are being taught how to measure the weather. Education is not just for children. Many adults take courses at home, or at colleges or universities.

Finding water

People in wealthy nations use around ten times more water per day than those in poor countries who have no water pipes and supplies. These women near Sukhana Lake in India are carrying their family's daily supply of drinking water in jars.

SCIENTIFIC INPUT

LIFESTRAW

For millions of people, stale, dirty rivers or lakes are the only source of water. Every day, more than 6,000 people in the world's poorest regions die because they have drunk water contaminated with dangerous diseases. The Lifestraw is an ingenious tube that contains filters and chemicals. Water sucked up through the Lifestraw is made safe to drink.

CELEBRATIONS

Around the world, peoples celebrate different events according to their local traditions. Many customs and celebrations developed out of religious beliefs.

CARNIVALS

Carnivals are holiday or festive seasons that may last from a few days up to several months. Most developed out of Christian religious festivals, and they are popular in many parts of Europe, the Caribbean, and South and Central America. The Rio Carnival in Brazil is the largest and most spectacular. There are giant parades of floats, powerful samba music, dancing and firework displays.

ANNUAL EVENTS

Every country has important holidays or annual events. Some, such as Halloween, honour the spirits of the dead. In Mexico, for the Day of the Dead, families dress in costumes, and leave food and other gifts called *ofrendas* for the spirits. Models of skeletons (left) and skulls are made from papier mâché and as items of food.

During Chinese New Year, giant paper dragons weave and dance their way through the streets.

CHINESE NEW YEAR

The arrival of the New Year according to the Chinese calendar is China's most important holiday. It is celebrated with lanterns, spectacular parades, special foods and events. Families exchange gifts, blessings and good wishes.

LOCAL CUSTOMS

The tradition of giving gifts to celebrate Saint Nicholas, a Greek bishop who lived over 1,600 years ago, is known as Sinterklass in the Netherlands (above). From this came the image of Santa Claus in the USA during the 19th century.

Religions of the world

A religion is a belief in something greater, for example spirits or gods. Millions around the world are devoted followers of a particular religion. Atheists do not believe in any religion.

There are many different religions. Most have holy writings or scriptures that provide followers of the religion with ways to lead a good life.

Christianity

Christians believe in the teachings of Jesus Christ, who they believe is the son of God. There are different forms of Christianity. The most popular is the Roman Catholic Church, which is led by the Pope.

Buddhism

Buddha founded Buddhism in India. Buddhists believe that they are reincarnated (born again) as another creature or human being. The monks are often brought offerings of food.

Islam

Islam was begun in the 7th century CE by the prophet Muhammad. Followers of Islam are called Muslims. They pray five times a day to one god called Allah, and follow the teachings contained in the Koran.

Hinduism

Hinduism is the oldest of the major religions, beginning 4,000 years ago. Hindus worship many different gods, including Vishnu, Shiva and the elephant god Ganesh (above). Hinduism's most important holy writings are called Vedas, which means 'books of knowledge'.

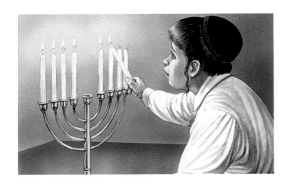

Judaism

Followers of Judaism are called Jews. They believe they have been chosen by God. Here, a Jewish boy lights a nine-branched candlestick called a menorah during one of the important Jewish holidays, Hannukah.

Shinto

Unlike many other religions, Shinto does not have a single major god. Instead, its followers believe that eternal truth is called *kami*, and that *kami* can be found everywhere in nature, from rivers to forests. People go to the Shinto shrines, mainly in Japan but also in other countries, when they want to pray and give thanks.

CULTURAL NOTE

ACTS OF WORSHIP

Acts of devotion or praise are known as worship. Some, such as praying or fasting, take place at home. Others happen in special buildings. Christians go to church, Muslims worship in mosques and Jews in synagogues. Followers of many religions, including Hinduism and Vietnam's Cao Dei religion (above), worship in temples.

Religious ceremonies

All religions have a variety of rituals and ceremonies performed by their followers. These may be about birth, becoming an adult or about death.

Some ceremonies celebrate a god or prophet's birthday, such as Christmas for Christians or the Buddha's birthday. Other ceremonies are designed to honour ancestors, or give thanks to gods or spirits.

Bar-mitzvah

This is a coming-of-age ritual for Jewish boys when they reach their 13th birthday. They read from the Torah, the sacred scroll containing the first five books of the Hebrew Bible. From this point on, the boy is expected to follow all the laws of Judaism.

The hajj

Islam calls on all Muslims to pray regularly, give charity to their community and fast during the month of Ramadan. Muslims also have a duty to make a pilgrimage to the most holy place in Islam, the city of Mecca in Saudi Arabia. This journey is called a hajj, and thousands of pilgrims visit the holy shrine of the Ka'bah there

Ganga Aarti ceremony

Some religious rituals are held once a year while others are held every day. The Ganga Aarti is an important daily ritual in Hinduism. It takes place beside the River Ganges in the Indian town of Varanasi. Lamps or dishes containing ghee butter and incense are set alight by young priests. They are then swung in circular movements to ward off evil spirits.

Sports

Most people take part in sport to get or stay fit, for the challenge, and also for fun and enjoyment.

Most people are amateurs – they play sports without being paid. Some people are paid to play and are called professionals.

The origins of sport

Many sports developed from skills needed for hunting and fighting. The ancient Egyptians played several sports, including forms of hockey, fencing and tug-of-war, while the ancient Sumerians held wrestling contests more than 4,500 years ago.

Basketball

Invented in 1891 by Dr James Naismith, basketball is a fast, five-a-side team sport. Players pass and dribble the ball around a court. They score points by shooting the ball through a 46cm–wide hoop attached to a backboard that is 3.05m off the ground.

Sumo wrestling

Influenced by wrestling in China and Korea, sumo wrestling developed in Japan between 300 and 200BCE. The wrestlers attempt to push each other out of a circle, the *dohyÿ*.

Sailing

Sailing is a sport that ranges from single-person boats like this dinghy to larger ocean-going yachts that compete in round-the-world events.

Tennis

Tennis pits individuals – singles – or pairs of players – doubles – against each other. The players use racquets to send a tennis ball around a court, trying to hit winning shots. They play on grass (above) or on hard courts.

Rowing

Rowing races are held for a range of different-sized craft. In a sculls event, individuals pull two oars each. The largest boats are rowing eights (above) which are around 19m long. They contain eight rowers, each pulling a single oar. A ninth person, the coxswain or cox, steers and helps the rowers keep their rhythm.

HISTORICAL DATA

FOOTBALL

The most popular team sport in the world, football developed out of a number of ancient ball sports and got its first sets of rules in the 19th century. Two teams of 11 players contest a match over two halves of 45 minutes, trying to score goals. The FIFA World Cup, held every four years, is the pinnacle of the sport, attracting hundreds of millions of TV viewers.

THE OLYMPICS

THE FIRST MODERN OLYMPICS WAS HELD IN 1896, IN ATHENS, AND ATTENDED BY JUST OVER 250 COMPETITORS. TODAY, IT IS THE SINGLE BIGGEST SPORTING EVENT ON EARTH.

A gold medal is given to the winner of an Olympic event. Second place receives silver and third place, bronze.

SWIMMING

Swimming is one of the most popular sports. The races take place over a range of distances, from 50m sprints to the 10km marathon which first appeared at the 2008 Beijing games. At the 1972 Olympics, American Mark Spitz won an astonishing seven swimming gold medals.

TRACK AND FIELD

Athletics events are mostly divided into throwing and jumping competitions called field events, and races run on a 400m-long oval track. Track events include sprints of 100m and 200m, hurdles races and relays such as the 4x400m which in 2004 was won by the US team (right). The USA has dominated track and field events, winning 313 gold medals between 1896 and 2008.

WINTER OLYMPICS

Since 1924, there has been a second major event for sports involving snow and ice. Called the Winter Olympics, it includes ice hockey, skating, snowboarding and many forms of skiing, including the giant slalom (above). In the slalom, competitors turn between sets of poles called gates, as they hurtle down the course trying to reach the end of the run in the fastest possible time.

Countries and nations

A country is an area of land run by a single government. There are more than 190 countries in the world. China has the most people, with a population of over 1.3 billion.

The land of a country does not have to be connected. For example, Alaska and the islands of Hawaii are not joined to the mainland USA, but are still a part of that country.

National borders

A national border is the point at which two countries' territory meets. Countries protect their borders with officials or soldiers who check travellers entering their country. The longest single border is between Canada and the USA (above) and is 8,891km long.

Colonies

Some parts of the world are controlled from a distance by a country. These are often known as colonies or dependencies. Many countries today were colonies or dependencies in the past. Australia (above) was a British colony from 1788 until 1901, when it became an independent country.

National anthems

Countries often have a particular piece of music, a national anthem, that represents their country. It is played to honour a leader of that country, or for an important event like this rugby match between South Africa (below) and Argentina.

Royal families

In the past, many countries were ruled by a king or queen. Their powers were often passed down to their son or daughter. Today, there are still royal families, but they are often figureheads with little or no say in running their country.

Independence

Independence happens when a colony or region of another country gets the freedom to make all of its own decisions and be counted as a nation. Many nations only became independent during the 20th century. In 1991, the Soviet Union split up, creating Russia and 14 other independent countries, including Ukraine and Belarus. In 2006, Montenegro (above) declared independence from Serbia.

Flags

Every country has a different national flag. They are flown from government buildings, and sometimes schools and private homes. These 15 children are each holding their country's rectangular flag. Only Switzerland and the Vatican City have square flags, while Nepal has a flag made of two triangles.

Government

Governments make laws, provide public services, and control trade and defence. The work is mainly funded by taxes paid by the people governed.

Most countries have a national government, and then one or more levels of local government. In some countries, local governments have the power to make some laws and to collect their own taxes.

Political parties

People of similar views band together in political parties. They campaign on issues and try to get members of their party elected. Pressure groups have strong views on one or a small number of issues. Pressure groups rarely seek to get elected. Instead, they try to influence public opinion and politicians.

Dictatorships

A dictatorship is where one or a few people have total control. Dictators do not usually hold elections and often rule until they die or are overthrown. Cuban leader Fidel Castro (left) took power in 1959, and was the longest serving dictator in the world. In 2008 his brother, Raúl (right), took over.

Parliaments and law-making

A parliament, or legislature, is a meeting of people to discuss and make a country's laws. Many legislatures, such as the Australian Parliament in Canberra (above), have two separate chambers with different duties.

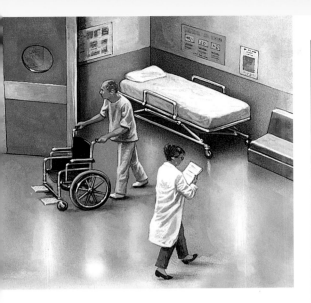

Public services

Modern governments spend enormous sums of money on defence, and on a wide range of public services from road- and bridge-building to education and healthcare (above). Many countries also spend a large part of their budget on social security schemes for the ill, elderly, the unemployed and the poor.

Elections

Elections give people a chance to choose a new government or leader. In many elections, people have to make their choice by selecting from a list of candidates on a ballot paper. Ballot papers are then posted in a sealed ballot box to be counted.

Power bases

There are three main branches of government: the legislature makes laws, the judiciary enforces laws and the executive carries out the daily running of the country. In the USA, these branches are completely separate. The legislature is the US Congress (above) and the executive branch is led by the US president.

HISTORICAL DATA

WINNING THE RIGHT TO VOTE

In South Africa, the policy of apartheid allowed the small white population of the country to control black South Africans and deny them many rights, including the right to vote. In 1994, the first election was held in which all South Africans, regardless of colour, could vote. Over 19.7 million people queued to vote in an election that saw Nelson Mandela become South Africa's first black president.

Law and human rights

For a society to run smoothly and in peace, it needs laws that everyone follows. These laws vary from country to country.

Most countries have criminal laws against acts such as murder and theft. Civil law deals with disagreements between people, for example whether or not a marriage ends in divorce.

Law and order

Most people obey the laws of their country all the time. But police, armed forces and other officials such as customs officers are on hand to enforce the laws, keep the peace and protect the public. Police try to solve crimes and bring criminals to justice in a court, where their guilt or innocence is decided.

Crime and punishment

A person found guilty of a crime faces punishment. They may be forced to pay a fine, be banned from doing something such as driving or sentenced to time they must serve in prison. In some countries, the punishments are physical. For example, they may be whipped in public (corporal punishment), or even lose their life (capital punishment).

In court

In court, one set of lawyers acts for the defendant and another set, the prosecution, argues the case against. The trial often takes place in front of a jury and a judge. The jury is made up of ordinary adult members of the public and they decide whether the defendant is guilty. If he or she is guilty, the judge decides on the exact sentence.

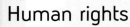

Human rights

Human rights are certain basic rights such as the right to observe a chosen religion and the right to be free from slavery. In many countries, people find their basic human rights abused because they are critics of a government or are of a different religious or racial group. Some are forced to flee their country and reach places of safety by whatever means they find (above).

Money

Money is a form of payment or method of exchange that is widely used to pay for goods people sell or work that they do.

In ancient times, people bartered or swapped goods, but then money was introduced and today is used in most cases. Money is also a way wealth can be stored or saved for future needs.

DIFFERENT 'MONIES'
Many different items have been used as forms of money.

Cowrie shells were used in ancient China, Africa and Arabia.

The ancient Chinese used bronze cast into a spade shape.

Strings of shells were used as money by native Americans.

Gold formed into large bars is another way to store wealth.

The first banknotes

Shortages of metals and the sheer weight of large amounts of coins led to the invention of paper banknotes. These were first produced in China in the 7th century CE. They are not valuable in themselves, but they are a promise to pay a sum of real money.

Currency

Currency is a form of money that people can use easily. Banknotes and metal coins are the most common forms today. Every country has its own currency system. The exchange rate is the cost of selling or buying a currency.

Rich and poor

Money is not shared out equally among people or countries. Some are much richer or poorer than average. Around 1.2 billion people – many in Africa, Asia and Latin America – live on less than $1 (50p) a day. They cannot afford to buy even basic items.

Electronic currency

Today, people use a card to access money. The card contains a microchip or magnetic strip that carries information about their identity and account. The Automated Teller Machines (ATMs) allow people to deposit or withdraw money by using the card and typing in their personal code which is called a PIN number.

Hyperinflation

Inflation is when prices of goods and services rise over time. Hyperinflation is when the prices rise by more than 50 per cent every month. In Germany in 1923, prices doubled every two days, making printed money worthless.

Financial institutions

There are many different institutions connected with money. Coins are made in a factory called a mint. Most countries have a central bank that controls the amount of coins and banknotes in circulation. Banks hold peoples' money for safekeeping in an account and make loans of money to individuals and businesses.

TRADE

PEOPLE HAVE BEEN TRADING FOR
THOUSANDS OF YEARS. TRADE IS THE
BUYING OR SELLING OF FINISHED GOODS,
RAW MATERIALS SUCH AS COAL, OIL OR
WOOD, OR SERVICES SUCH AS BANKING.

BUYING AND SELLING

Trade allows people and companies to obtain
things that they do not have and to sell a surplus of
something they do. Farmers, for example, cannot
grow every type of crop. So they bring any surplus
of their crops to a market, such as this floating
market in Bangkok, Thailand (right). Here, they
sell their goods and buy items that they need.

MOVING FREIGHT

For trade to work, raw materials and goods have
to be moved to places where they are needed.
Freight trains are made up of a locomotive and
a long series of wagons or freight
cars. They carry goods and
raw materials such as
iron ore and coal
to factories.

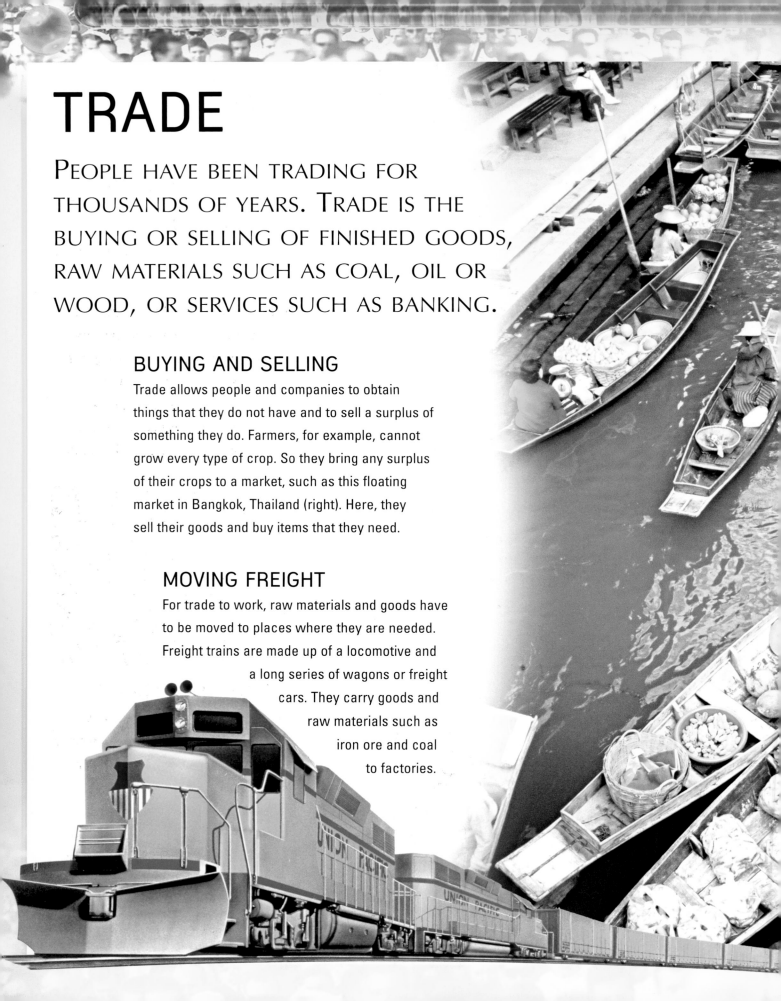

INTERNATIONAL TRADE

Goods sold to foreign customers are called exports, and imports are goods or services bought from another country. Giant container ships and planes transport millions of tonnes of imports and exports around the world.

FINANCIAL MARKETS

Financial markets are places where shares in a company or large quantities of commodities (goods) such as gold, oil, wheat or sugar are bought and sold. The prices of the shares and commodities go up and down. These traders at the London Stock Exchange (above) are trying to buy goods or shares at a lower price than they will eventually sell at, thus making a profit.

Warfare

People go to war to win territory, to capture riches or hostages, or to defend their borders and the population.

Many wars are short or confined to a local area. Some wars take place in distant places and last many years. A war continues until one side surrenders or both sides sign a peace treaty.

Guerrilla warfare

In this kind of fighting, small groups carry out hit-and-run attacks and sabotage enemy equipment and buildings. Many rebel groups, such as these rebels in Guatemala, resort to using guerrilla warfare tactics.

War at sea

A navy consists of many different craft, from submarines to giant aircraft carriers (above), the decks of which serve as mobile runways for dozens of jet aircraft. The navy protects a country's coastline and shipping, and transports troops, equipment and supplies.

Motorized military

In the past, wars and battles were fought mainly by infantry on foot and cavalry on horseback. The invention of motor vehicles, and from 1915 onwards, heavily armoured tanks, changed military tactics completely. Today, tanks and lighter, faster armoured vehicles such as these US Army Humvees serving in Iraq, often lead an army's forces in battles and invasions.

War in the air

Air forces sometimes attack targets on the ground using bombs and missiles, or fight enemy aircraft in the air. They also patrol skies, act as transporters and drop supplies and troops into battle areas.

Military intelligence

Intelligence is information that is thought of as vital to a country's security. Spies on the ground seek out top-secret intelligence. Spy planes such as this SR71 Blackbird operate at very high altitudes, using powerful zoom cameras to photograph the ground below.

Civil war

Many wars are caused by one nation invading its neighbours to extend territory. However, conflicts also take place inside a country. During these civil wars, people who share the same culture or politics fight against one another for political power.

AMAZING FACTS

HIGH-TECH WARFARE

Military machines no longer need a driver to risk death or injury in risky situations. In the air, pilotless drones and Unmanned Aerial Vehicles (UAVs) can be controlled from hundreds of kilometres away. On the ground, mobile crawler robots such as the Packbot (above) can be sent ahead of troops to scout out dangers such as unexploded mines.

International organizations

International organizations have been formed to allow countries to discuss ideas and share information on global issues.

Some international organizations exist to tackle a specific problem. These include WADA, which fights drugs in sport, and Interpol, which helps police forces from different countries work together efficiently.

Worldwide charities

Major charities, such as the Red Cross and Oxfam, collect money and goods. They use these to improve the lives of people in poor countries hit by famine, war and disease.

Peacekeepers

These soldiers, police and other officials work with peacekeepers from other countries to restore calm to war-torn areas. These men (right) are blue-helmeted United Nations peacekeepers.

NATO

Countries sometimes group together in military alliances. The North Atlantic Treaty Organization (NATO) was formed in 1949 by the USA and 11 other countries. Today NATO has representatives of 28 countries in its headquarters in Brussels, Belgium.

United Nations

The United Nations (UN) was formed in 1945 after the end of World War II. Its aim is still to keep peace in the world, and to improve peoples' lives. The UN General Assembly in New York (pictured) provides every member country (nearly 200 now) with a chance to air its views. Each nation gets one vote on all decisions.

Society facts

The different countries in the world vary in many ways, including in size. The smallest country of all, Vatican City, the home of the Pope, has an area of just 0.44km², while the largest, Russia, covers a massive 17,075,200km².

LARGEST URBAN POPULATIONS

Tokyo/Yokohama, Japan	34,450,000
New York City, USA	20,420,000
Seoul/Incheon, South Korea	20,090,000
Mumbai, India	19,380,000
Jakarta, Indonesia	19,300,000
Delhi, India	18,560,000
Mexico City/Toluca, Mexico	18,410,000
São Paulo, Brazil	18,130,000
Manila, Philippines	17,320,000
Osaka/Kobe/Kyoto, Japan	17,280,000
Cairo, Egypt	16,000,000
Los Angeles, USA	15,350,000
Kolkata, India	14,580,000
Shanghai, China	14,530,000
Moscow, Russia	14,100,000

AVERAGE LIFE EXPECTANCY (HIGHEST AND LOWEST)

1	Japan	82.6 years
2	Hong Kong SAR	82.2 years
3	Iceland	81.8 years
4	Switzerland	81.7 years
5	Australia	81.2 years
6	Spain	80.9 years
7	Sweden	80.9 years
188	Afghanistan	43.8 years
189	Zimbabwe	43.5 years
190	Angola	42.7 years
191	Lesotho	42.6 years
192	Sierra Leone	42.6 years
193	Zambia	42.4 years
194	Mozambique	42.1 years
195	Swaziland	39.6 years

LARGEST ORGANIZED RELIGIONS

Christianity	2.1 billion
Islam	1.3 billion
Hinduism	851 million
Buddhism	375 million
Sikhism	25 million
Judaism	15 million
Baha'ism	7.5 million
Confucianism	6.4 million
Jainism	4.5 million
Shintoism	2.8 million

MOST POPULOUS COUNTRIES

China	1,322,570,000
India	1,129,291,310
USA	303,475,518
Indonesia	231,627,000

Portland in Oregon, USA, at twilight

USEFUL WEBSITES

http://cyberschoolbus.un.org/ Facts about every country, the UN and world issues.

www.timeforkids.com/around-the-world Information about 35 countries and language tips.

www.christianaid.org.uk/resources/games/ A look at different lives and cultures around the world.

www.bbc.co.uk/religion/religions/ A detailed guide to religious beliefs and ceremonies.

Arts and Entertainment

People have always wanted to be entertained, to express themselves and find out what others have to say. They do this in many ways in different cultures – through art, design, music, dancing and acting. Many of the arts bring these elements together – for example, a theatrical show might include acting, dance and music, all performed in front of painted scenery.

Architecture

Architecture is the process of designing buildings and other structures. Architects choose the materials and styles that allow us to live, work and play in comfort and safety.

There are many different architectural styles, from basic 'box' homes to curved, glass-walled skyscrapers.

Built for a purpose

Every building has a purpose, but some look interesting, too. Australia's Sydney Opera House (above) has a roof of concrete panels that look like shells or sails, to fit in with Sydney Harbour.

Bridge design

Bridges are structures created by architects and engineers to cross an open space or gap such as a valley. One of the most impressive is the 300m-high Millau Bridge, in France, with its web of steel cables stretching from tall masts.

Taller and taller

Skyscrapers began to dominate city views from the 1890s. The invention of safe elevators made it possible for people to reach the high storeys without running out of breath.

| Eiffel Tower, France | Empire State, USA | Petronas Towers, Malaysia | Taipei 101, Taiwan | CN Tower, Canada | Burj Dubai, Dubai |

The old and the new

Old and new buildings sit side by side in many cities. This tall building in London is 30 St Mary Axe, better known as 'The Gherkin' because of its curved shape. It has 24,000m^2 of glass that allow in plenty of natural light and warmth. This, together with other energy-saving design elements, means it uses half the power of similar buildings.

Dance

Dance is movement that is used to show feelings and ideas. It is full of rhythm and often accompanied by music. Most people dance from the time they learn to walk.

Ancient carvings and drawings show that dance has been part of human rituals and ceremonies for thousands of years. Dance is a truly international art form because it needs no words.

Folk dance
Groups of people sometimes develop their own style of dance. They wear costumes, and use movement and music to tell stories about their culture.

Flamenco
This dramatic style of dance comes from Andalusia in Spain. Dancers respond to the powerful rhythms of flamenco guitar music. They perform intricate toe- and heel-clicking steps (mostly the men) and graceful body and hand movements (mainly the women).

Ballet
This classical style of dance began hundreds of years ago and is often set to orchestral music. It needs precise movements, and dancers train for years to learn the technique. They wear special shoes with wooden blocks at the toe to help them stand tall. Ballet usually has solo dancers backed by a 'chorus' of other dancers.

Tap

Tap dancing started in the USA, and gets its name from the clicking sound that is made by metal plates on the dancer's shoes striking the ground. Many types of dance make use of the sounds made by the feet.

Telling a story

Many classical Indian dances tell stories, usually either religious or epic. The story can be told through mime or by set gestures, with the hands sometimes used for a kind of sign language to add extra expression. Costumes are often very elaborate and brightly coloured.

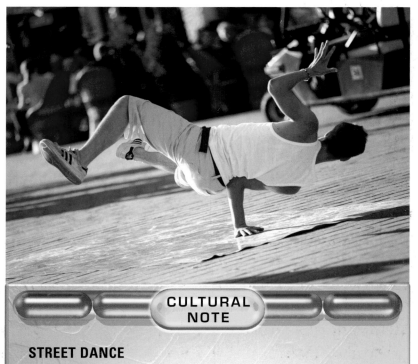

Jazz dance

In modern jazz dance, performers make a wide range of movements, set to lively music. There are standard jazz moves, but the performers use these to create their own personal style. Jazz dance is faster and freer than ballet, and is often performed in groups.

CULTURAL NOTE

STREET DANCE

This modern dance style is performed to music such as rap, hip hop and funk. It often involves break dancing, in which dancers improvise a series of movements to show off their skill and flexibility. They might start with some standing steps (toprock) before performing moves with hands and feet on the floor (downrock). Another element is the freeze, when the dancer holds a stylish pose before continuing a movement.

Decorative arts

Some artists make attractive objects out of ceramics, wood, glass, metal or textiles. The finished work, such as a vase, may be useful or simply made to be beautiful.

GLASS-BLOWING
In this ancient craft, the raw materials are mixed and melted at high temperatures.

1 The artist blows in air to form a bubble.

2 The molten glass is pulled into shape.

3 Unwanted glass is then cut away.

4 The glass is decorated using a cutter.

Some people do decorative art as a job, but others enjoy making attractive objects as a hobby. The materials can be cheap, but often great skill is needed to produce the object.

Ceramics

Ceramics, or pottery, involves shaping clay, for example to make a pot. The shape is heated (or 'fired') in a kiln to make it solid. Here, a pot is being shaped on a revolving stand. The finished object can be decorated or left its natural colour.

Wood-carving

People have been carving wood since the introduction of sharp tools thousands of years ago. The wood might be made into pieces for a chess set or a fish (above). Turning the wood while cutting it creates rounded shapes such as lamp stands.

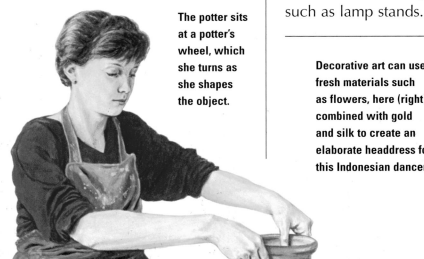

The potter sits at a potter's wheel, which she turns as she shapes the object.

Decorative art can use fresh materials such as flowers, here (right) combined with gold and silk to create an elaborate headdress for this Indonesian dancer.

Weaving

Weavers use wooden looms to turn thread or yarn into cloth. The fabric can be plain or patterned, and will become a rug (below), tapestry or maybe an item of clothing.

Cross-stitch

This is one of the oldest forms of embroidery. It creates pictures using X-shaped stitches of thread. For centuries, people have used this method to sew samplers showing the alphabet or phrases such as 'Home sweet home'.

Jewellery

Simple jewellery may be stringing beads along a thread to make a necklace or bracelet. More complicated jewellery combines precious metals such as gold or silver with gemstones. The end product could be a wedding ring, an intricate brooch, a royal tiara, or a child's first pair of earrings.

GAMES

GAMES HAVE LONG BEEN PART OF HUMAN CULTURE BECAUSE THEY ENTERTAIN AND ARE A GOOD WORKOUT FOR THE BRAIN. SOME GAMES ARE THOUSANDS OF YEARS OLD – DICE CARVED FROM BONES HAVE BEEN FOUND AT MANY ANCIENT SITES.

The players in this 19th-century Japanese print are taking their game of Go very seriously!

BOARD GAMES

Simple games such as Snakes and Ladders rely on luck to win, but more complicated games need a good strategy. Many board games are based around our everyday lives, for example the property-dealing game Monopoly, or Scrabble, where players create words. Some, such as chess (below) were based on warfare. The pieces are moved to get an advantage and capture the most important piece, the king. Online versions of board games allow you to play against anyone in the world, anytime.

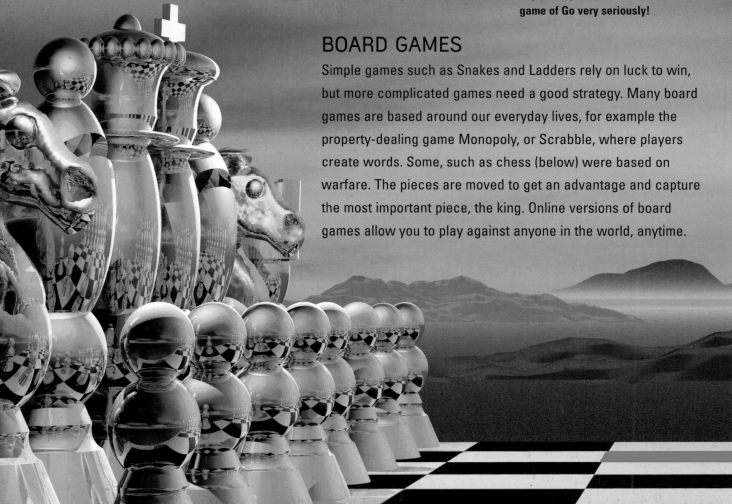

This 'hand' is part of the standard 'deck', which consists of 52 cards in four suits.

CARD GAMES

Card games began in China about 2,000 years ago using paper money. There are thousands of card games, ranging from those for a solo player to games for large groups. Some games, such as Uno, have their own special sets of cards.

EARLY BOARD GAMES

The first board games probably involved moving pebbles around in the dirt. Then dried beans or clay tablets were used for counters, and boards were introduced. A 4,000-year-old papyrus board was once used by the ancient Egyptians to play senet, which resembles the modern game backgammon.

Chess as we know it today is about 2,000 years old, when it developed from an earlier Indian game. Some chess sets are beautifully carved.

Film and television

Films use moving pictures to tell stories. Film cameras take 24 pictures a second. When the images are shown at that speed in a cinema or on television, it looks as if they are moving.

The first 'motion pictures' were made in Hollywood, USA, where the natural light was ideal for filming. Today, top film actors earn millions of dollars.

Making a movie

Filming can take place at studios, where massive sets are built to look like real places. It also happens 'on location' – on real city streets or in the countryside. A huge crew is needed to make a movie, with different teams responsible for pictures, sound, lighting and acting.

Silent movies

Until the 1920s, films were silent as there was no way to record sound. Musicians would play along to them in the cinema. They were also shot in black and white until colour filming became possible in the 1930s.

Animation

In animated films, each frame is photographed, either as a drawn picture or a figure that is moved slightly and photographed again, like Wallace and Gromit (right). It takes a very long time to make an animated movie.

Series

Some films are made as part of a series, using the same characters who have different adventures. Examples are space sagas such as *Star Trek* (above) or *Star Wars*, and the James Bond action movies.

Bollywood

The massive Indian film industry produces about 1,000 films every year, and they are bursting with colourful costumes, singing and dancing. Bollywood film plots are always romances with some comedy and thrills.

Films in the home

Most films are made to be shown in the cinema, but after a short time are then available as DVDs to be watched in the home. Later, they may be broadcast on network television. Some less popular films never make it to the cinema and are known as 'straight to DVD' films.

AMAZING FACTS

THE OSCARS

Since 1929, the film industry has given annual awards at a special ceremony. The Academy Awards – better known as the Oscars after the small golden statuettes presented as trophies – are given for categories such as Best Actor, Best Film and Best Director. A winning film is likely to attract a much larger audience and earn more money.

Special effects

Special effects are tricks that convince the audience something is happening. They range from special stunts to the blending of images to make people 'fly'.

During live action filming, scenery effects can transform the set, while mechanical effects create illusions, for example that a dinosaur is attacking.

Bluescreen technique
Also known as a travelling matte, this is a technique in which actors are filmed against a blue or green backdrop (above left). The colour is later replaced with scenery to make it appear that the action is taking place at sea, in space or at some other location.

Models in action
If something is too complicated to film, or does not exist, it may be created as a model. It can then be moved about like a giant puppet – this is called animatronics. Or it may be filmed in stop motion as an animation (*see p.234*). Models are usually created on a small scale and made to move in front of a miniature or computerized backdrop.

Out of a fireball!

There are several ways to make a plane appear to fly through an explosion (above). One is to actually do it – although often an optical illusion is created and the plane is really at a distance from the flames. Another is to film the plane and fire separately, then fit the images together. Alternatively, a model plane could be used, or the whole event could be created on a computer!

Classical music

Classical music is usually played by orchestral instruments, or sung. Much of the music written in the past is still played today because it is good at expressing ideas and feelings.

TYPES OF INSTRUMENT

A symphony orchestra has four sections.

Percussion instruments are hit to make sounds and include the piano.

Most string instruments are played with a bow and include the violin.

Brass instruments such as trumpets are made of metal and are blown.

Woodwind instruments include the clarinet, oboe and flute (above).

Music developed through performance in churches and at royal courts. It changed as new instruments were invented, and is still developing. Some modern pieces use electronics.

Solo performers

Classical musicians train for years to become good performers. Some may have the chance to perform solos, for example in a concerto, when single instruments are accompanied by the orchestra.

Early music

In the many centuries before music could be recorded, it had to be played live. Musicians such as Johann Sebastian Bach (below) made their living by performing in churches and composing new music.

Famous composers

Some composers such as Mozart became big stars. The young pianist Beethoven even travelled to Vienna in 1787 to try to meet him (left). Beethoven went on to achieve great fame himself.

Chamber music

Not all classical music is played by orchestras or solo instruments. Small groups of between 2 and 40 play chamber music. For example, a string quartet of two violins, viola and cello is known as a quartet. With no conductor, chamber groups have to listen carefully to each other.

The orchestra

A symphony orchestra can have about 100 players in sections. The music is usually very complex, and melodies and rhythms move between the instruments. The conductor stands at the front, moving his body and arms to show how he wants the musicians to play.

Opera

Opera began in Italy in the 1500s. It is a dramatic story with singing that is set to music played by the orchestra. The players sit low down in front of the stage in an area called the 'pit'. Opera singers act the story and use their powerful voices to fill the theatre, expressing the emotions of their characters. All the characters' conversations are sung. Modern musical shows are a kind of opera.

Modern music

There are numerous types of modern music, from relaxing ambient to exotic world music, and they often influence each other. Many of them are used to accompany dance.

Much of modern popular music developed from the rock and roll music that began in the USA in the 1950s. The basic equipment for modern music is guitar, bass, keyboard and drums.

Rock

Rock music can be songs or longer pieces, usually with a heavy beat and featuring energetic electric guitar solos. Really loud, insistent rock is called 'heavy metal', while the quieter, more melodic kind is called 'soft rock'. There are many other types.

Pop

Pop is short for 'popular 'and aims to appeal to the largest possible number of listeners, who are mainly young. It is generally written to be good to dance to, and comes in the form of short, fairly simple songs that have a memorable tune.

Hip hop

Hip hop is rap music, in which rhyming lyrics, mainly about city life, are rhythmically spoken or chanted. The backing is in many styles, usually electronic, and has a very strong beat.

Reggae

This began in Jamaica in the 1960s, and has a distinctive chopped-up beat often strummed on electric guitar. The most famous and popular reggae star was Bob Marley (above).

World music

This is traditional music made by people anywhere in the world. For example, Indonesian gamelan music (above) is played on drums, gongs, xylophones and chimes, and is part of the country's culture. Its magical, rhythmic, tinkling sound can now be heard right around the globe.

Jazz

Jazz has its origins in New Orleans, USA, early in the 20th century. It can be very complicated, sophisticated music in which the players make up, or improvise, some of what they play.

HISTORICAL DATA

BLUES

Developed in the USA early in the 20th century, blues music influenced many other kinds of music, especially rock. The lyrics are about the bad things that can happen in life, and the singer is often simply accompanied by a guitar or harmonica. Bessie Smith (above) was a major blues star in the 1920s and 1930s who sang about poverty and sadness.

Painting

Painting is putting colours onto a surface such as paper or a canvas. Some of the earliest paintings are hunting illustrations on the walls of caves.

Some painters have been successful in their lifetime. But many of the artists we enjoy today struggled to make a living, and would be amazed to see people queuing to see their pictures in art galleries.

Subject matter
Early paintings were often religious, but then artists began to paint landscapes, still lives and portraits. The portraits could be of important people such as a king, or perhaps the artist themselves (right).

Perspective
Early paintings had no perspective and so look flat, with no depth. During the Renaissance (from the 1400s), painters learned to use angled lines to create depth (below).

Paints and painting
The main painting materials used by artists are oil, acrylic and watercolour (above), although others including chalk, pastels and inks are also used. Oil paints can be very thick and some artists paint it in layers on the canvas to add texture to their work. The oils also dry slowly, allowing colours to be mixed on the canvas. This technique is also used with watercolours.

Abstract art

Abstract art does not try to show objects, but rather to express ideas or explore new processes. Jackson Pollock created some of his works (left) by pouring paint onto a canvas lying on the floor in an 'action painting'.

Different techniques

This woodblock image was created by cutting shapes into a block of wood. The wood was then inked and used to print an image. This technique is very popular in China and Japan.

Other art forms

Not all painters use an easel and brushes. There is digital art, where images are drawn or photographic images changed using a computer. In video art, moving images are put together to create a 'piece' that is usually viewed as a picture, not a film.

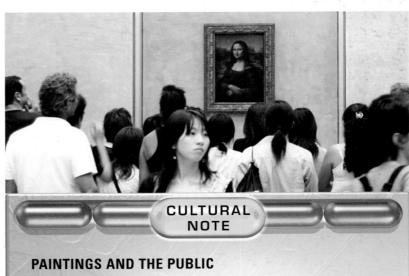

CULTURAL NOTE

PAINTINGS AND THE PUBLIC

Each year, millions of people go to view famous works such as Leonardo da Vinci's 'Mona Lisa' (above), which hangs in the Louvre in Paris and is the world's most visited painting. And many people are prepared to pay very high prices in order to own works of art. In 1987, one of Van Gogh's paintings of sunflowers was sold for an amazing $49 million.

Sculpture

Sculpture is three-dimensional art that we can look at, move round and sometimes touch.

Sculptures are made with materials such as stone, metal, wood, plastic and glass. Some sculptures are carved out of the material. In other cases, the material is melted before being moulded or cast.

Sculpting in stone
On Easter Island in the south Pacific, there are 3,000-year-old stone statues. They represent ancestors who were believed to be gods. Some are 10m tall.

Sculpting in metal
Metal sculptures are cast from a mould. The technique has been used for centuries, but this bronze bull, head lowered ready to charge, is a modern sculpture in New York. It weighs 3,200kg.

Art and contrast

Old and new sculptures sit side by side in London's Trafalgar Square. On the right is the 50m-high stone column and statue of Nelson, dating from 1843. On the left is a modern sculpture in coloured glass, called 'Model for a Hotel', by Thomas Schutte, which sat in Trafalgar Square from 2007–09. Its 21 storeys rose 5m from a stone plinth, and were designed to reflect the changing lights of the area.

Ship in a bottle

Trafalgar Square's Fourth Plinth has been occupied by 'Nelson's Ship in a Bottle', by the British-Nigerian artist Yinka Shonibare, since May 2010.

Photography

Photography is the recording of still images with a camera. It is used for many businesses, especially advertising and newspapers, as well as in art, and to take holiday snaps.

Camera technology

A camera is basically a box with a hole that lets in light. Today, black and white and colour film is being replaced by digital technology that uses an electronic sensor instead. We can even take moving pictures on many mobile phones.

The lens is a special piece of glass that can magnify or change the shape of the image.

Zoom ring

Focus ring

Lens hood stops stray light getting in.

Wide angle: a wide angle lens shows more than an eye can see, capturing everything over a large area, even things that are nearly out of sight; it is great for shots of big buildings.

Fish eye: this special lens gives a special effect by bending the image so that the foreground is pushed towards the viewer and the background forced away.

Zoom: a zoom lens on the camera acts as a powerful magnifier that allows the photographer to zero in on objects that are a long way away.

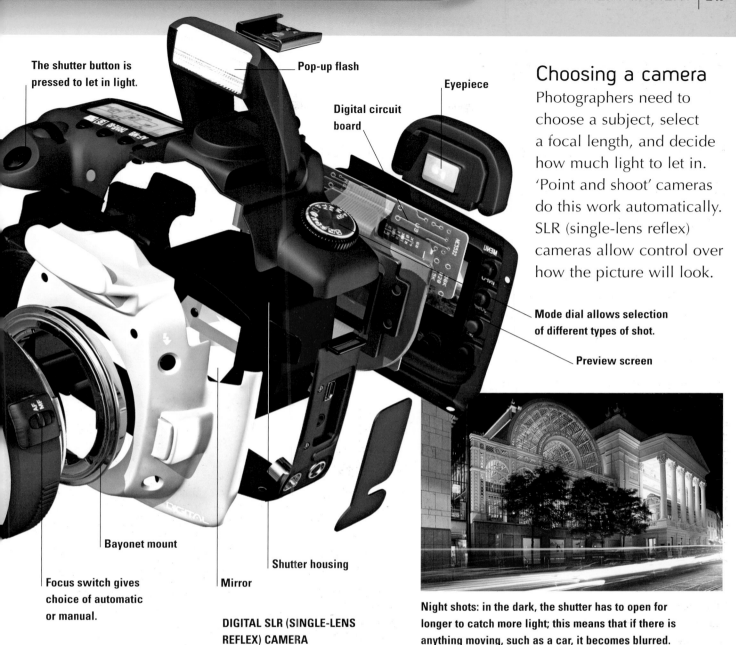

The shutter button is pressed to let in light.

Pop-up flash

Eyepiece

Digital circuit board

Choosing a camera

Photographers need to choose a subject, select a focal length, and decide how much light to let in. 'Point and shoot' cameras do this work automatically. SLR (single-lens reflex) cameras allow control over how the picture will look.

Mode dial allows selection of different types of shot.

Preview screen

Bayonet mount

Focus switch gives choice of automatic or manual.

Mirror

Shutter housing

DIGITAL SLR (SINGLE-LENS REFLEX) CAMERA

Night shots: in the dark, the shutter has to open for longer to catch more light; this means that if there is anything moving, such as a car, it becomes blurred.

Portrait: pictures of people are called portraits, and are often deliberately posed for the camera.

Landscape: these pictures are often very dramatic, portraying an environment such as a park in a city (above), or fields and mountains in the countryside.

Macro photography: these close-up shots often reveal details that cannot be seen with the naked eye.

Print

Printing is the process of putting words and images onto paper. For the last 500 years, printing has been the most effective way of communicating ideas to a wide audience.

The Chinese were the first to print material, in the 7th century CE, by rubbing impressions from a wood block. The method was being used in Europe to decorate cloth by the year 1300.

Story-telling

Before printed books, a popular method of communication was story-telling. The role of the story-teller was often passed down from generation to generation.

Early writing

Early writing was done by scratching symbols onto clay tablets. Later, scrolls (rolls of papyrus or parchment) were used. The writing was done by hand, so there were no standard books. Texts such as the Bible were hand-copied by monks, so each one was different from the other.

Printing revolution

Mechanical printing began in Germany in the 1450s after Johannes Gutenberg developed the printing press from a machine for crushing grapes to make wine. He employed his knowledge of metals to create moveable type that could be used again and again, allowing the cheap, fast production of quality books. By 1500, there were 9 million books in circulation.

Modern printing

Today's books and newspapers are made with offset lithography, where the ink image is transferred from a rolling plate onto the final surface. This process is fast, and good for large quantities of print.

Newspapers and magazines

The first daily newspapers appeared in the 17th century. Today's papers are printed on cheap, off-white paper known as newsprint, which is often partly made up of recycled paper. Magazines are general- or special-interest publications circulated regularly, usually every week or month.

Fiction and non-fiction

Printed books are either fiction (stories and poetry) or non-fiction (information books like this one). Fiction publishers are offered many more stories than they can sell, so it can be very hard to get new work into print. The best-selling single book in the world is the Bible.

CULTURAL NOTE

COMICS

Comics combine words and cartoon-style illustrations to tell stories. There are many types of comic, including those telling tales of superheroes such as Batman and Superman. Comics use speech bubbles and text in panels to convey extra information, but the most important element is the drawings. Japanese comics known as 'manga' (above) are colourful, and their stories often become TV shows or movies.

Theatre

Theatre is the performing of plays by actors, usually in a special building, but sometimes in parks or on the street. The stories can be about feelings or ideas.

The action usually takes place on the stage, with the audience sitting in front. Some plays are performed by one actor; others need a huge cast and complicated scenery.

The Greek masks represent tragedy and comedy.

Kabuki plays are about historical events and people.

Early theatres

The Greeks invented theatre thousands of years ago, building open-air arenas where thousands of people watched plays. The actors wore masks (above) to show their character, and very little scenery was used. A 'chorus' group at the side also told some of the story.

Japanese theatre

Kabuki is a traditional Japanese theatre style dating from the 16th century. All the actors are men. They wear elaborate make-up and costumes and perform stories by singing, dancing and speaking. A Kabuki show lasts a whole day and is very popular.

Puppets

Plays can be performed by puppets. People who live on the island of Java in Indonesia use shadow puppets. The figures are moved behind white screens lit from behind.

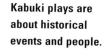

Mime

Mime is performing without speaking. Instead, mime artists tell a story using gestures and facial expressions. Mime has a very long history, but the most famous silent performer was Frenchman Marcel Marceau with his painted white face.

Musicals

Musicals, such as *Starlight Express* (above), combine songs, dance and dialogue to tell a story in a lively and entertaining way. Some musicals need a huge cast and many special effects. Some are turned into films.

Pantomime

This is a type of theatre usually performed around Christmas. The stories are generally traditional, such as Cinderella, or Jack and the Beanstalk. The main male character is played by an actress, while a man portrays the older woman – the dame (right). Pantomimes have lots of silly jokes and singing.

CULTURAL NOTE

STREET THEATRE

These performances take place in an outdoor space such as a park or shopping centre. Sometimes street theatre is part of a festival. There is little or no scenery, and the actors do not usually have microphones. They have to project their voices further than usual, and they need to use big gestures that can be seen across a crowded square.

THE GLOBE THEATRE

THE GLOBE THEATRE WAS BUILT IN 1599 BUT DESTROYED BY FIRE IN 1613. IT WAS ONE OF LONDON'S FIRST PUBLIC THEATRES. HERE, EVERYONE, NOT JUST THE RICH, COULD SEE PLAYS BY WRITERS SUCH AS SHAKESPEARE.

THE PEOPLE'S THEATRE

People could pay a penny to stand in the 'pit' in front of the stage. Known as 'groundlings', they were sometimes a noisy and difficult crowd. They bought nuts and oranges from passing sellers to eat – or throw at the stage if the actors were not thought good enough.

It cost two pennies for a seat higher up in the galleries under the roof, and the richest people paid four pennies to sit behind the stage.

SHAKESPEARE THE BARD

William Shakespeare (1564–1616) is one of the world's greatest playwrights. He began as an actor and became part-owner of the Globe. He is most famous for his 38 plays, which included histories, comedies and tragedies. His works, including *Romeo and Juliet* and *Macbeth*, are full of clever word-play and are still performed today.

The Globe was a three-storey building that could hold up to 3,000 people.

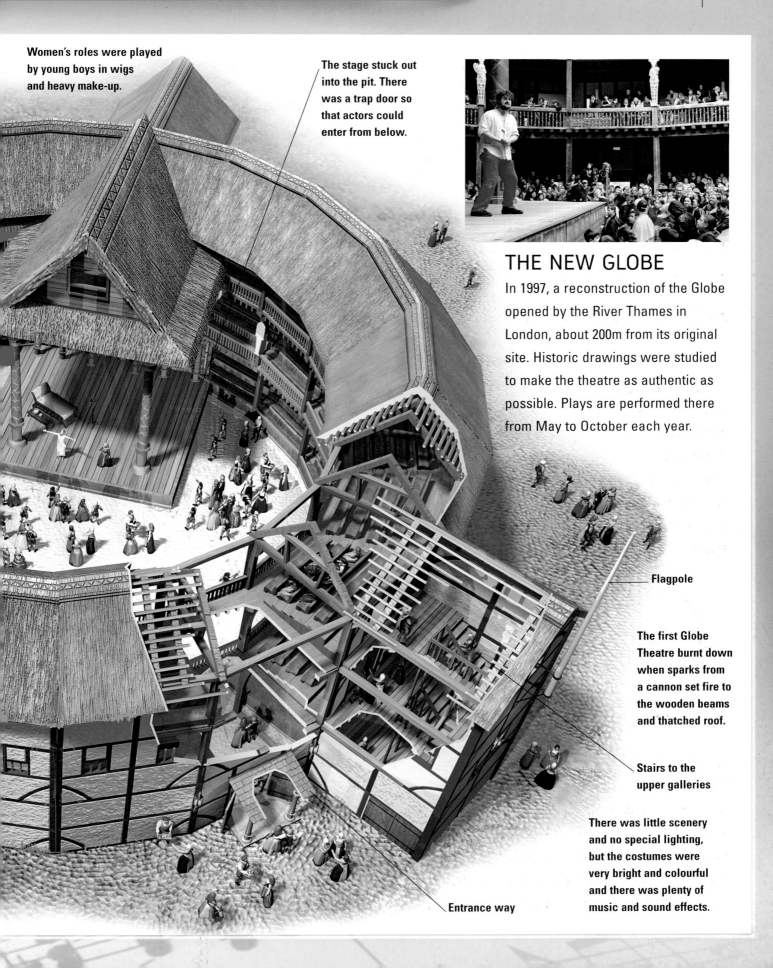

Women's roles were played by young boys in wigs and heavy make-up.

The stage stuck out into the pit. There was a trap door so that actors could enter from below.

THE NEW GLOBE

In 1997, a reconstruction of the Globe opened by the River Thames in London, about 200m from its original site. Historic drawings were studied to make the theatre as authentic as possible. Plays are performed there from May to October each year.

Flagpole

The first Globe Theatre burnt down when sparks from a cannon set fire to the wooden beams and thatched roof.

Stairs to the upper galleries

There was little scenery and no special lighting, but the costumes were very bright and colourful and there was plenty of music and sound effects.

Entrance way

Out and about

People want to enjoy themselves and are willing to travel to find new experiences. Devising and operating places of entertainment is now a massive industry around the world.

The Guggenheim in New York is a famous modern art gallery.

The Louvre in Paris houses one of the finest art collections.

The Altes ('old') Museum in Berlin is built in the classical style.

The Hermitage in St Petersburg has 3 million works of art.

While there have never been more home entertainment choices – television, DVDs, radio, computer and online games – there are also many places that are fun to visit.

Theme parks

Theme or amusement parks developed from fairgrounds and offer many rides and other fun events. Top attractions are 'thrill rides' where people travel very fast – and sometimes upside down – for example, on a rollercoaster (below) or on water.

Art galleries

These are buildings with exhibitions of art, sometimes by one artist or by artists who belong to one particular art movement. More often, there are many kinds of art through the ages. In addition to paintings, there may be sculptures and photographs, as well as other media, such as textiles.

Circuses

A group of travelling performers set up a 'big top' (tent) and perform shows. The ringmaster introduces popular acts such as acrobats, clowns, jugglers and trained animals.

Zoos and safari parks

Before films and television, zoos were often the only place where people could safely see animals from around the world. Wild animal parks (above), or safari parks, are toured by car.

Arcades

'Gamers' battle on coin-operated machines in street arcades. Typical arcade games include racing or fighting video games, pinball and slot machines.

Museums

Museums contain different collections to do with themes such as science, history or transport. They show us how our world developed. Museums employ experts to study a subject and buy in new exhibits. Many museums are interactive, letting visitors experience objects in action.

AMAZING FACTS

THE OLYMPICS

Many people love to watch sport, and the most famous event of all is the Olympic Games. Since 1896, the Olympics (*see pp.208–9*) have been run in a different place around the world every four years. More than 300 contests are held each time, with 28 different sports from archery to wrestling.

Arts and entertainment facts

Many countries are recognized for their enthusiasm for particular art forms. Italy is famous as the home of opera. Russian ballet dancers are known throughout the world. And Chinese and Indian art and sculpture have flourished for millennia.

MOST-SEEN MOVIES (mi = million)
Gone with the Wind (1940) 35 mi
The Sound of Music (1965) 30 mi
Snow White and the Seven Dwarfs
   (1938) 28 mi
Star Wars (1977) 20.76 mi
Spring in Park Lane (1948) 20.5 mi
The Best Years of Our Lives (1947) 20.4 mi
The Jungle Book (1968) 19.8 mi
Titanic (1998) 18.9 mi
The Wicked Lady (1946) 18.4 mi
The Seventh Veil (1945) 17.9 mi

BIGGEST-SELLING SINGLES
*Candle In The Wind (Princess Diana
   Tribute)* Elton John 37 mi
White Christmas Bing Crosby 30 mi

Rock around the Clock Bill Haley
   and His Comets 17 mi
I Want to Hold Your Hand
   The Beatles 12 mi
Hey Jude The Beatles 10 mi
It's Now or Never Elvis Presley 10 mi
I Will Always Love You Whitney
   Houston 10 mi
Hound Dog Elvis Presley 9 mi
Diana Paul Anka 9 mi
(Everything I Do) I Do It For You
   Bryan Adams 8 mi
I'm a Believer The Monkees 8 mi

BEST-SELLING BOOKS SERIES
Perry Rhodan (German science
   fiction), began 1961 1 billion

Star Wars, began 1977 750 mi
Harry Potter, began 1997 535 mi
The New Park Street Pulpit and the
   Metropolitan Tabernacle Pulpit,
   began 1854 300 mi
Goosebumps, began 1992 300 mi
Choose Your Own Adventure, began
   1979 250 mi
Noddy, began 1949 200 mi
Nancy Drew, began 1930 200 mi
Peter Rabbit, began 1902 150 mi
Dirk Pitt, began 1973 120 mi

MOST POPULAR BOARD GAMES
1 Monopoly   4 Scrabble
2 Risk   5 Beyblades
3 Mah Jongg   6 Backgammon

On stage in the musical *A Chorus Line*

USEFUL WEBSITES

www.shakespearesglobe.org The Globe Theatre and links to theatres worldwide.
www.nga.gov/kids/zone/zone.htm   Interactive site where kids can make pictures.
www.creatingmusic.com/   Interactive site where kids can compose and hear their music.
www.rudimentsofwisdom.com/   Full of cartoons that relate to arts and entertainment.

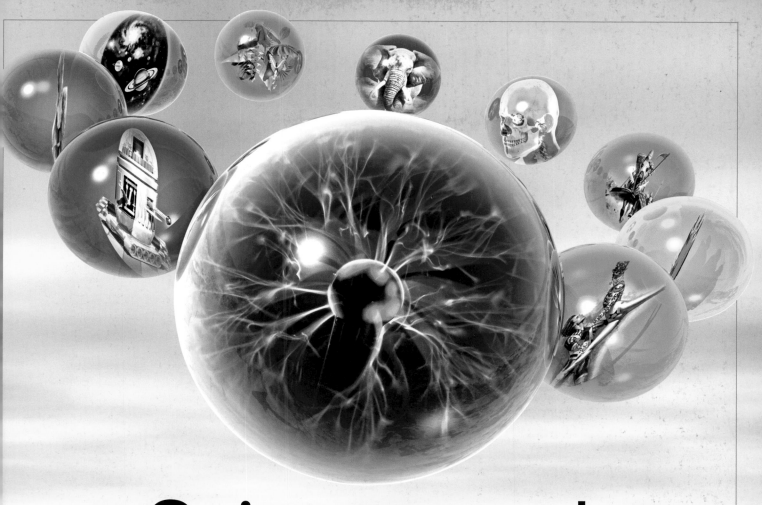

Science and Technology

Science is a powerful tool for understanding how and why things happen. Through technology, that understanding has given people enormous power, and changed the whole world. Though science is a vast and complex subject, it is based on quite a small number of laws which took centuries of study to discover. However, there are still many mysteries to explain.

What is science?

Science is a way of finding out about the Universe, and using that knowledge to control the world around us.

GREAT SCIENTISTS

In the past, individuals developed new areas of knowledge. Today, science relies on teams.

Galileo Galilei
(1564–1642)
First to work out the mathematics of motion.

Isaac Newton
(1642–1727)
Formulated the laws of motion and gravity.

Charles Darwin
(1809–1882)
Discovered how species evolve.

Albert Einstein
(1879–1955)
Linked gravity, time and space.

Areas of science include mathematics (the science of numbers), physics (the study of matter, energy, time and space), chemistry (the study of different substances and their interaction), biology (the science of living things) and astronomy (the investigation of the Universe).

Ancient science

Science has its roots in Greece. Over 2,000 years ago, Greek philosophers debated the nature of the Universe and developed many different theories about it. But they did not experiment to test their ideas, so they could not be sure who was right.

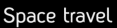

Space travel

The exploration of space is one of the great achievements of science. Isaac Newton's laws are used to work out the motion of planets and spaceships. Advanced technology is used to build and control spacecraft.

Mathematics and computers

Mathematics is used to work out the details of a theory and to make predictions that can be tested. Usually, computers are needed to carry out the complex calculations.

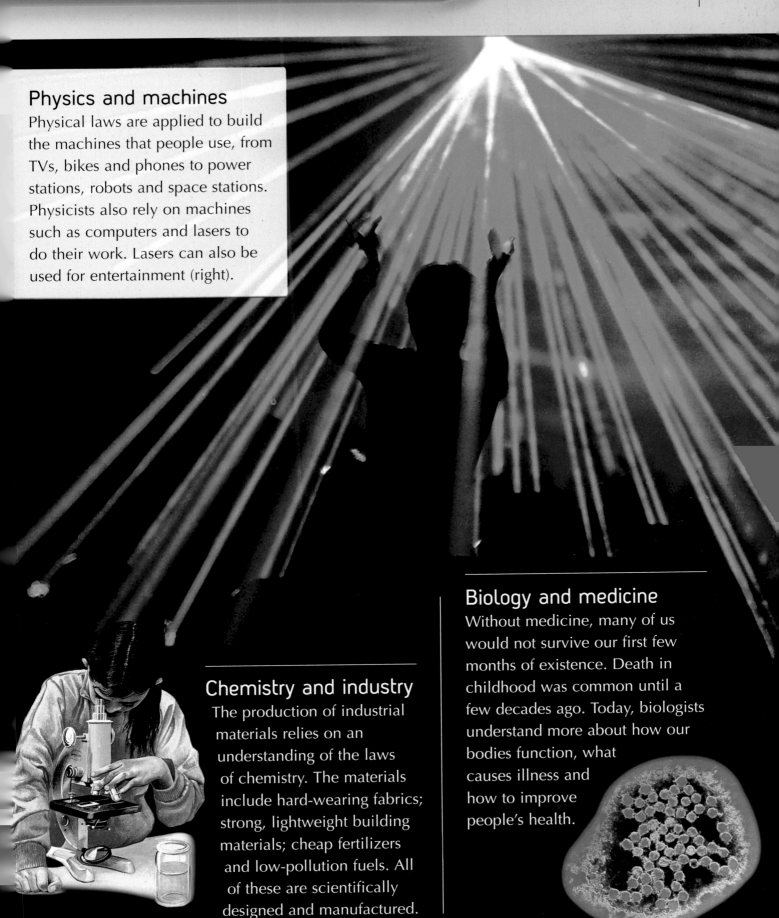

Physics and machines

Physical laws are applied to build the machines that people use, from TVs, bikes and phones to power stations, robots and space stations. Physicists also rely on machines such as computers and lasers to do their work. Lasers can also be used for entertainment (right).

Chemistry and industry

The production of industrial materials relies on an understanding of the laws of chemistry. The materials include hard-wearing fabrics; strong, lightweight building materials; cheap fertilizers and low-pollution fuels. All of these are scientifically designed and manufactured.

Biology and medicine

Without medicine, many of us would not survive our first few months of existence. Death in childhood was common until a few decades ago. Today, biologists understand more about how our bodies function, what causes illness and how to improve people's health.

How science works

Science starts with thinking up explanations for the way things happen. To test these, scientists make predictions they can check.

Gradually, the explanations that the scientists have thought up are developed into theories which are both complete and accurate.

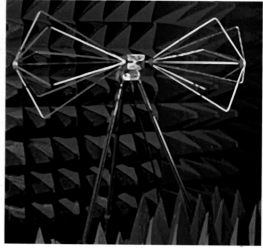
Radio waves can be measured very accurately in this special chamber.

The scientific method

Scientists apply a logical approach, in which ideas are tested and developed into theories and laws. For instance, it was once believed that heavy objects fall faster than light objects. But after observing hailstones falling, Galileo questioned this belief. He experimented with falling objects to discover the mathematical law of fall.

Observing phenomena

Science starts with observing as wide a range of phenomena as possible and trying to explain them. Microscopes, spectroscopes and telescopes allow us to observe things that cannot otherwise be sensed.

Science in action

Some things, such as the motions of planets, can be predicted centuries ahead. 'Chaotic' systems, such as weather, can only be predicted roughly. In a chaotic system, any one of many small changes may lead to big effects, such as a hurricane.

Measurement

We can see light, hear sound, taste and smell some chemicals, and feel heat, force and electricity. But without machines we would neither be able to make the accurate measurements needed to test theories, or detect things such as radio waves or X-rays.

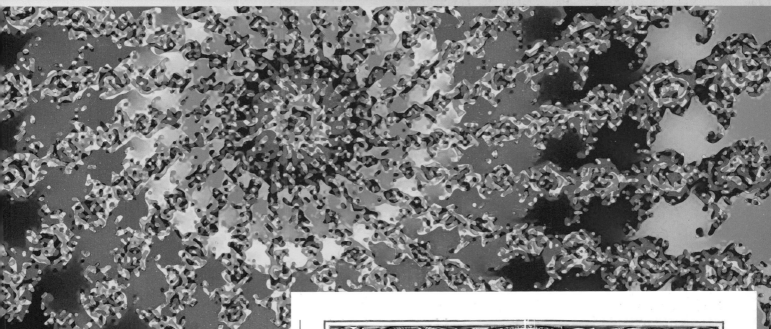

This computer-generated picture is of a fractal, an endless mathematical pattern that occurs in nature.

Mathematical models

Using powerful computers, scientists can make mathematical models of things such as stars, germs or transport systems. These models are used by them to predict what will happen in different situations.

Big science

Modern science is expensive, whether it is a planet or the inside of an atom that is being studied. This huge underground laboratory in Switzerland is called CERN. It uses powerful blasts of energy to break apart atomic particles.

HISTORICAL DATA

REVOLUTIONS IN SCIENCE

Science does not move forwards steadily. Successful theories explain most things for a while, then new evidence mounts up until a new and more powerful theory replaces the old one. For centuries, it was believed that the Sun went round the Earth – until Copernicus' theory, that the Earth goes round the Sun (above), replaced it. Similarly, in the 20th century, Einstein's powerful new theories replaced those of Newton.

A sundial

The world's time system is based on the moment at which the Sun is at its highest, when seen from the prime meridian.

It is 11am in western Africa, and the class is hard at work.

It is 4am in western USA, and time to sleep.

Most time zones are one hour later than the neighbouring zone to the west.

TIME

WE ALL KNOW WHAT TIME IS, BUT TRY PUTTING IT INTO WORDS! TIME IS CLOSELY LINKED TO SPACE – NEITHER CAN EXIST WITHOUT THE OTHER. BUT, WHILE WE CAN MOVE AS WE WISH THROUGH SPACE, WE CAN ONLY MOVE IN ONE DIRECTION THROUGH TIME.

TIME ZONES

The Earth is divided up into time zones. Within each zone, the clocks are set to the same time. The edges of the zones often follow the frontiers of the different countries.

A mechanical pendulum clock

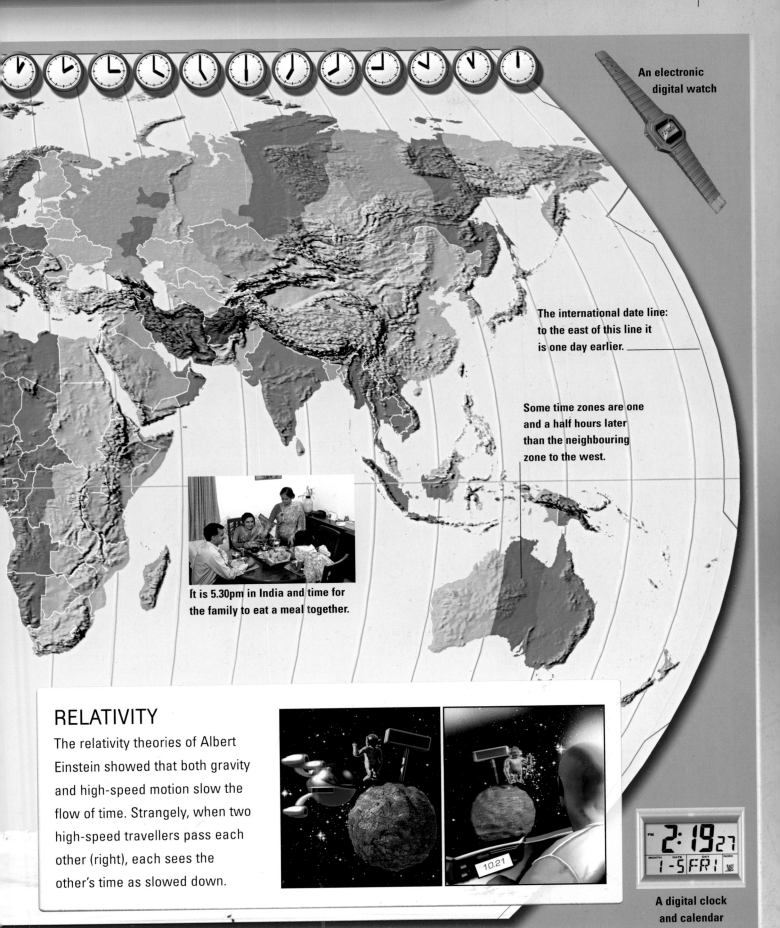

An electronic digital watch

The international date line: to the east of this line it is one day earlier.

Some time zones are one and a half hours later than the neighbouring zone to the west.

It is 5.30pm in India and time for the family to eat a meal together.

RELATIVITY

The relativity theories of Albert Einstein showed that both gravity and high-speed motion slow the flow of time. Strangely, when two high-speed travellers pass each other (right), each sees the other's time as slowed down.

10.21

2:19 27

PM

MONTH   DATE   DAY   PACIFIC
1-5 FRI

A digital clock and calendar

Matter and atoms

Everything, including you, is made of matter. All matter is made of atoms, less than a millionth of a millimetre across.

Matter exists in four forms (states or phases): solid, liquid, gas and plasma. The atoms that make up matter behave differently in each state, and matter can change from one state to another.

Atoms and molecules

Atoms are the building blocks of matter, and they are usually bonded to other atoms in groups called molecules. Some molecules, such as the oxygen that we need to breathe, contain just two atoms. Complex molecules, such as the DNA that tells our bodies how to grow, contain millions.

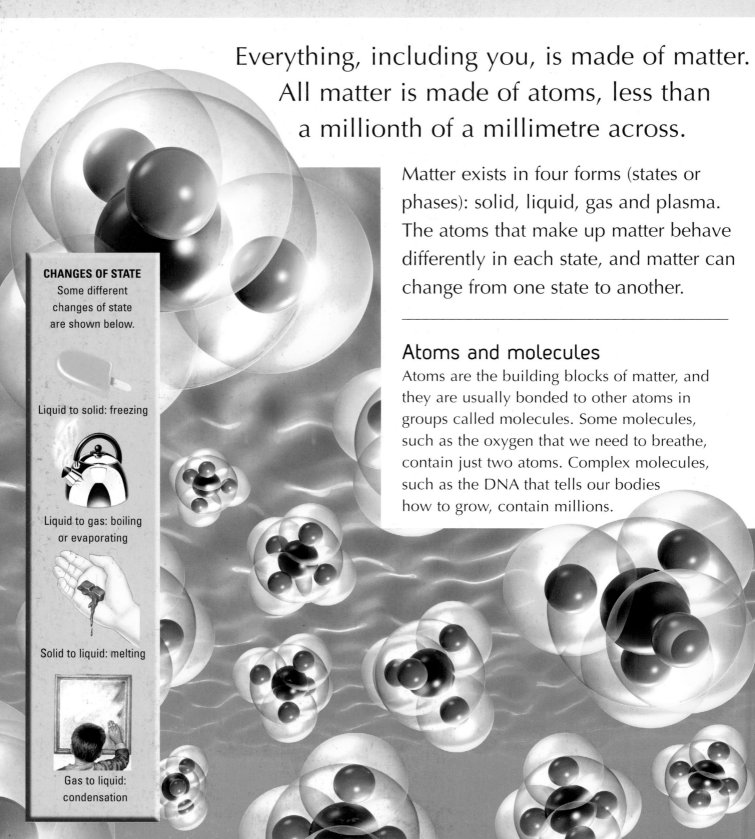

CHANGES OF STATE
Some different changes of state are shown below.

Liquid to solid: freezing

Liquid to gas: boiling or evaporating

Solid to liquid: melting

Gas to liquid: condensation

Solids, liquids and gases

In a solid, the molecules are held together and cannot move easily. In liquids they can move past each other but still remain close. In gases, the molecules can move freely, and in plasmas they are broken down into atomic nuclei and electrons.

Atomic nuclei

Atoms are mostly empty space, with a tiny, dense core called the nucleus at the centre. Nuclei are made of particles called neutrons and protons. Nuclei have diameters 100,000 times smaller than an atom's.

Electrons and ions

Atomic nuclei are surrounded by particles called electrons. Electrons have a negative electric charge which usually balances the positive charge of the protons. An atom with an unequal number of electrons and protons is called an ion.

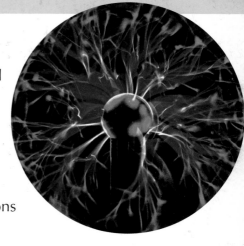

Isotopes

The atoms of a chemical element all have the same number of protons, but not always the same number of neutrons. Atoms of the same element with different numbers of neutrons are called isotopes.

Normal hydrogen nucleus

Deuterium nucleus

Tritium nucleus

Isotopes of hydrogen used in nuclear reactors

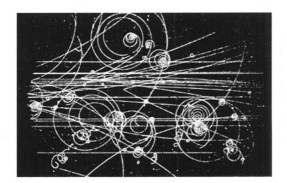

Sub-atomic particles

Protons and neutrons are made of even smaller particles called quarks. These are held together by particles called gluons. To study nuclei, quarks are smashed to pieces in particle accelerators, and special instruments show how they move (above). Their masses, electric charges and other properties can be worked out from these images.

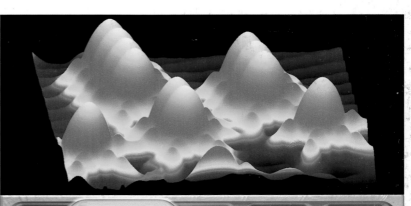

AMAZING FACTS

QUANTUM PHYSICS

Tiny things such as electrons do not behave like the larger objects that we are used to in our everyday lives. Electrons do not have exact speeds and positions. In the group of atoms above, the electrons can only be defined as being somewhere in the red and yellow areas. And they behave like light waves as well as particles. The study of these strange properties is called quantum physics.

Elements and compounds

An element is a substance made of atoms, each of which has the same number of protons. Everything in the Universe is composed of around 100 different elements.

The atoms of different elements can join together. The resulting substance is called a compound, and usually has very different properties to the original elements.

Elements and atoms
The properties of an element depend on the properties of its atoms. So hydrogen and helium, which are made of very small atoms, are both very light gases. Lead, which is very heavy, is made of much larger atoms.

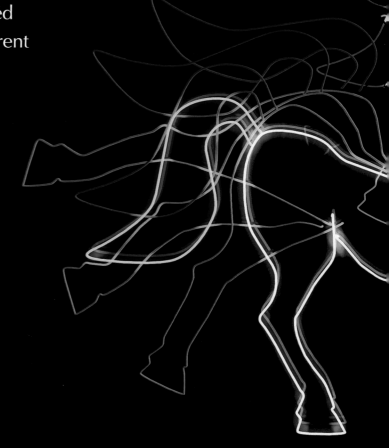

Metals
Metals are a very useful group of elements, partly because they conduct electricity and heat. Metal atoms all share their outer electrons. This makes it easy for electrical or thermal energy to move between them. Some metals react easily with oxygen to form oxides. Rust, for example, is iron oxide.

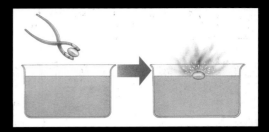

Reactive elements

Elements whose atoms have a single outer electron are all highly reactive, combining easily with other elements. A small amount of potassium reacts violently with water (above), releasing hydrogen and forming a compound called a hydroxide.

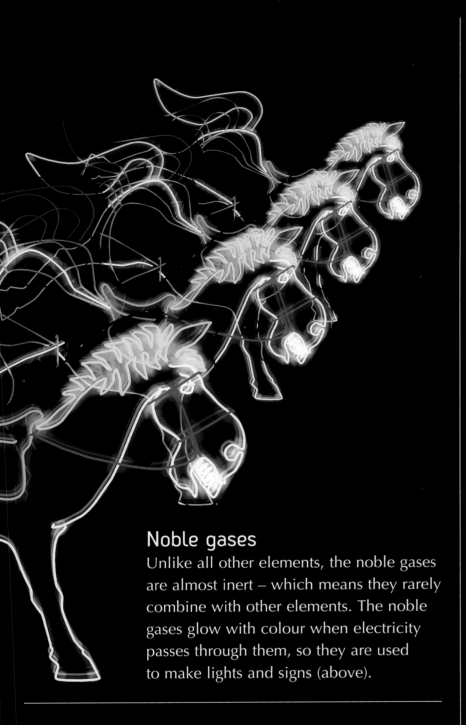

Noble gases

Unlike all other elements, the noble gases are almost inert – which means they rarely combine with other elements. The noble gases glow with colour when electricity passes through them, so they are used to make lights and signs (above).

Radioactive elements

The atoms that make up some heavy elements, such as uranium, are unstable. They break apart unpredictably and release energy in the form of intense radiation (gamma rays) and particles (alpha and beta particles). Radioactive elements can both cause and cure some forms of cancer, and are used in nuclear weapons and power stations.

Compounds

Often, heating will cause elements to combine into compounds. When the elements hydrogen and oxygen are mixed and heated, they produce water. The symbol of water is H_2O, because its molecules contain two hydrogen atoms and one of oxygen.

Materials

Some of the materials we use are natural, such as wool, wood and stone. But most things are made from artificial (synthetic) materials, such as concrete, glass and plastic.

Today, people design materials with the properties they need, such as building materials that are strong and lightweight.

Wood

Wood is used all over the world for building, and for making paper and furniture too. Different types have different properties: balsa is light, oak is strong, and teak is hard.

Plastics

Most plastics are made from oil-based chemicals and they are easy to mould, shape and colour. They can be flexible and transparent for food packaging, or hard and tough for vehicles.

Metals

Metals have many useful properties. They can be shaped when heated, and many are tough and hard-wearing. Alloys are mixtures of metals and sometimes other materials. The most useful alloy is steel, which is iron with carbon added to harden it.

OIL PRODUCTS
Oil from the Earth can be made into many useful everyday items.

Paint

Candles

Petrol

Lubricating fluid

Glass

Glass is made from sand and can be shaped by blowing, moulding or rolling. Though naturally brittle, it can be toughened to resist heat or impact. Metallic chemicals are used to colour it.

Adhesives

Adhesives are substances that stick objects together. Some are made from natural materials. The strongest and longest-lasting adhesives are artificial.

Smart materials

It is possible to change the properties of some artificial materials by applying heat, electricity or magnetism to them: these 'smart materials' can change shape or turn into a liquid at the press of a button. Objects made of 'Shape Memory Alloys' (SMAs) spring back to their original shapes when heated.

ENERGY

ENERGY IS THE ABILITY TO DO WORK: SO WITHOUT IT, NOTHING COULD HAPPEN. ENERGY CANNOT BE DESTROYED, AND EXISTS IN MANY FORMS, INCLUDING MASS.

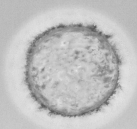

Inside the Sun, hydrogen nuclei are crushed together to form helium nuclei. The process releases enormous amounts of energy, and is called nuclear fusion. We see this energy as sunlight.

TYPES OF ENERGY

The many forms of energy can be converted into each other. Sunlight is converted to chemical energy by plants and to electrical energy by solar cells. Televisions convert electrical energy to sound and light. Animals convert the chemical energy in food into kinetic energy when they move. All these energy changes also produce heat (thermal energy).

Surplus natural gas is burned off as a flare.

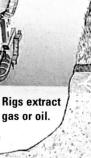

Rigs extract gas or oil.

Excavator working on opencast mine, where coal lies on surface

Gas and oil

NUCLEAR ENERGY

Some large atoms are unstable and disintegrate naturally, releasing energy (nuclear fission). In a nuclear power station, these disintegrations are kept under control and used to produce electrical energy.

FOSSIL FUELS

Plants use the energy of sunlight to bind together water and carbon dioxide to make their leaves and other structures. The remains of whole forests of plants which lived more than 200 million years ago, crushed deep underground, change gradually to coal, oil and gas. When these fossil fuels are burned, the energy of ancient sunlight is released again.

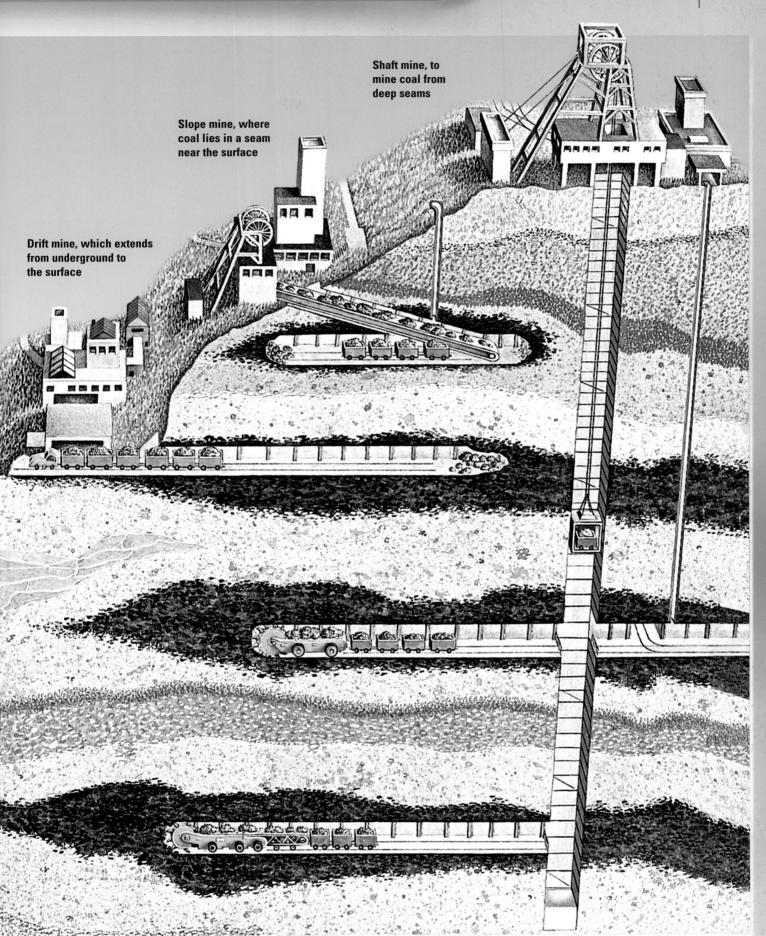

Shaft mine, to mine coal from deep seams

Slope mine, where coal lies in a seam near the surface

Drift mine, which extends from underground to the surface

Sound, light and colour

Most of our information about the world comes to us as sound or light. Both are flows of energy that travel in the form of waves.

There are sound waves we cannot hear and light waves we cannot see. Infrasound and infrared frequencies are too low for us, and ultrasound and ultraviolet are too high.

Sound

Sound usually starts as a vibration in an object. It travels through air, water or solids as longitudinal (backwards and forwards) waves of pressure. Sound travels much faster in solids and liquids than in air.

Noise

Noise is unwanted sound, whether it comes from cars, planes or radios. Even quiet noise can be annoying, and high levels can damage hearing.

Pitch and frequency

Frequency is the number of backwards and forwards motions of a sound wave per second. Sounds of higher frequency are higher-pitched. Most of the sounds we hear are a mixture of many frequencies.

Light

Light travels at 299,792,458m per second through empty space, but slightly slower in liquids and solids. Light, like radio signals and X-rays, travels as a rapidly changing electromagnetic field.

Colour

We see different light frequencies as different colours, from low-frequency red, through the colours of the rainbow to high-frequency violet. Mixes of different frequencies can be seen as further colours, such as pink. When light of all colours is mixed, we see white.

Fibre optic cables inside a telephone wire

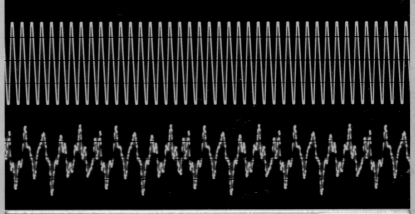

Optics

Optics is the science of light. Geometrical optics describes how light bounces and scatters. Physical optics studies the nature of the photons of which light is composed. The photons behave as particles in some ways and as waves in others.

SCIENTIFIC INPUT

SOUND WAVES AND LIGHT WAVES

Sound and light are very different. Light travels about a million times faster than sound. Even the shortest sound waves we can hear are many thousands of times longer than light waves. Sound needs a medium (air, for example) to travel in; light does not. Machines called oscilloscopes (above) can display the rapidly changing pressures of sound waves as rising and falling lines of light.

Heat

Heat is a form of energy consisting of the random motion of particles. It is generated by all processes. Even refrigerators heat the air around them.

The melting and then boiling of substances as they are heated happens because the increasing energy of molecules allows them to break their bonds. They then escape from each other. Even more heat breaks down the molecules themselves.

KINETIC ENERGY
As temperature rises, the energy of molecules increases until they break free, causing changes of state.

In a solid, molecules are locked together.

A solid melts when the molecules have enough energy to break their bonds.

A liquid boils when the molecules can move freely, filling their container.

Heat and temperature
Heat is a type of energy, and temperature describes the 'concentration' of that energy. A lake contains more heat than a cup of tea. However, it has a lower temperature because the energy is spread out more thinly over its large volume.

Heating and cooling
Usually, heating a solid substance causes it first to melt (or 'thaw') and then turn into a gas (called boiling if the change is rapid, or evaporation if slow). Cooling a gas usually causes it to condense and then freeze (left). But sometimes the liquid phase is missed out – frost in sunlight can 'sublime', changing directly to gas.

Heat transfer

Heat moves in three ways. It passes through solids by conduction (the metal bucket would burn anyone it touches). It moves through liquids and gases by convection (like the draught of hot air rising from the bucket). And it is transferred through gases or space by radiation (the molten metal is glowing with invisible infrared heat radiation as well as light).

Electricity and magnetism

Electricity and magnetism are vital to the way we live. Streetlights and phones are electrically powered, while motors and credit cards need magnets to work.

Both electricity and magnetism depend on the motion of electrons. Force fields around magnetic or electrically charged objects push or pull other similar objects.

Natural electricity

Our brains and nerves use tiny amounts of electricity in order to function and to control our bodies. Very much larger amounts of electricity can be seen when lightning strikes during a thunderstorm.

Electronics

Materials which allow electricity to pass easily are called conductors, and those through which electricity cannot pass are insulators. Semiconductors allow a variable amount of electricity to pass and are used to control the flow of electricity in electronic circuits.

Electric circuits

A battery is a device which produces electricity. It has two 'poles'. If these are connected by a wire, electricity flows from the negative pole to the positive pole. It can be made to do work on the way, by powering a bulb or motor.

Static and current electricity

When an object loses or gains electrons, it becomes electrically charged. This charge is called static electricity, because it stays where it is. When areas with different amounts of charge are connected by a metal wire, electricity flows along the wire and is called an electric current.

Magnets

Magnets attract other magnets. They also attract iron and some other metals. All magnets have a 'north' and a 'south' pole, and each pole attracts poles of the opposite type and repels poles of its own type.

Electromagnetism

A current-carrying conductor generates a magnetic field. If the conductor is wound around an iron core, the field can be very strong. Devices like this are called electromagnets and provide controllable magnetic fields.

EARTH EVIDENCE

THE EARTH AS A MAGNET

Movements of molten metal deep inside the Earth generate a worldwide magnetic field. This magnetic field protects life on Earth from harmful radiation from space. In a compass, a small, thin magnet lines up with the Earth's field, pointing the way to the north and south poles and helping people navigate.

FORCES AND MOTION

A MOVING OBJECT IS SAID TO HAVE KINETIC ENERGY — THE FASTER IT MOVES, OR THE MORE MASS IT HAS, THE HIGHER ITS KINETIC ENERGY. THE VELOCITY OF AN OBJECT IS ITS SPEED IN A PARTICULAR DIRECTION. ACCELERATION IS CHANGE OF VELOCITY.

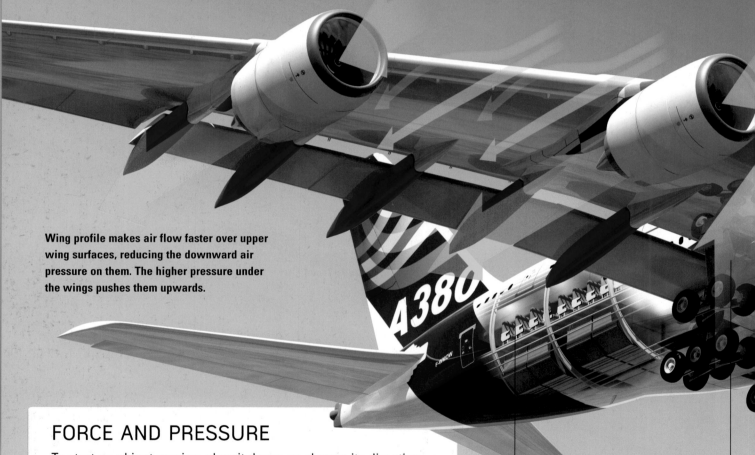

Wing profile makes air flow faster over upper wing surfaces, reducing the downward air pressure on them. The higher pressure under the wings pushes them upwards.

FORCE AND PRESSURE

To start an object moving, slow it down, or change its direction, a force (a push or pull) is required. When air resistance or friction is present, force is required to keep the object moving. Where there is no air resistance or friction — in space, for instance — objects will continue to move with no force present. Pressure is the amount of force applied to a particular area.

The A380 can seat 525 people because it has 50 per cent more floor space than any other passenger airliner.

The upwards force on the wings opposes the downwards force of gravity.

WORK AND POWER

When an object is moved by a force, work is achieved. The higher the force, or the greater the distance, the more work is done. Power measures how quickly this happens. Whether you walk or run upstairs, you do the same amount of work, but running needs more power.

The inertia of the air molecules means that they resist being moved aside by the plane. This resistance would slow the plane if it were not constantly pushed forwards by its engines.

The upper deck extends the entire length of the fuselage.

The flight deck has liquid crystal displays.

The A380 has a cruising speed of Mach 0.85 (about 900km/h).

Air is drawn into the engines.

Engines use chemical energy from fuel to speed up the air, increasing its momentum and pushing the plane forwards.

Force of gravity pulls plane down

MOMENTUM AND INERTIA

Momentum is the tendency of a moving object to keep moving, while inertia is the tendency of a stationary object to remain still. The larger the mass of an object, the more inertia or momentum it has. The momentum of a moving object increases with its speed.

Engineering

Engineering is the application of science to the construction of the systems and structures we use.

DEVELOPMENT OF AIRCRAFT

Aircraft have developed rapidly over the last 100 years.

Biplanes were invented in the 1900s.

Monoplanes replaced them in the 1930s.

The first successful jet plane flew in 1939.

The first supersonic flight was in 1947.

Rocket planes reached the edge of space in 1963.

We live in an engineered world. Cities can be thought of as vast machines, containing many smaller machines and systems.

Civil engineering

Over thousands of years, civil engineers have gradually developed materials, designs and methods to build roads, bridges and buildings. Today, computer models are essential to all civil engineering projects.

Mining

Mining engineers organize the extraction and transport of minerals (such as coal or salt) and metal ores (such as iron) from mines. They are responsible for miners' safety too.

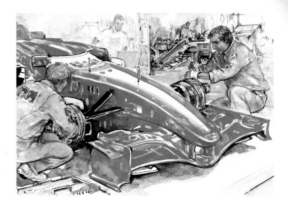

Machines and vehicles

Mechanical engineers design, build and test machines, from factory robots to trains. Cars, motor bikes and lorries are designed by automotive engineers.

Electrical engineering

Electrical engineers develop electrical and electronic devices and systems. These include electricity distribution systems, computer hardware, and telecommunication systems such as phone networks and television.

Aerospace

Aerospace engineers design and build aircraft and spacecraft, which are some of the most challenging and complex machines of all. They have to be able to keep passengers safe while they travel through environments that may change rapidly and unpredictably.

Software engineering

Software has to be engineered not only to perform a function – for example, transferring money between banks – but also to be fast, efficient and reliable. It is often necessary for it to run properly on different types of computer system.

AMAZING FACTS

RECORD-BREAKING TUNNEL

Nearly 13,000 people, including mining, mechanical, civil, software and electrical engineers, were needed to construct the 50-km Channel Tunnel (above), which connects the UK and France. It is the longest undersea tunnel in the world, and it is air-conditioned by a system that is equivalent to 260,000 domestic refrigerators. Some of the tunnel-boring machines used were the length of two football fields.

Industry and manufacturing

Over the last few centuries the application of science through technology has transformed the world. It is used to produce all kinds of things, from food to cars.

Almost every part of our lives depends on industry and manufacturing – the vehicles we travel in, the books and computers we use, our homes, food, and clothes. Many products are built where they can be made cheaply, and transported all over the world.

Food production

Industry affects every stage of the food production process. Biological expertise is used to develop improved vegetables and fruit. Chemicals are used to fertilize seedlings and keep them free from weeds and pests. And the crops are harvested, processed, preserved, packaged and transported by machinery.

Industrial chemistry

Many of the things you use every day, including plastics, fuel and many fabrics, were made chemically in industrial plants. The increasing use of robots and computers in these plants has gradually reduced the numbers of human workers involved in the process. Safety has been improved because machines have taken over work that was often unpleasant and dangerous.

Mass production

Most machines are made by other machines, in large numbers and with very limited human involvement. Standard-sized, accurately machine-made parts mean that different components of large machines can be made in different countries and will still work together correctly when assembled. This amazing storage facility for newly completed cars is in Wolfsburg, Germany. It is fully automated – a robot arm moves the cars up and down when needed.

Medicine

Medicine is one of the greatest triumphs of science, giving most of us many more years of life than our ancestors had.

TYPES OF MEDICINE

Medicine is a wide-ranging field of science and includes the skill areas below.

First aid delivers rapid help at the scene of an accident.

Surgery involves operating on the body, usually in a hospital.

Minor ailments are treated at a local doctor's surgery.

Medical research develops new cures and treatments.

Early doctors tried different cures to see what worked. Today, the discovery of germs and a greater understanding of the way the body works have led to much more effective treatments of illnesses.

Health and illness

Modern medicine recognizes that it is as important to encourage health through good diet, exercise and living conditions, as it is to cure illness. Good health does not just mean a fit body – the mind too can become ill. Care of the whole person is called holistic medicine.

Injuries and healing

The body is capable of healing most injuries itself, if it is protected while it recovers. Antiseptics stop wounds becoming infected and bandages support injuries. Good diet and a desire to get better are important.

Operations and antiseptics

To replace organs, remove tumours and install artificial body parts, it is necessary to operate on the body. To avoid pain, local anaesthetics numb body parts. For major surgery, general anaesthetics cause unconsciousness.

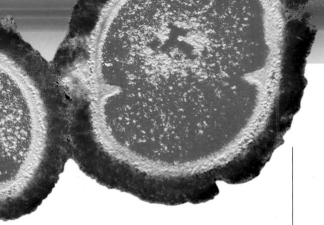

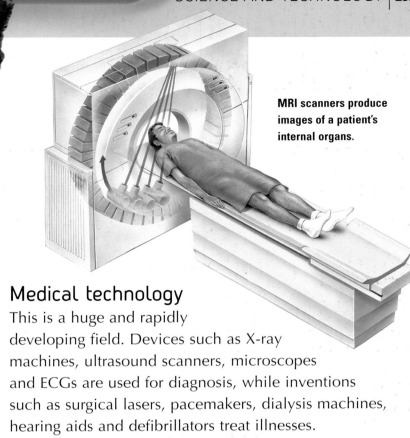

MRI scanners produce images of a patient's internal organs.

Microbes

Diseases are spread by microbes (germs). Microbes include large molecules called prions; viruses; single-celled creatures called bacteria and protozoa; parasites and fungi. The picture above is of MRSA bacteria, which are resistant to many of the common antibiotics.

Medical technology

This is a huge and rapidly developing field. Devices such as X-ray machines, ultrasound scanners, microscopes and ECGs are used for diagnosis, while inventions such as surgical lasers, pacemakers, dialysis machines, hearing aids and defibrillators treat illnesses.

Antibiotics and vaccines

Antibiotics are one of the most important weapons against disease. 'Broad-spectrum' antibiotics such as penicillin are capable of destroying almost any type of bacterium. In many cases, if a person is vaccinated with a weakened version of a virus, their body's immune system can adapt to fight the full-strength virus.

HISTORICAL DATA

DISCOVERY OF GERMS

In the 1670s, Anthony van Leeuwenhoek used microscopes to discover nearly invisible living organisms, later called germs or microbes. In the 1860s, Louis Pasteur's experiments (above) proved that germs came only from other germs, not rotting meat or other non-living materials. In 1877, Robert Koch showed that particular types of germ cause particular diseases when he identified the type that causes anthrax.

Biotechnology

Biotechnology is the scientific design and alteration of living things to benefit human beings.

Farmers have been developing animals and plants for food and other uses for thousands of years. Today, research into the chemical basis of life has led to rapid developments.

Making medicine

Making drugs in laboratories is an important application of biotechnology. Today, insulin can be produced from genetically modified bacteria cheaply and effectively.

Fermentation

Fermentation is the biological process that changes fruit juice into wine, and flour dough into bread. To make wine, yeast (a type of fungus) is added to the juice. If the temperature and other conditions are right, the yeast multiplies, feeding on sugar in the juice and producing alcohol as a waste product.

Genetic engineering

Genetic engineering is the modification of genes. It is used to improve food crops, to develop drug-producing bacteria and breed new types of experimental mice for research. Genetically modified crops may be designed to stay fresh or to resist pests and disease.

DNA and genes

Modern advances in biotechnology rely on modifying genes. Genes are structures that form parts of enormous molecules of DNA (deoxyribonucleic acid). Genes are the instructions, found in every cell, which tell that cell how to grow and function.

DNA coils up, and then the coil is itself coiled into a structure called a chromosome.

Identity cards in the future may carry DNA information.

Genetic fingerprinting

Every person's genes are unique. Because they are in all our cells, this means that each of us can be identified from a tiny trace of blood, skin or even sweat. As our genes resemble those of our relatives, family relationships can also be explored by our genetic fingerprints.

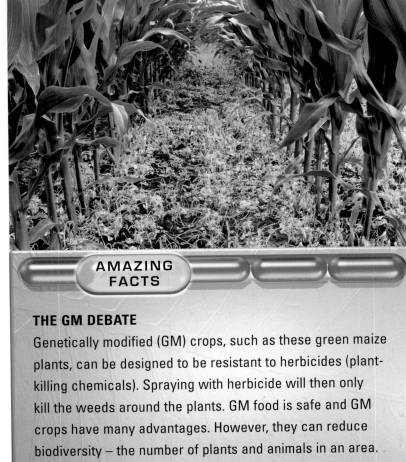

AMAZING FACTS

THE GM DEBATE

Genetically modified (GM) crops, such as these green maize plants, can be designed to be resistant to herbicides (plant-killing chemicals). Spraying with herbicide will then only kill the weeds around the plants. GM food is safe and GM crops have many advantages. However, they can reduce biodiversity — the number of plants and animals in an area.

Each 'rung' of DNA is made of two out of four bases — adenine, cytosine, guanine and thymine.

Guanine (blue) always pairs with cytosine (yellow).

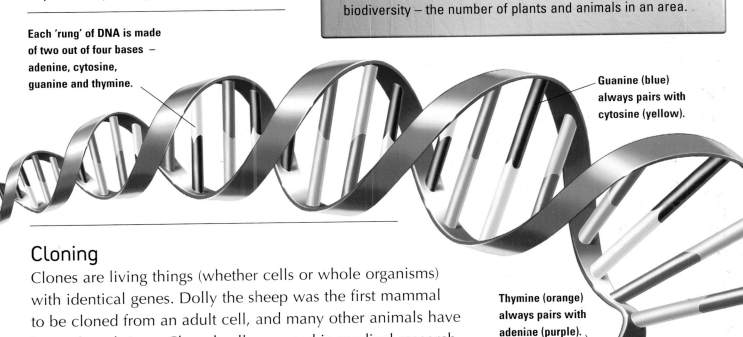

Cloning

Clones are living things (whether cells or whole organisms) with identical genes. Dolly the sheep was the first mammal to be cloned from an adult cell, and many other animals have been cloned since. Cloned cells are used in medical research.

Thymine (orange) always pairs with adenine (purple).

Science facts

People in different countries use different units to measure things – for example, inches, hands, yards, metres, fathoms, feet and kilometres all measure lengths. But scientists always use the same set of units, some of which are given below.

UNITS OF MEASUREMENT

Base units

Mass: kilograms

Length: metres

Time: seconds

Temperature: kelvins

Amount of substance: moles

Electric current: amperes

Luminous intensity: candelas

Units combining base units

Frequency: hertz (cycles per second)

Speed: metres per second

Volume: cubic metres

Energy: joules

Pressure: pascals

Force: newtons

Power: watts

VALUES

Speed of light: 299,792.458m per second

Charge on electron or proton:
  1.602×10^{-19} coulomb

Mass of an electron: 9.109×10^{-31} kg

Mass of a proton: 1,836 times more than an electron

At normal air pressure, pure water boils at 100°C (373.15 kelvins) and freezes at 0°C (273.15 kelvins)

Power of a kettle: about 2,500 watts

Energy required to heat a litre of water to boiling point: about 330,000 joules

Force with which an apple pushes down on the hand: about 1 newton

Piano notes range: 27.5–4,186 hertz

Normal air pressure: 101,323 pascals

ELECTROMAGNETIC SPECTRUM

In order of shortening wavelength and rising frequency

Radio waves

Microwaves

Infrared

Visible light:
  Red
  Orange
  Yellow
  Green
  Blue
  Violet

Ultraviolet

X-rays

Gamma-rays

Speed of light = wavelength x frequency

Jug of ice melting over four-hour period

USEFUL WEBSITES

www.sciencenewsforkids.org/ The latest science news geared to kids, games and more.

www.physics4kids.com/ Kids website full of information and facts about physics.

www.bbc.co.uk/schools/ks2bitesize/ The science of living things, materials and processes.

http://library.thinkquest.org/J001539/ Everything you need to know about chemistry.

Communications

Communication is the sharing of information, instructions and ideas between people. It can happen face-to-face or, using technology, with people thousands of kilometres away. Today, there are more ways of communicating than ever before. They range from television and electronic media to improved transport technologies that enable people to travel the world.

Messages and the media

A message is the information that is to be communicated. The transmitter is the person or thing sending the message, and the audience is the person who receives the message.

Methods of communicating, from sending an email to speaking over a telephone, are known as media.

Short or long

Messages can be very short, for example a stop sign or whistle blast. Books contain many thousands of words. The longest novel, by Frenchman Marcel Proust, has nearly 1.5 million words.

Targeting an audience

Some messages are aimed at large numbers of people, for example a neon sign in a city or a pop concert in front of a big audience. Here, a large crowd is at a rally to hear Archbishop Desmond Tutu speak.

Holospot is sprayed on belongings, for example a car, and can only be read in ultraviolet light.

Private messages

Some messages are private or only intended for a specific audience. Secret letters written in invisible ink are an example. This Holospot (above) is a tiny dot containing security information about a car.

Mass media

Some forms of media reach many people in different places at the same time. They are called mass media. Television, newspapers, magazines, radio, cinema and giant advertising billboards are all examples of this.

Without words

Many messages can be sent without language. Visual communication includes road signs, photographs and posters. People communicate without words by using signs and gestures. Here, a member of the US Air Force uses hand signals to give the pilot messages.

Sending a message

Messages carried by hand or by messengers on horseback used to take weeks to reach their audiences. Today, texting and emails are almost instantaneous. Around 25 billion emails alone are sent every day. The amount and major locations of internet traffic (emails and other electronic information) are represented on this map.

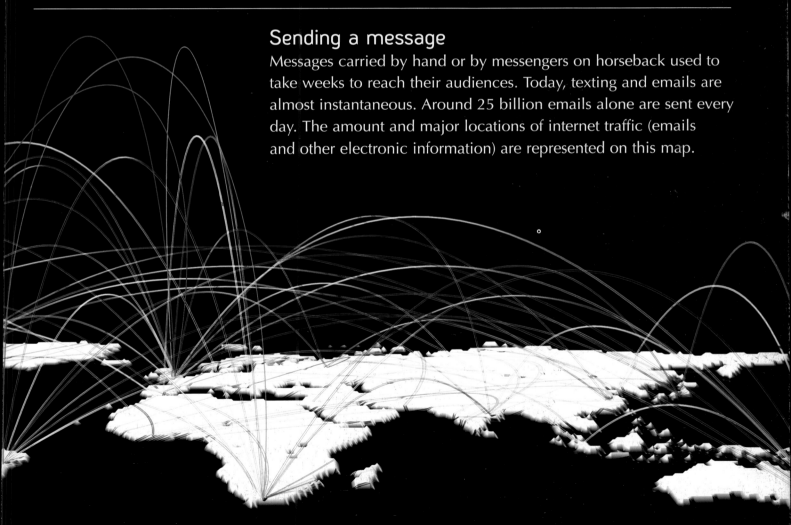

Why we communicate

Every time you choose to communicate you do so for a reason. It may be for fun, for example telling a story, or to give information to someone.

People also communicate to express their feelings and to try to influence the feelings or decisions of other people.

Warning

One of the oldest communications is to warn another person or creature. Warnings can be verbal (spoken) or non-verbal (using a sign). Here, a referee shows a football player a yellow card to warn him about his play.

Instructions

Communication can be used to instruct someone how to perform a task or order them not to do something (above). Leaflets and frequently asked questions (FAQs) on websites also provide instruction.

Information and education

One of the most important uses of communication is to provide help and information to others. Land maps, for example, communicate vital details about the terrain to allow people to find their way.

Propaganda

Propaganda is information that influences people's beliefs. The propaganda posters above glorify a leader. Other propaganda may blame people for things they did not do, or contain lies or exaggerations.

Entertainment

From telling a joke to listening to music, communication often entertains an audience. This can be live – for example, going to the theatre or a concert – or through recorded media such as a CD, a book or a DVD.

Advertising

Advertising uses communication to promote the sale of a company's goods or services. Advertisers use many forms of media from giant displays in cities (above) to TV, web and newspaper adverts to persuade people to buy their products.

SCIENTIFIC INPUT

CREATING AN ILLUSION

Special effects (FX) are techniques used in television and movies to create the illusion of something happening that is not real. This includes moving physical models and computer generated imagery (CGI). This image of the Human Torch – a superhero covered in fire – was created using CGI graphics for the movie *Fantastic Four* (2005).

Long-distance communication

In the past, people have blown horns, beaten drums and sent smoke signals to send messages over distances.

Telecommunications are more modern ways of communicating long distance, using electrical signals, radio waves, satellites and other electronic devices.

Warning lights

Lighthouses shine their lights to warn sailors of rocks or other threats to their boat or ship. These tall towers are usually built on platforms out at sea or on coastal outcrops. Modern lighthouses are equipped with radios and computers, as well as foghorns to blast sound over many kilometres.

Long-distance delivery

Postal systems transport letters, books, magazines and other items over great distances. Many operate light aircraft which deliver letters and packages to isolated parts of a country, such as Australia (above).

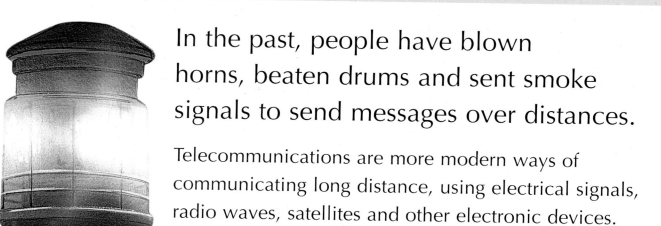

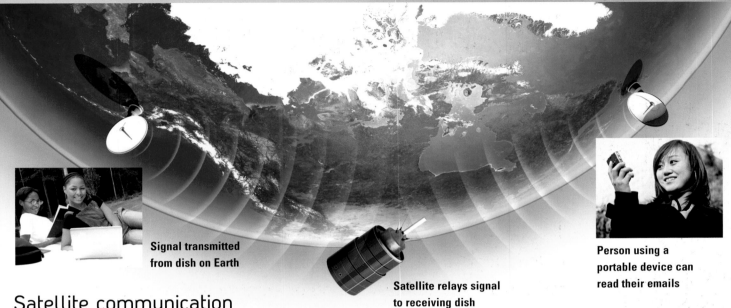

Signal transmitted
from dish on Earth

Satellite relays signal
to receiving dish

Person using a
portable device can
read their emails

Satellite communication

Most communication satellites orbit approximately 35,900km above the equator. Telephone, radio, computer and television signals can be beamed to and from the satellite in only fractions of a second.

Speaker

Microphone

1687485124

LCD screen

Dial pad

Telephone

Telephones convert sound and speech into electrical signals that travel along wires to a telephone exchange. Computers direct the call along fast cables or use radio waves to beam the signal via a satellite.

Radio

Communications can be sent through the air as radio waves. Some radios are used by people on the move, such as pilots, police and truck drivers (right). Broadcasted speech, music and computer data can be collected by a household radio receiver.

Mobile phones

Mobile phones transmit their signals wirelessly using radio waves. Users can make voice calls, and send and receive text messages, photos and videos. Many mobile phones can now connect to the World Wide Web and send and receive emails.

TELEVISION

THE CAPTURING OF SOUND AND IMAGES WITH
CAMERAS AND SOUND RECORDING EQUIPMENT
CHANGED EVERYBODY'S LIVES. TODAY, BROADCAST
TELEVISION PROGRAMMES REACH PEOPLE
IN EVERY COUNTRY OF THE WORLD.

IN THE STUDIO

Programmes are usually produced in television studios. A show may be recorded in advance or filmed as it happens. There may also be some outside broadcast – footage filmed outside the studio. The studio floor (below) is where TV cameras film the action. The images and sound are sent to a control room (left), where the different camera angles are displayed so that a director and their assistants can select the ones they need to make the programme.

TRANSMITTING AND RECEIVING

Television signals are broadcast using transmitters that send the signals via radio waves. Many long-distance broadcasts are made using communications satellites that orbit the Earth to relay the signals. The signals are picked up by aerials or small satellite dishes, or sent along a cable connection buried underground. Modern televisions are often the centre of a complete home entertainment sytem that can record, store and even pause live television.

Languages

Languages are collections of sounds or symbols forming words that have meanings. Children learn at least one language as they grow up.

Most languages, such as French, Hindi and German, have a spoken and a written form. Some spoken languages also include sighs, grunts, laughter and other noises.

Body language

This is the collection of signals given out by a person's facial expressions, gestures and how they stand or sit. Some body language is obvious, for example the angry faces and finger-pointing of two people arguing.

Verbal language

Verbal communication has existed for tens of thousands of years. Before there were written or recorded languages, history, legends and teachings were passed from parent to child through stories and speeches. Today, story-telling is still an important method of communication.

Languages of the world

Experts estimate there are as many as 6,000 different spoken languages around the world. There are many more dialects (different versions of the same language). The most used languages are English, Hindi, Mandarin Chinese, Spanish and Arabic.

Sign language

Languages have been developed to make communication easier for people with special needs. Braille, for instance, uses raised dots on a page to represent letters for blind or sight-impaired people. This teacher is using a sign language for the deaf and hard of hearing, where hand gestures represent letters, numbers and whole words.

The written word

Writing is a way of recording information using signs or symbols to represent words and meanings.

Russian		Greek		Arabic
А	а	А	α	ا
Б	б	В	β	ب
В	в	Г	γ	ت
Г	г	Δ	δ	ث
Д	д	Е	ε	ج
Е	е	Z	ζ	ح
Ж	ж	Н	η	خ
З	з	Θ	θ	د
И	и	I	ι	ذ
Й	й	К	κ	ر
К	к	Λ	λ	ز
Л	л	М	μ	س
М	м	N	ν	ش
Н	н	Ξ	ξ	ص
О	о	О	ο	ض
П	п	П	π	ط
Р	р	Р	ρ	ظ
С	с	Σ	σ	ع
Т	т	Т	τ	غ
У	у	Υ	υ	ف
Ф	ф	Ф	φ	ق
Х	х	Х	χ	ك
Ц	ц	Ψ	ψ	ل
Ч	ч	Ω	ω	م
Ш	ш			ن
Щ	щ			ه
Ъ	ъ			و
Ы	ы			ي
Ь	ь			
Э	э			
Ю	ю			
Я	я			

The Russian, Greek and Arabic alphabets look very different.

The oldest example of writing so far discovered is a 5,100-year-old clay tablet from the Sumerian city of Uruk.

Alphabets

An alphabet is a system of symbols or characters that allow a language's sounds to be written down. Usually, each symbol represents one sound and can be combined with other symbols to form all the words.

Books and publishing

Today, a book goes through many stages including writing, editing, design, illustration and production before its pages are printed and bound together. It is published when it is finally available for sale (above).

Printing presses

Printing presses were invented in China and first used in Europe by Johannes Gutenberg around 1450. They originally featured metal letter shapes arranged in trays to form a page. This was then covered in ink and pressed on sheets of paper. Modern printing presses use computers and can output tens of thousands of pages per hour.

Journalism

Journalists collect information so that they can write news stories, which are published in newspapers or magazines, or broadcast on radio, television or the internet. They interview people on the spot. Some risk injury working in war zones (above) to report the news.

Newspapers

Newspapers communicate news and features of interest to their readers. A newspaper earns money from selling space for adverts. The circulation of a newspaper is the total number of copies of a newspaper sold.

Today's large industrial printing presses are powered by electricity and can produce the vast numbers of magazines, newspapers or books that the public demand.

Electronic books

More and more books are being published in electronic formats as well as, or instead of, on paper. Some of these can be read on the internet, or can be downloaded and viewed on a portable eBook reader. These electronic devices can hold many books at one time.

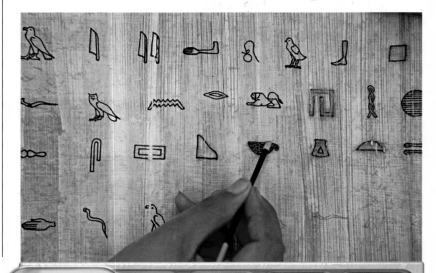

HISTORICAL DATA

THE WRITING SYSTEM OF ANCIENT EGYPT

Around 5,000 years ago, the ancient Egyptians developed one of the first writing systems. Each symbol or picture, called a hieroglyph, represented an object (such as 'boat' or 'bread') or an idea (such as 'hot' or 'powerful'). More than 2,000 symbols were developed. The symbols were carved into stone or they were painted with brushes on wood, or on scrolls called papyrus. Papyrus was made of flattened fibres of reeds.

COMPUTERS

Computers are machines that perform hundreds of different jobs. Their microprocessors allow them to gather in information, process it and then output the results.

PROGRAMS

Computers need instructions – computer programs or software – to perform tasks. The operating system (OS) is a collection of programs that control and organize the computer. Useful programs known as applications include wordprocessing, graphics programs and games.

A wireless mouse beams its instructions to the computer using an infrared light beam.

INPUT AND OUTPUT

A computer uses input devices such as a keyboard, joystick or mouse to let users enter information and commands. Once these have been processed, the results are usually displayed using an output device such as a monitor or a printer.

Each of a keyboard's keys acts as a small switch. When it is pushed down, a tiny electric current tells the computer which key has been pressed.

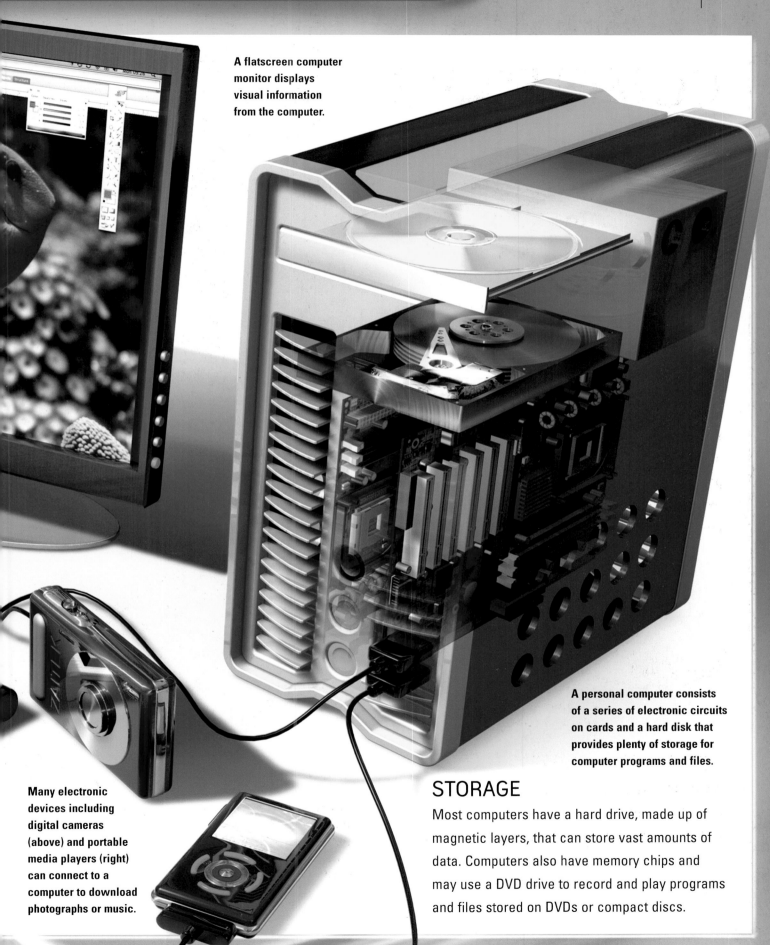

A flatscreen computer monitor displays visual information from the computer.

A personal computer consists of a series of electronic circuits on cards and a hard disk that provides plenty of storage for computer programs and files.

Many electronic devices including digital cameras (above) and portable media players (right) can connect to a computer to download photographs or music.

STORAGE

Most computers have a hard drive, made up of magnetic layers, that can store vast amounts of data. Computers also have memory chips and may use a DVD drive to record and play programs and files stored on DVDs or compact discs.

Land transport

Land transport is the most common means of carrying people and goods from one place to another.

Today, there are more than 800 million trucks, buses and cars on the world's roads. Railways carry millions of passengers and vast quantities of freight such as coal and chemicals.

Moving goods
Milllions of tonnes of raw materials and finished goods are transported every day on roads. The freight is carried by vans, lorries and giant articulated trucks pulling trailers.

Bicycles
Today, one of the most popular, healthy and environmentally friendly methods of transport is the bicycle. It has a rear wheel driven by a chain. The chain is connected to pedals that the cyclist turns.

Trains
Railways are large networks of steel tracks on which trains run. Trains were first pulled by steam engines but today are mostly electric or powered by diesel engines. High-speed train systems, such as this Japanese JR500 train, can cruise at speeds of up to 300km/h.

Special transport

Some conditions on land require special vehicles. Off-road vehicles often have large, chunky tyres for extra grip. This snow scooter runs on caterpillar tracks driven by an engine. It balances on two small skis.

AMAZING FACTS

LAND SPEED RECORDS

In 1898, Gaston de Chasseloup-Laubat set the first land speed world record of 63.15km/h in France. Advances in technology have today sent the record soaring. In 1997, Thrust SSC (above), driven by Andy Green, set a new land speed world record travelling at an incredible 1,228km/h.

Underground systems

Many large cities now have transport systems running deep underground. Known as metro, subway or tube systems, they carry millions of commuters and tourists around.

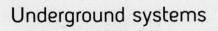

Safety and modern vehicles

Modern cars, trains and trucks are packed full of safety features that are tested thoroughly. These cars are being crash-tested to check that their bodies crumple on impact in the right way, channelling the energy from the crash around the vehicle and away from the driver and passengers.

WATER TRANSPORT

PEOPLE HAVE BUILT BOATS FOR THOUSANDS OF YEARS. THEY USE THEM TO FERRY PASSENGERS FROM PLACE TO PLACE, TO CARRY HEAVY GOODS FROM CONTINENT TO CONTINENT, OR SIMPLY FOR THE JOY OF TRAVELLING ON WATER.

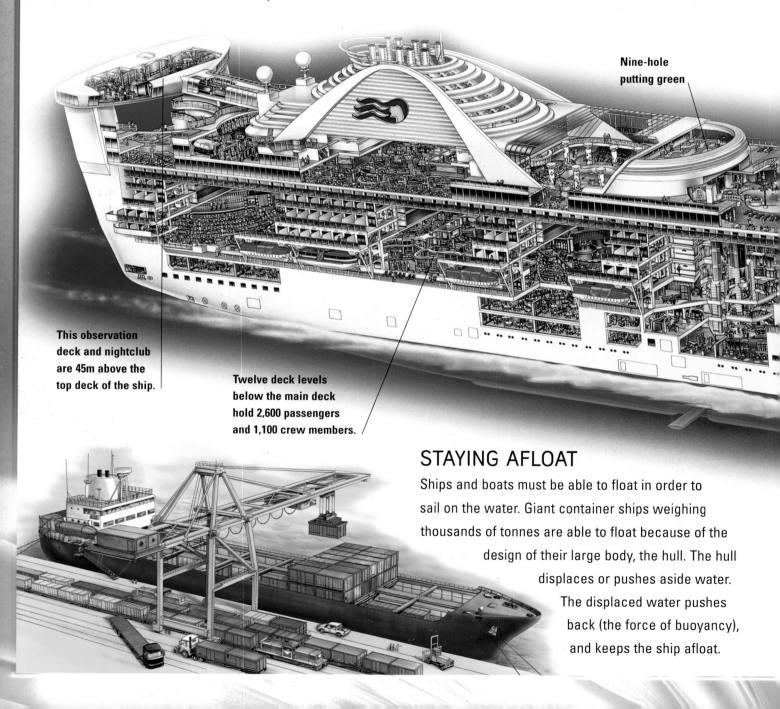

Nine-hole putting green

This observation deck and nightclub are 45m above the top deck of the ship.

Twelve deck levels below the main deck hold 2,600 passengers and 1,100 crew members.

STAYING AFLOAT

Ships and boats must be able to float in order to sail on the water. Giant container ships weighing thousands of tonnes are able to float because of the design of their large body, the hull. The hull displaces or pushes aside water. The displaced water pushes back (the force of buoyancy), and keeps the ship afloat.

SMALL AND LARGE

Boats and ships vary in size from the smallest one-person kayak or canoe to giant cruise liners and navy aircraft carriers carrying thousands of people. Whatever their size, they need some form of propulsion (power to move them forwards). A kayak uses human effort to push a paddle through the water. Other boats use large sails to catch winds. The fastest ships use engines to turn large propellers in the water. The propeller drives water backwards, thrusting the vessel forwards.

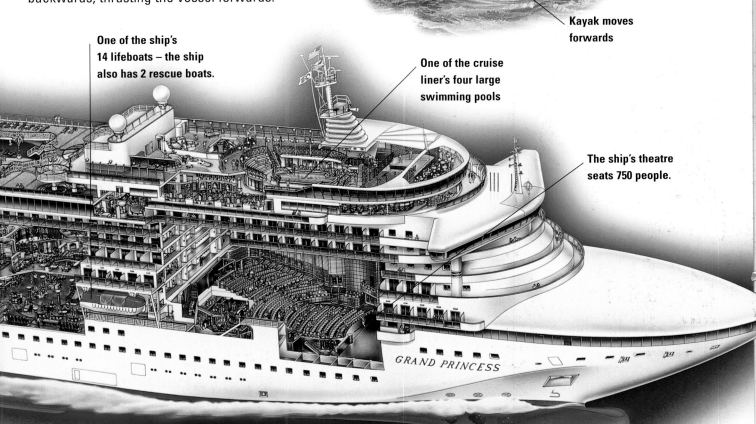

Paddle pushes back against water

Kayak moves forwards

One of the ship's 14 lifeboats – the ship also has 2 rescue boats.

One of the cruise liner's four large swimming pools

The ship's theatre seats 750 people.

GRAND PRINCESS

The ship is powered by six giant electrical generators. These power engines that turn two large propellers. The typical cruising speed of the liner is 41km/h.

CRUISING THE SEAS

Millions of people travel on water using canal boats, ferries and cruise ships. The Grand Princess (above) is one of the world's largest passenger ships. It is 290m long and taller than the Statue of Liberty. At the same time, thousands of millions of tonnes of food, raw materials for industry (such as coal, oil and metals) and finished goods, are carried in tankers and container ships.

Air transport

Aircraft can fly through the air. As an aircraft moves forwards, its wings generate lift, helping it rise.

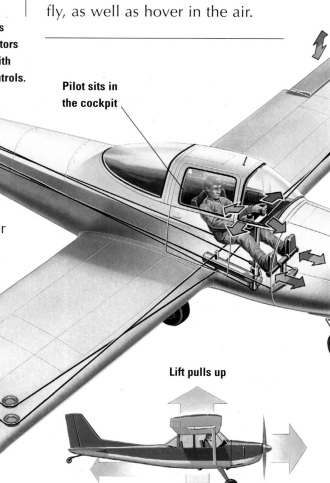

Most aircraft are powered by either jet engines or engines which drive propellers round.

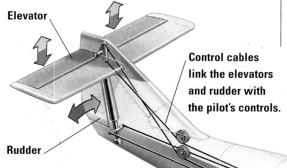

Elevator

Control cables link the elevators and rudder with the pilot's controls.

Rudder

Helicopters

Helicopters have a series of rapidly spinning rotor blades. As these spin, they act like wings. They generate lift and allow the helicopter to fly, as well as hover in the air.

Pilot sits in the cockpit

Basic controls

Aircraft have moving parts on their wings and tails to help the pilot steer in different directions. Ailerons on the wings and the rudder on the tail make the plane turn. Elevators on the horizontal tail plane tilt the aircraft's nose up or down.

Ailerons are controlled from the cockpit

Four forces act on an aircraft as it flies: lift, gravity, thrust and drag.

Lift pulls up

Drag slows down

Thrust pulls or pushes forwards

Gravity pulls down

Flying boats

Some aircraft are capable of floating in water. These flying boats have stabilizing floats fitted to their wings. Some have been modified to fight forest fires. They skim the surface of a lake or sea to gather up water which they drop on the fire.

Jet propulsion

The development of jet engines in the 1930s allowed aircraft to fly faster. Jet engines draw in large amounts of air. This is mixed and burnt with fuel to generate huge amounts of thrust, which propels the aircraft forwards.

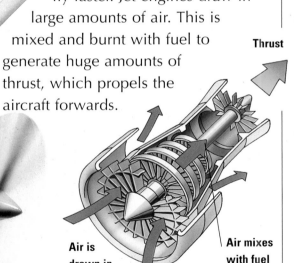

Thrust

Air is drawn in

Air mixes with fuel

SCIENTIFIC INPUT

HOT AIR BALLOONS

Balloons consist of a giant bag, called an envelope, that is filled with gas and has a basket suspended underneath. Some balloons are filled with helium gas, but many are filled with hot air. A gas burner heats the air inside to make the balloon lighter than the air around it. This makes it rise.

Airliners and airports

In 2007, more than 4,400 million people flew on aircraft, mostly in giant airliners carrying up to 500 passengers. These airliners and smaller light aircraft take off and land at airports. The busiest airports have to handle hundreds of airliners every day.

Future communication

Over the last century, there have been amazing advances with the arrival of television, computers, the internet, cars and aircraft.

Future advances in technology may see machines take an increasingly active role in the everyday lives of people around the world.

Newer technologies

Mobile communications will continue to develop. Wearable computers will shrink to the size of a tiny box but with all the power of a home computer. They may work with voice and touch commands and project their display onto a tiny screen in front of the user.

Cyborg implants

In the future, tiny microprocessors may be implanted in the human body (above). These will communicate directly with other computers, acting as identity devices and translating foreign languages instantaneously.

Robot workers

Robots will work alongside humans performing tasks with perfect accuracy. They can be sent into danger areas to rescue people, or act as war reporters, like this Afghan Explorer.

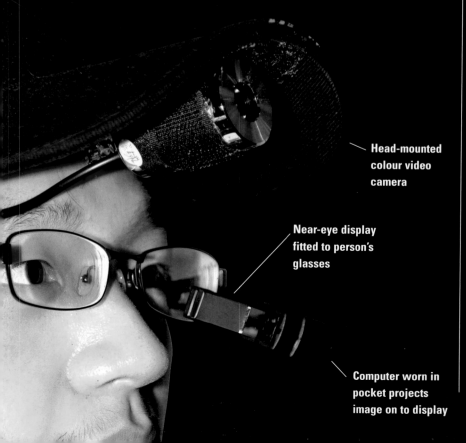

Head-mounted colour video camera

Near-eye display fitted to person's glasses

Computer worn in pocket projects image on to display

Robot interaction

Robots are being developed that can recognize faces, words and phrases, and communicate directly with people. Future robots may act as smart playmates and teachers for young children as they grow.

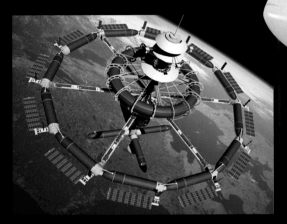

Space tourism

A handful of people have already paid to travel into space. The future may see a major increase in space tourism, with people staying in space hotels orbiting high above Earth.

Contacting aliens

Extraterrestrial life may or may not exist. Schemes such as SETI (the Search for Extraterrestrial Intelligence) have beamed radio signals deep into space. There has been no answer yet, but there may be in the future.

A humanoid (human-like) robot kicks a football. This robot can recognize voice commands, dance, climb stairs and jog at a speed of 6km/h.

Communications facts

As populations have risen, transport and communications systems have grown. The World Wide Web, which contained only a few hundred webpages in the early 1990s, is now estimated by some to consist of up to one trillion webpages.

INTERNET GROWTH
Approximate number of regular internet users

1995	16 million
1996	37 million
1997	70 million
1998	147 million
1999	248 million
2000	361 million
2001	513 million
2002	587 million
2003	719 million
2005	1,018 million
2007	1,262 million
2009	1,637 million
2011	2,095 million

MOST TV STATIONS
7,306 – Russia, 1998

LONGEST-RUNNING TV SHOWS
Meet The Press, NBC, first broadcast November 1947, still on air 2011.
Children's TV show: Blue Peter, BBC, first broadcast in 1958.

BUSIEST INTERNATIONAL AIRPORTS
London Heathrow LHR (UK)
  61,348,340 passengers per year
Paris CDG (France) 51,888,936
Amsterdam AMS (Netherlands)
  45,940,939
Frankfurt FRA (Germany) 45,697,160
Hong Kong HKG (China)
  43,274,765
Tokyo NRT (Japan) 33,860,094
Singapore SIN (Singapore) 33,368,099
London Gatwick LGW (UK) 30,016,837
Bangkok BKK (Thailand) 29,587,773
Dubai DXB (UAE) 27,925,522

LARGEST PASSENGER SHIP
RCI Oasis of the Seas: 360m long and carries up to 6,300 passengers and 2,165 crew members.

BIGGEST ROAD NETWORK
USA: a network of 6.4 million km of graded roads throughout its land.

Shinkansen Bullet train speeding past Mount Fuji

USEFUL WEBSITES

www.gutenberg.org/wiki/Main_Page More than 20,000 eBooks to read for free.
http://transition.fcc.gov/cgb/kidszone Information about every aspect of communications.
www.bbc.co.uk/worldservice/programmes/bbc_journalism/ Learn how to be a journalist.
www.howacarworks.com/ Comprehensive site about how a car works.

Glossary

acid rain Rain containing toxins from factory and car fumes that falls and poisons trees and plants.

adaptation The way in which a plant or animal changes over generations to suit a different environment.

adrenaline A hormone released into the bloodstream in response to physical or mental stress.

amoeba A tiny, single-celled animal with no fixed shape that lives in water.

amphibian A cold-blooded, smooth-skinned vertebrate that begins life in the water, but can live on land when it is an adult. Frogs, toads and salamanders are amphibians.

antibiotic A medicine used to kill the bacteria that cause disease.

apartheid An official government policy formerly practised in South Africa involving discrimination against non-whites.

arachnid An animal that has four pairs of segmented legs and a body divided into two parts. Spiders and scorpions are arachnids.

asteroid A rocky body that circles the Sun. Most asteroids are between Mars and Jupiter in the asteroid belt.

astronomer A person who studies the stars and planets, as well as other bodies in space.

atmosphere The layers of gases and clouds that surround a planet, star or moon.

atoll A ring-shaped coral reef, or a ring of small coral islands, enclosing a shallow lagoon.

bacterium (pl. bacteria) A microscopic single-celled organism. Some bacteria can cause diseases.

Big Bang The starting point to our Universe, according to modern theory.

biodiversity The number and variety of animals found in a particular area.

biome A community of living organisms found in a particular ecological area, such as a desert.

biotechnology The use of living organisms to generate useful products.

black hole The remains of a star that pulls in any object around it in space, even rays of light, so that it appears black from Earth.

blood pressure The pressure of the circulating blood against the inner walls of blood vessels.

camouflage The colour, markings or body shape that helps to hide an animal in its surroundings.

carbohydrate An energy-giving substance made by green plants, found in foods such as potatoes and bread.

cartilage Gristly material that is found in some parts of the body, such as the joints and outer ear.

cell The basic unit from which all living things – plants and animals – are made up.

cephalopod A mollusc with a beaked head and tentacles, i.e. an octopus.

ceramics Objects made by firing clay or porcelain.

chemical Any substance that can change when joined or mixed with another substance.

chlorophyll The green pigment found in most plants that absorbs light and gives energy for photosynthesis.

chromosome A thread-like part of the nucleus of a cell that contains genetic information.

civil war A war fought between groups from and in the same country or region.

civilization A human society that has reached a high state of cultural, political, social and intellectual development.

climate The meteorological conditions, for example rainfall and temperature, of a particular area.

comet A ball of frozen gas and dust that travels around the Sun. Some of the dust streams out behind the comet to make a 'tail'.

communism A political and economic movement that seeks to establish a system in which all property is held equally.

coniferous Describes trees or shrubs that bear cones and evergreen leaves.

conservation The preservation and careful management of natural resources and the environment.

cosmology The study of the structure and origin of the Universe.

crusades The European campaigns to recover Palestine from Muslim rule that took place from 1095 to 1192.

crustacean Usually aquatic group of animals, with segmented bodies and paired, jointed limbs. Lobsters, crabs and woodlice are crustaceans.

culture The knowledge, values and way of life of the people of a country or region.

deciduous Describes trees and shrubs that shed their leaves annually.

democracy Government based on rule by the people, usually through elected representatives.

digestion The process by which food is broken down so the nutrients can be absorbed.

DNA Deoxyribonucleic acid, a substance in cells that carries all the genetic information in the form of a chemical code.

dynasty Generations of rulers from the same family.

echolocation A way of finding objects by sending out sounds, then listening for the echo. Bats use echolocation to navigate.

ecosystem A self-contained community of plants and animals and their environment, such as a rainforest.

election The selection of someone for public office by voting.

electron A tiny particle that has a negative electrical charge, and that usually orbits the nucleus of an atom.

endangered Describes animals threatened with extinction.

equator An imaginary circle on the surface of a planet or star, at equal distances from its two poles.

erosion The wearing away of the Earth's surface by water, wind, ice or gravity.

ethnic Describes the cultural, racial, religious or linguistic tradition of a group of people or society.

evolution A gradual process of change in the genetic make-up of a species over generations.

exile A person banished from his or her native land.

extinct No longer existing or living.

fossil The ancient remains, impression or trace of an animal or plant, usually found in rocks.

fossil fuel An energy-containing substance – coal, oil or gas – that is formed from the remains of prehistoric plants or animals.

galaxy A collection of millions or billions of stars, planets, gas and dust, bound together by gravity.

gene A section of DNA in a chromosome that carries information about an inherited characteristic.

geological Relating to the scientific study of the origin, history and structure of the Earth.

geothermal Energy produced by harnessing the heat from inside Earth.

germination In plants, when seeds or spores sprout.

gland An organ or group of cells in the body that produces a specific substance, such as a hormone.

gravity The force that pulls everything towards the centre of the Earth, making objects fall and giving them weight.

habitat The place where an animal or plant normally lives or grows.

haemoglobin An oxygen-carrying, iron-containing protein found in red blood cells.

hieroglyphs The ancient Egyptian writing system that used pictures to represent objects, ideas and sounds.

hormone A chemical messenger produced in a gland to control processes of the body, such as growth.

humidity Dampness in the air.

independence Freedom from control and influence.

invertebrate An animal that does not have a backbone.

larva The second stage in the life of an insect, between egg and adult.

law A system or collection of rules that people must obey.

literacy The ability to read and write.

magma Liquid molten rock found underneath the Earth's crust.

magnetism Having the power to attract objects made of iron or steel, or force them away.

mammals Warm-blooded vertebrates that have a covering of hair on the skin, give birth to live young and nourish their young with milk.

marsupial A mammal that has a pouch on the outside of its body in which its young develop.

media The communication with and influence on people, by radio, television, newspapers and magazines etc.

metamorphosis The transformation of an animal during growth, for example from a caterpillar to a butterfly.

meteorite A piece of rock or metal from space that manages to pass through a planet's atmosphere without burning up.

microwaves Radio waves of very short wavelength that are used for communication, radar and cooking.

migration The movement of animals, birds and some sea creatures from one place to another to find food, warm weather or produce young.

mineral A natural substance that has not been formed from plant or animal life, for example rocks, metals and salt.

molecule The smallest unit of an element or chemical compound, made up of at least two atoms.

mollusc An animal with a soft body that usually lives in a shell, for example a snail or a limpet.

monotreme One of a group of egg-laying animals that live in Australia and New Guinea, for example the platypus or the echidna.

moraine An area covered by rocks and debris dropped by a glacier.

mummification To preserve a body by embalming and drying it, as practised by the ancient Egyptians.

nebula A cloud of dust and gas found in space.

nocturnal Active at night.

nuclear Operated or powered by atomic energy.

nutrients The parts of a food that can be used by animals or plants for health and growth.

observatory A building or spacecraft that astronomers use to watch space.

orbit The path of one body around another, such as the Moon's path around the Earth.

ozone A gas that absorbs harmful ultraviolet radiation from the Sun.

photosynthesis The chemical process in which plants use the energy in sunlight to turn carbon dioxide and water into food (glucose sugar).

pitch How high or low a musical note sounds to the ear.

plague A disease that causes high numbers of deaths.

pollination The transfer of pollen from one flower to another (ie by an insect) to help make seeds.

pollution Substances such as chemicals from factories that poison the air, land or water.

predator An animal that lives by hunting and eating other animals.

prehistory Human history in the period before recorded events.

prey An animal that is hunted or eaten by another animal.

propaganda News and information designed to persuade people to adopt a particular point of view.

radar A way of finding the position of an object using radio waves.

radiation Anything that radiates from its source. It could be waves, such as light or sound, or a beam of invisible particles, such as neutrons.

revolution The overthrow of a government by the people.

ritual Ceremonial acts or rites used in an act of religious worship.

robot A machine that can do work automatically.

seismograph An instrument for measuring and recording earthquakes.

species A group of organisms that look alike and breed with each other.

superpower An enormously powerful state with influence around the world, for example the USA.

temperate Describes a climate that has mild summers and cool winters.

temperature The measure of how hot or cold something is.

vertebrate An animal with a bony skeleton and a backbone. Fish, reptiles, birds, amphibians and mammals are all vertebrates.

virus A tiny microbe that can invade and take over living cells.

Index

KINGFISHER

First published 2008 as *Explore* by Kingfisher
This edition published 2012 by Kingfisher
an imprint of Macmillan Children's Books
a division of Macmillan Publishers Limited
20 New Wharf Road, London N1 9RR
Basingstoke and Oxford
Associated companies throughout the world
www.panmacmillan.com

ISBN 978-0-7534-3342-3

1 3 5 7 9 8 6 4 2
ITR/1011/UTD(SCHOY)/WKT/140MA

A CIP catalogue record for this book is available from the British Library.

Printed in China

Acknowledgements

The Publisher would like to thank the following for permission to reproduce their material. Every care has been taken to trace copyright holders. However, if there have been unintentional omissions or failure to trace copyright holders, we apologise and will, if informed, endeavour to make corrections in any future edition.

Top = t; Bottom = b; Centre = c; Left = l; Right = r

Cover all images courtesy of Shutterstock.com **Pages** 11tr Getty/National Geographic Society; 11cr Corbis/Sygma; 15tr Corbis/Reuters; 18tr Alamy/Mike Greenslade; 21cr Science Photo Library (SPL)/Adam Hart-Davies; 22-23 Getty/National Geographic Society; 31t Digital Vision; 32 Getty/Stone; 35tl SPL/Mark Garlick; 41cr Bridgeman Art Library(BAL)/National Gallery; 43cr SPL/Mark Garlick; 48 SPL/RIA Novosti; 51cr SPL/Julian Baum; 56 NASA/Wally Pacholka; 60cl NASA/Stanford University; 61cl Kobal Collection/Columbia Pictures; 63tl SPL/Larry Landolfi; 64 Getty/Panoramic Images; 69cr SPL/Dr Keith Wheeler; 73tr Getty/Stone; 73cr Alamy/Scott Hortop; 74-75 Corbis/Scott Stulberg; 78bl Naturepl/Stephen David Miller; 83tr Corbis/Phil Schermeister; 86cr Corbis/Kazuyoshi Nomachi; 90-91 Corbis/Frans Lanting; 93tr Corbis/Keren Su; 93br Corbis/Wayne Lawler/Ecoscene; 94b Corbis/Du Huaju/Xinhua Press; 95cr Corbis/Paul A. Souders; 96 Corbis/Kazuyoshi Nomachi; 99cr Naturepl/Meul/ARCO; 106-107 Photolibrary/Michael Duva; 113cr Corbis/Daniel J. Cox; 117tr Corbis/Joe McDonald; 119c Getty/Jeff Lapore; 124-125 Corbis/Patricia Fogden; 127cr Corbis/Alexander Demianchuk; 128 NHPA/Stephen Dalton; 131tr SPL/Zephyr; 133 Alamy/Jupiter/Brand X; 137tr SPL/AJ Photo/Hop Americain; 137cl Alamy/Horizon International; 138-139 SPL/Philippe Psaila; 139tr BAL/Menil Collection /Giraudon; 140cl Corbis/Keren Su; 141tr Alamy/Eddie Linsson; 142cl Getty/Angelo Cavalli; 143cr Corbis/Mediscan; 145 SPL/Susumu Nishinaga; 147tr Alamy/Medical; 148br SPL/Steve Gschmeissner; 149tr Alamy/Sinibomb Images; 149cr SPL/Alfred Pasieka; 150c SPL/Robert Brocksmith; 150bl SPL/Tek Image; 151tr SPL/Dept of Clinical Cytogenetics, Addenbrookes Hospital; 151cr SPL/Dr Jeremy Burgess; 153 SPL/Medi-mation; 155tl Corbis/Anna Peisl/zefa; 155bl Corbis/Don Hammond/Design Pics; 155tr. SPL/Helen McCardle; 155br SPL/Helen McCardle; 156-157 SPL; 160 Corbis/Bo Bridges; 163 BAL/National Museum, Aleppo/Giraudon; 177cr AKG Images; 178l Corbis/Michael Nicholson; 178-179 Corbis/Gianni Dagli Orti; 181cl BAL/Charmet Archive; 181cr Corbis/Bettmann; 181b SPL/David Ducros; 182cl Alamy/Mary Evans Picture Library; 183 Getty/Edwin Levick/FPG; 186br Corbis/Hulton; 187tr Corbis/Hulton; 189t BAL; 189b Corbis/Wolfgang Kumm/dpa; 190tl Corbis/Reuters; 190br Getty/Courtney Kealy ; 191cl Getty/Jaafar Ashtiyeh/AFP; 191tr Corbis/Hubert Boesi/dpa; 191crl Corbis/Reuters; 192 Corbis/Jacques Langevin; 194b Alamy/Chad Ehlers; 195tr Haiduc; 195cr Corbis/Gideon Mendel; 195cl Alamy/Sebastian Green; 196 Getty/Christopher Pillitz/Reportage; 197 Alamy/Alan Gignoux; 198tr Corbis/Les Stone/Sygma; 198cr Corbis/Robert Garvey; 199l Corbis/Ajay Verma/Reuters; 199br Perrinpost; 200cl Sergio Luiz; 200bl Tomascastelazo; 200l Sengkang; 203cr Corbis/Jose Fuste Raga/zefa; 204b Corbis/Kazuyoshi Nomachi; 205 Corbis/Jon Hicks; 206cr Getty/Popperfoto; 207c Alamy/Richard Wareham; 208tl Corbis/Tim Wimbourne/Reuters; 208-209 Corbis/Gary Hershorn/Reuters; 209tr Corbis/Duomo; 210tr Corbis/Joe Travers/Reuters; 211tl Getty/David Rogers; 211tr Getty Images/Dimitar Dilkoff/AFP; 212 Corbis/Claudia Daut/Reuters; 213t Photolibrary/Hisham F. Ibrahim; 213c Corbis/Peter Turnley; 214cl Alamy/Jim West; 214bl Alamy/Jupiter/Brand X; 215 Alamy/David R. Frazier; 217b Getty/Romeo Gacad/AFP; 218-219 Getty/Robert Harding; 219cr Alamy/John Sturrock; 220cl Alamy/Guatebrian; 220b Corbis/Kai Pfaffenbach/Reuters; 221tl Alamy/Jeff Gynane; 222cl Alamy/Jenny Matthews; 223 Alamy/Vario Images; 224 Corbis/Steve Terrill; 227 Pete Clayman; 229tr Corbis/Paue Seux/Hemis; 229cr Alamy/JoeFoxKrakow; 230tr Corbis/Randy M. Ury; 231 Corbis/Al Rod; 234tr Kobal Collection/Hal Roach/Pathe Exchange; 234-235 Kobal Collectio/Dreamworks/Aardman Animations; 235tr Corbis/Sharie Kennedy; 235cl Getty/Stewart Cohen; 235b Corbis/David Brabyn; 236cl Kobal Collection/Walt Disney Pictures/Elliot Marks; 236bl Corbis/Louie Psihoyos; 237t Corbis/Keith Hamshere/Paramount Pictures; 237b Corbis/Mark Dye/Star Ledger; 238c Alamy/Janine Weidel; 239tr Corbis/Robbie Jack; 239b Corbis/Eddy Risch/epa; 240tr Alamy/Redferns Music Picture Library; 240b Getty/Robert Mizono/Photonica; 241t Corbis/Jeff Albertson; 241cr Range Pictures; 242cl Alamy/Uppercut Images; 242br Art Archive/Musee du Louvre; 242-243t BAL/Musee National d'Art Moderne, Centre Pompidou/Giraudon; 234tc Alamy/The Print Collector; 243cr Art Archive/Claude Debussy Centre, St Germain en Laye; 243b Alamy/Alex Segre; 244cl Alamy/Vario Images; 245 Pete Clayman; 246-247 Pete Clayman; 248c Corbis/Gideon Mendel; 249tr Corbis/VIP Production; 249cr Digital Vision; 249bl Pete Clayman; 250bl Getty/Koichi Kamoshida; 251tl Getty/Michel Boutefeu; 251tr Corbis/Gideon Mendel; 251cl Alamy/Jerome Yeats; 251cr Alamy/The Photolibrary Wales; 253tr Alamy/Vehbi Koca; 254cr Alamy/Barry Mason; 254bl Photolibrary/Robin Smith; 254b Alamy/Wildscape; 255tr Pete Clayman; 255cr Corbis/Elizabeth Kreutz/Newsport; 255b Alamy/Paul Broadbent; 256 Corbis/Gary Hershorn/Reuters; 258br Corbis/Louie Psihoyos; 259t Corbis/Julian Smith; 259br SPL/A.B. Dowsett; 261cr BAL/BL; 262tl Corbis/Kelley Mooney; 262cr Alamy/Ulrich Doering; 263c Alamy/David R. Frazier; 265cr SPL/Drs A. Yazdani & D.J. Hornbaker; 266cl Photolibrary/Imagesource; 267cr Nicky Studdart; 268tr SPL/Geoff Tompkinson; 268c Alamy/Ace Stock; 269t Corbis/Richard Cummins; 269bl SPL/Klaus Guldbransen; 270cl Corbis/Roger Ressmeyer; 272tr SPL/Robert Brook; 272-273 SPL/Lawrence Lawry; 273tr Digital Vision; 273cr SPL/Andrew Lambert; 275 Corbis/William Taufic; 276c Photolibrary; 277bl SPL/Peter Menzel; 280cr Alamy/Horizon International; 281bl SPL/Scott Bauer/Dept of Agriculture; 281cr Alamy/Roger Bamber; 283 Corbis/Christian Charisius/Reuters; 284-285t SPL/Dr Kari Lounatmaa; 285cr Corbis/Hulton; 286cl Corbis/George Steinmetz; 286bl Alamy/AWPhoto; 287t SPL/AGS; 288 SPL/Ted Kinsman; 290tr Corbis/David Turnley; 291tl Pete Clayman; 282b Corbis/Brand X; 293tr Corbis/Image 100; 293cl Getty/Stephen Shaver/AFP; 293cr Corbis/Kerry Hayes/Twentieth Century Fox; 294c Alamy/Bill Bachman; 295tl Getty/DK Stock; 295tr Getty/Taxi; 295cr Alamy/Radius Images; 295br Digital Vision; 296 Getty/Science Faction; 297 MDR Kripo; 298b Alamy/Danita Delimont; 299 Corbis/Gabe Palmer; 300 Pete Clayman; 301tl Alamy/Eddie Gerald; 301cr Corbis/Richard T. Nowitz; 305tr Getty/David Taylor; 305cr Corbis/Yuriko Nakao/Reuters; 309cr Alamy/Buzz Pictures; 310bl Rex Pictures/Sipa Press; 310tr SPL/James King-Holmes; 312 Photolibrary/Vidler Vidler

The Publishers would like to thank the following artists for original material commissioned for this book:
Mark Bergin; Peter Bull; Ray Bryant; Stuart Lafford, Patricia Ludlow, Sebastian Quigley, Sam Weston, Steve Weston (Linden Artists)